Crowned With Glory

Recommendation Page

"I highly recommend Dr. Holland's boxivok *Crowned With Glory* not only for the Christian Educator and Pastor, but for the lay person as well. A tremendous amount of information has been gathered together into one easily accessible source."
-Dr. Thomas Cassidy, President,
San Diego Baptist Theological Seminary San Diego, California, USA

"I am honored to recommend this book. For years, my students have taken classes from Dr. Holland, and they have consistently stood out in classroom discussions and in their research assignments. So much, in fact, that eventually I took some of his courses myself. Dr. Holland has been a tireless servant with a love for truth and character, a true Philosopher. Thank you for making this book available to us."
-Dr. John Harbaugh, President
Bible Institute of Naples, Italy and Kentucky Bible Institute

"Much of what has been written regarding the KJV over the past century has been superficial and partisan, intent on finding fault with the version of 1611 and without any real awareness of its deep and continuing significance. Dr. Thomas Holland has gone a long way toward returning to the KJV its due in this book. His scholarship is solid, his tone is that of a true gentleman, and his perspective is historically sound. It is my hope that a book of this caliber and substance will do much good, and that it will counteract some of the straw and chaff on this subject already in the marketplace."
-Thomas L. Hubeart Jr.
Ft. Lauderdale, Florida

"Dr. Thomas Holland is unquestionably one of the finest scholars I have ever encountered. Tom Holland leaves nothing to chance, nor does he ride on the coattails of other pundits. Rather, Dr. Holland unravels the fabric of each subject strand by strand until the material is thoroughly exposed. Laymen and scholar alike are fortunate to be the recipient of Dr. Holland's labors in such a critical discipline. This book is a must read for every Christian."

-Scott Jones
Author of *Heaven's War*

"*Crowned with Glory* by Thomas Holland, helps to defend the Greek Received Text. Noteworthy of many features in this book is his defense of the two most attacked passages, 1 John 5:7-8 and the last six verses of Revelation."

-Michael Maynard,
Author of *A History of the Debate Over 1 John 5:7-8*

"It is with great enthusiasm and gratitude that I recommend the writings of Dr. Thomas Holland. With enthusiasm because it is time for a book of this nature. With gratitude because Bible-believing Christians are in great need of scholarly writings that express God's ability to preserve his Word. This book will become one of the most valued study resources for any serious student of Scripture."

-Pastor Dan Parton
Timberline Baptist Church
Manitou Springs, Colorado

Crowned With Glory

The Bible from Ancient Text to Authorized Version

Dr. Thomas Holland

CROWNED WITH GLORY
The Bible from Ancient Text to Authorized Version

Copyright © 2000 Dr. Thomas Holland.

Writers Club Press
an imprint of iUniverse.com, Inc.

iUniverse books may be ordered through booksellers or by contacting:

iUniverse
1663 Liberty Drive
Bloomington, IN 47403
www.iuniverse.com
1-800-Authors (1-800-288-4677)

ISBN: 978-0-5951-4617-8 (sc)

Print information available on the last page.

iUniverse rev. date: 10/28/2015

Dedication

"Thou shalt also be a crown of glory in the hand of the LORD, and a royal diadem in the hand of thy God."

-Isaiah 62:3

Contents

Foreword

Due to the great popularity enjoyed by the King James Version of the Bible, discussions about whether it is or is not a completely faithful rendering of the original languages into English are often heated. One side of the discussion is typically dominated by persons who rant about how antiquated the KJV is, asserting without proof the superiority of most modern versions. From the other camp, we typically hear attacks on nineteenth century textual criticism and on the defective state of all modern translations. Surprisingly, most of the arguments presented by both sides are done second-hand and without a knowledge of the issues of textual criticism, but here, Dr. Holland attempts the very difficult task of keeping the debate on a scholarly level.

This book does not provide absolute proof that God preserved his Word in English through the translators of the Authorized (King James) Version, but it does present evidence for the text types that support the KJV, and it does make known to the modern generation the level of scholarship that went into completing the translation of 1611. Such is Dr. Holland's attempt to raise levels of awareness. As a mathematician and scientist himself, this reviewer appreciates the approach taken here.

This reviewer does not subscribe to the views expressed in Dr. Holland's book; however, he is impressed with the level of discussion that such a book will hopefully bring about. Other recent and popular attempts at presenting a foundation for the discussion have occasionally betrayed their own ignorance, but Dr. Holland pulls every scrap of evidence—for and against his view—out from the closet of the certainty of the modern paradigm and reopens an honest discussion of the issues themselves. For this he is to be commended, and there should be no doubt that any modern debate on the subject of Biblical preservation should include a thorough examination of the evidence presented in this volume.

Frank Daniels, PhD (Mathematics)
Translator, "A Non-Ecclesiastical New Testament"

Acknowledgements

Throughout the course of presenting my lessons on textual criticism, several have provided suggestions and insight into this subject, making what is complex more reader friendly. To all who have contributed, I am greatly indebted. There are, nevertheless, certain individuals who have directly helped with the preparation of this book; it is their assistance with proof-reading, editing, and research that have made this book possible. Therefore, thank you to my wife Amy, Thomas Hubeart Jr., Scott Jones, Dr. Frank Daniels, Sonny Pate, and Myrtle Pond. Your efforts have not gone unnoticed and are greatly appreciated.

Editorial Method

The majority of Greek and Hebrew words found within this volume have been transliterated for the convenience of those who do not read either Hebrew or Greek. Additionally, orthography has been modernized in regard to early English versions of the Bible and identification of early Greek papyri. When church fathers are mentioned followed by a specific date, the date given is that of their death and not the work cited.

Introduction

"A thing of beauty is a joy for ever:
Its loveliness increases; it will never
Pass into nothingness;"

-John Keats, *Endymion: A Poetic Romance* (1817)

There are a myriad of books available today that analyze, criticize, and debate the issues of biblical preservation and textual criticism. After all, there is much to explore in this vital area of Christianity. It has been nearly two thousand years since the completion of the New Testament. Since then, the Bible has been copied over and over by hand, translated into other languages, and massively produced in the electronic age. From our perspective in the twenty-first century, it is natural to inquire if what was given originally has passed through time unaltered. Is it possible that changes were made, inadvertently or intentionally, to some or part of the text over the centuries? Could it be that some of the original words have been lost during this long process of transmission, or have they been preserved so that we have exactly what was originally penned? Have modern discoveries such as the Dead Sea Scrolls or ancient manuscripts shed any light on these questions? Can we fully trust any translation of Scripture, or must we conclude that all are faulty?

Crowned With Glory seeks to address these and other questions relating to the Bible and its transmission over time. Its goal is to scholastically and scripturally present textual and historical evidence while remaining true to the premise that God has provided for us today the words he faithfully gave us in the beginning. It will examine the many textual differences found among manuscripts of the Old and New Testaments and attempt to explain why some variants have permeated these manuscripts. *Crowned With Glory* will also discuss ancient and current translations of Scripture, providing analytical and biblical reasoning for the readings found in the traditional texts.

My hope is that the information gleaned from the pages of this book will encourage the Christian in growth and faith. The reader may not always agree with my conclusions, but hopefully he or she will recognize the spirit of love and truth in which my statements are presented. And for those of like-mindedness on the issue of biblical preservation, I trust that this book will be a valuable resource for understanding and edification.

Perhaps my greatest desire is that the reader might gain a new appreciation for the value, beauty and wealth found in the pages of the Authorized Version. That which was given to us so long ago is well worth defending and believing today. While it is understandable that progress brings change, we must bear in mind that cultural, societal, or spiritual advancement should never take place by sacrificing time-tested treasures. In this book we will explore how throughout history people have thirsted for the springs of truth and salvation found in God's written word. Today, those who turn to the Authorized Version find this old well still produces sweet and living waters.

Thomas Holland
Summer, 2000

Chapter 1

The Monarch Of Books

"Both read the Bible day and night,
But thou read'st black where I read white."

-William Blake, *The Everlasting Gospel* (1818)

For the past two thousand years the world has been blessed with the monarch of books, the Holy Bible. It has been loved, read, and written about more than any other book in history. Today, the Bible has been printed, published, recorded, placed on CD-ROM, and videotaped. It has been translated in whole or part into every major language throughout the world. Many languages have several translations available. In English, for example, there have been over one hundred versions of the New Testament in the past century.

Of all the books of antiquity the Bible stands as the most attested. There are over five thousand ancient Greek manuscripts of the New Testament alone. Although the contents of these manuscripts mostly agree, there are some differences. Such variants are the subject of this book. Were these variants accidental or deliberate? Is it possible to know the original wording of the Scriptures? Or, despite the passage of time and inclusion of textual variants, have the very words of Scripture been preserved for all generations?

For a number of years there has been a controversy brewing among the Bible reading public. Some believe that the Bible, especially the New Testament, needs to be reconstructed in light of recent textual discoveries. The reconstruction of the New Testament is known as the science of textual criticism. Others believe the original text of the Bible has been preserved over time. This is known as the doctrine of biblical preservation. Neither side is without bias, nor is this book offered in an unbiased fashion. What it does seek to do is to inform those who are interested in this debate from both a scholastic and scriptural perspective.

Reconstruction And Biblical Preservation

The starting point of contemporary scholarship is the evidence of textual criticism. Through the ages several corrections in transmission (the copying of manuscripts over the generations) have crept into the various manuscripts. The place where one manuscript differs from another is called a textual variant. The vast majority of these textual variants came into existence before the beginning of the third century;[1] this is significant because the majority of existing manuscripts date after this period. Therefore, the age of a textual variant is not limited to the age of its parent manuscript. Whether these variants were deliberate or simply cases of copying the text incorrectly is open for debate. Most likely examples of both can be found in the numerous manuscripts.

The textual scholar's job is one of sifting through these various manuscripts, comparing textual variants, and determining what is the most likely reading. This is a difficult process so naturally researchers differ as to the final consideration. Textual scholars often are certain they are right but uncertain as to the final product. From an evangelical and conservative perspective, it seems amazing that God gave his words without error (*inspiration*) and provided the knowledge as to which books are Scripture (*canonicity*), only to produce uncertainly in the final analysis or lose a portion of them in the process of transmission.

---

[1] George D. Kilpatrick, *The Principles And Practice Of New Testament Textual Criticism* (Belgium: Leuven University Press, 1990), 34.

To offset this, conservative and evangelical scholars will incorporate the doctrine of preservation into the process of transmission. They will state that somewhere in the host of textual evidence the original reading remains. It is left to the scholar and student to discover the original reading. Unfortunately, biblical scholarship and biblical preservation are not easily compatible.

To begin with, many of the manuscripts currently known were unknown until the middle of the nineteenth century. Since these manuscripts are usually favored by modern scholarship (liberal or conservative) and considered the original reading, we must logically conclude that what is determined to be original was hidden from the church throughout the majority of its existence. Also, it is reasonable to assume that more manuscripts will be discovered with more variants, making it increasingly difficult to proclaim biblical preservation using this definition.

Additionally, modern scholarship suggests that some of the original readings have forever disappeared. In 1 Samuel 13:1, scholars believe the original reading of the verse has been lost in the process of transmission.[2] In the New Testament, we have the example of Mark 16:9-20. Most scholars believe the original ending to Mark's gospel was lost and that the current longer and shorter endings were added in the second century.[3] Obviously, redefining preservation leaves us on shaky ground. If the Scriptures teach the preservation of God's words, we must either accept the truth of preservation or reject the testimony of Scripture. The following passages are often used to support the doctrine of biblical preservation

---

[2] The Revised Standard Version reads: "Saul was…years old when he began to reign; and he reigned…and two years over Israel." The footnotes for these omissions informs us that, "The number is lacking in Heb[rew]" and "Two is not the entire number. Something has dropped out."

[3] Bruce Metzger, *A Textual Commentary On The Greek New Testament*, 2nd ed. (New York: United Bible Societies, 1994), 102-106.

(1 Samuel 3:19; Psalm 12:6-7; 105:8; 119:89, 160; 138:2; Ecclesiastes 3:14; Isaiah 40:8; Matthew 4:4; 24:35; 1 Peter 1:23-25).

Rudiments Of Textual Criticism

Biblical preservation does not demand the rejection of textual criticism. It is just as essential for the student of biblical preservation to be aware of the textual evidence as it is for any student of textual criticism. The biblical preservationist, however, first approaches the subject theologically and then considers the existing textual evidence, usually in light of the promise of preservation.

Because there are variants within all the existing manuscripts, the science of textual criticism is conjectural. Different scholars examining the same manuscripts will produce differing Greek texts. This is why there are now three basic Greek texts of the New Testament in circulation: the *Critical Text*, the *Majority Text*, and the *Textus Receptus*.

The Critical Text is the basis for the majority of modern Bible translations today. It is currently reflected in the Greek New Testament of the UBS-4 (United Bible Societies fourth edition) and the NA-27 (Nestle-Aland twenty-seventh edition). These two texts are now identical in regard to their Greek text, but differ in regard to their critical apparatus (the footnotes discussing the different textual variants). Generally, the Critical Text reflects a textual line called *Alexandrian*, a name that is explained later in this chapter.

The Majority Text is a work in progress. As the name suggests, it catalogs the majority of the existing Greek manuscripts and reflects a consensus of these manuscripts. However, it does not use all of the existing manuscripts; instead, it uses only a portion of those manuscripts that would reflect what is considered the majority.[4]

---

[4] There are currently two editions of the Majority Text: *The Greek New Testament According to the Majority Text* (Nelson, 1985) by Zane C. Hodges and Arthur L. Farstad, and *The New Testament in the Original Greek According to the Byzantine/Majority Textform* (Original Word Publishers, 1991) by Maurice A. Robinson, William G. Pierpont, and William David McBrayer.

The Textus Receptus was the standard Greek text for centuries. It was used by Protestant translators during the Reformation, and is responsible for the Authorized Version and its English forerunners.[5] The Majority Text and the Textus Receptus are very similar (except in the book of Revelation) because both reflect the majority of existing Greek manuscripts.

The history of New Testament manuscripts is divided, roughly, into three periods: papyrus, vellum, and paper. The manuscripts we have were usually written on one of these three and often reflect the date of the manuscript. Papyrus[6] is made from papyrus plants that grew abundantly in Egypt. The inner bark of the plant was cut into thin strips, which were laid side by side and crossed with other strips. They were then pressed together and sun-dried. The papyrus was, for the most part, written only on one side and bound together in rolls. The custom was to write in very narrow columns that had no separation of words, accents marks, or punctuation. Paragraphs were marked with a line in the margin of the text.[7] The papyrus manuscripts are very fragile, and most of what we have are fragments. This period of manuscript production lasted until the seventh century. Philippians 1:1-2, in Greek, would read something like this:

ΠΑΥΛΟΣΚΑΙΤΙΜΟΘΕΟΣΔΟΥΛΟΙΙΗΣΟΥΧΡΙΣΤΟΥΠΑΣΙΤΟ
ΙΣΑΓΙΟΙΣΕΝΧΡΙΣΤΩΙΗΣΟΥΤΟΙΣΟΥΣΙΝΕΝΦΙΛΙΠΠΟΙΣ
ΣΥΝΕΠΙΣΚΟΠΟΙΣΚΑΙΔΙΑΚΟΝΟΙΣΧΑΡΙΣΥΜΙΝΚΑΙΕΙΡΗΝ
ΗΑΠΟΘΕΟΥΠΑΤΡΟΣΗΜΩΝΚΑΙΚΥΡΙΟΥΙΗΣΟΥΧΡΙΣΤΟΥ

---

[5] The Textus Receptus used by the translators of the King James Version was that of Theodore de Beza (1589 and 1598). The basic text of this edition has been reproduced by The Trinitarian Bible Society (1976) and is entitled, *The New Testament: The Greek Text Underlying the English Authorized Version of 1611*. This was based on the work by F. H. A. Scrivener, *The New Testament in the Original Greek according to the text followed in the Authorized Version* (Cambridge University Press, 1894 and 1902).

[6] There are about 100 Greek papyri manuscripts.

[7] The Greek word *para* means *beside*. The Greek word *grafo* means *writing*. Thus, *paragraph*.

Even when translated into English, the reading is difficult.
PAULANDTIMOTHEUSTHESERVANTSOFJESUS
CHRISTTOALLTHESAINTSINCHRISTJESUSWHI
CHAREATPHILIPPIWITHTHEBISHOPSANDDEA
CONSGRACEBEUNTOYOUANDPEACEFROMGOD
OURFATHERANDFROMTHELORDJESUSCHRIST

Manuscripts written on vellum (or in some cases, parchment) replaced papyrus manuscripts during the period from about the end of the third century to the fifteenth century. The narrow columns used in the papyrus manuscripts were maintained in the vellum manuscripts. Vellum is made of dried animal skins that were cut into leaves and formed into a book called a codex.[8] Some vellum manuscripts maintain the same style of writing used in papyrus manuscripts. Manuscripts that use this style are referred to as uncials,[9] which consist of all capital letters written without accent marks, with no separation of words or sentences, and typically no punctuation. Later, around the ninth century, small letters were also used in manuscripts, with spacing between the words. These manuscripts are referred to as minuscules or cursives.[10]

Manuscripts written on paper date from about the fourteenth century to the present. Until this period, it was rare to have a complete Bible in one book. Most of the papyrus and vellum manuscripts are fragments, passages, or maybe a book of the New Testament. But, in the thirteenth century whole books containing all or most of the New Testament became common.

---

[8] Some scholars believe that a codex (book) may have been used during the time of the New Testament. The redating of P64 to before 66 AD, if correct, would provide historical support for this. In passages such as Revelation 5:1, the Greek word *biblion* (book) is used of something with writing on both sides. Although most understand this to mean a scroll, the discovery of an early codex would certainly give weight to a literal interpretation of this and other passages.

[9] There are currently over 300 known Greek uncial manuscripts.

[10] There are about 2,800 Greek minuscules manuscripts.

Sources For New Testament Texts

There are three classes of evidence used by textual critics in the reconstruction of the New Testament. First, the main sources for reconstructing the New Testament are the extant Greek manuscripts, which exist in papyrus, vellum, or paper and contain variants. These manuscripts are classified under one of four textual types.

The Byzantine Text. The name is derived from the Byzantine Empire, as it is the type of text copied by Byzantine monks. There are more manuscripts of this text-type than of the other three combined. This line of manuscripts would reflect the Greek Textus Receptus that was used to produce the King James Version. It is also known as the Traditional Text or the Syrian Text.

The Alexandrian Text. The name refers to Alexandria, Egypt where scribes prepared most of these texts. Most contemporary versions are derived from this textual line. The three most important manuscripts that reflect this text-type are Alexandrinus[11] (also known as Codex A, fifth century), Sinaiticus (also known as Codex Alpha, fourth century), and Vaticanus (also known as Codex B, fourth century).[12]

The Western Text. Some scholars debate whether this is a real text-type or not. Most believe it is, while others deny its existence as a text-type because of the vast diversity within its representative manuscripts.[13] This line has several sub-groups of manuscripts or families within it. The text is longer than the Alexandrian, sometimes given to paraphrases, and is closer

---

[11] Codex Alexandrinus is of the Alexandrian textual line except in the four Gospels. There it reflects the Byzantine textual line.

[12] Most scholars today only recognize two text-types: The Alexandrian and the Byzantine.

[13] Frederic *Kenyon, Handbook to the Textual Criticism of the New Testament* (Grand Rapids: Eerdmans, 1912), 356. E. C. Colwell, "The Greek New Testament with a Limited Critical Apparatus: its Nature and Uses," in *Studies in New Testament and Early Christian Literature*, ed. D. E. Aune (Leiden: E. J. Brill, 1972), 33.

to the Byzantine Text. Some have considered this the oldest textual line.[14] Codex Bezae (also known as Codex D05) in the Gospels and Acts and Codex Claromontanus (also known as Codex D06) in the Epistles reflect the Western Text. The majority of the Old Latin manuscripts are usually classified as Western.

The Caesarean Text. This text-type seems to be a mixture of the Western and Alexandrian line of manuscripts. It is represented in a few manuscripts (Θ, 22, 28, 565, 700, family 1, and family 13).[15] Some believe it was derived in Egypt by Origen and brought to Caesarea. Because it is a mixture, some question if this should be classified as a separate text-type.[16]

The second source for making a Greek text is the testimony of ancient versions. These versions, usually translated from Greek, are used as a source for establishing a Greek text. Like the Greek manuscripts, there are a variety of ancient versions that do not agree. Among these are the Latin versions (including both the Old Latin and Jerome's Latin Vulgate), Syrian (including the Old Syriac and the Peshitta), Coptic (Egyptian), Gothic (early German), Armenian, Ethiopic, and others. These are useful in demonstrating what the non-Greek reading world used.

The third source is the quotations of the early church fathers, called *patristic citations*. Again, we have differences in several of the quotations that demonstrate differences in New Testament texts. More will be given about some of the early church fathers in later chapters.

---

[14] Bruce Metzger, *The Text Of The New Testament*, 3rd ed. (New York: Oxford University Press, 1992), 213-214.

[15] A "family" is a cluster of manuscripts that reflect the same characteristics and therefore are grouped together.

[16] At the beginning of the twentieth century, Kirsopp Lake expounded the possible existence of the Caesarean textual line. Others, such as B. H. Streeter, suggested that this was a new text-type. However, the textual line lacks pure representatives, most demonstrating a significant mixture with the Byzantine text. Larry W. Hurtado has argued against the Caesarean text, *Text-Critical Methodology and the Pre-Caesarean Text: Codex W in the Gospel of Mark* (Studies and Documents 43, Eerdmans, 1981).

Other sources used in reconstruction include lectionaries[17] and extra biblical writings such as apocryphal works. Lectionaries were books used by the early church that contained lessons, hymns, and citations from passages of Scripture. These would show that certain Scriptures were in use at a given time and substantiate a questioned text. Apocryphal and extra biblical writings would be citations from books contemporary with the New Testament or works written within the first few hundred years of Christianity. Although not inspired, they often quote Scripture. The following are a few examples.

In Romans 14:10, the King James Version reads, "For we shall all stand before the judgment seat of Christ." Modern versions tend to read, "judgment seat of God" instead of "judgment seat of Christ." *The Epistle of Polycarp to the Philippians* quotes the verse as saying:

> If then we entreat the Lord that He would forgive us, we also ought to forgive: for we are before the eyes of our Lord and God, and we must all stand at the judgment-seat of Christ, and each man must give an account of himself. (*Philippians* 6:2).

This reading, which dates to 150 AD, would offer support in favor of the Traditional Text and the Authorized (King James) Version of 1611.

The same is true of 1 John 4:3; "And every spirit that confesseth not that Jesus Christ is come in the flesh is not of God: and this is that spirit of antichrist, whereof ye have heard that it should come; and even now already is it in the world." The phrase "is come in the flesh" is not found in many of the ancient Greek texts and therefore is not contained in the Critical Text and many contemporary English versions. Once more, in Polycarp's *Philippians* we read:

---

[17] There are about 2,200 Greek lectionary manuscripts.

For every one who shall not confess that Jesus Christ is come in the flesh, is antichrist: and whosoever shall not confess the testimony of the Cross, is of the devil; and whosoever shall pervert the oracles of the Lord to his own lusts and say that there is neither resurrection nor judgment, that man is the first-born of Satan. (*Philippians* 7:1).[18]

This apocryphal passage offers some evidence supporting the Traditional Text.

The Textus Receptus And Preservation

Until the early 1800's, the Textus Receptus was the only Greek text used, at least where Protestant scholarship was concerned. Dr. Kurt Aland, who helped with the Critical Text, wrote: "Finally it is undisputed that from the 16th to the 18th century orthodoxy's doctrine of verbal inspiration assumed this Textus Receptus. It was the only Greek text they knew, and they regarded it as the 'original text'."[19]

Critics of the Textus Receptus believe that its readings are recent and not reflective of early manuscripts. However, there is early support favoring the Byzantine line and thus the Textus Receptus. The Chester Beatty Papyri (P45, P46, and P66) all have readings that reflect the Byzantine line, although they are mixed and have Alexandrian readings as well. These papyri date to the second century or before. The now famous P64 (also known as the Magdalen Papyrus) has been listed by some as the earliest known manuscript, dating to before 66 AD.[20] The textual variants

---

[18] Some have suggested that Polycarp was not citing 1 John 4:3 but instead was citing 2 John 1:7. J. B. Lightfoot and others have listed this citation of Polycarp as coming from 1 John 4:3, and the Greek of Polycarp matches better with the Greek in 1 John 4:3 than it does with the Greek in 2 John 1:7.

[19] Kurt Aland, "The Text of the Church," *Trinity Journal*, Fall (1987): 131.

[20] Carsten Peter Thiede and Matthew D'Ancona, *Eyewitness to Jesus* (New York: Doubleday, 1996), 125.

within this manuscript support the Byzantine line with no textual support for the Alexandrian line.

Codex W dates from the fourth to early fifth century. It contains the Gospels, yet uses several of the various lines of manuscripts. While most of Mark and part of John reflect the Alexandrian and Western lines, all of Matthew and Luke 8:13-24:25 support the Textus Receptus.[21] Even Codex Alexandrinus, dating around 450 AD, reflects the Byzantine line and the Textus Receptus in the Gospels while the epistles reflect the Alexandrian line.

Likewise, early translations such as the Peshitta (second century) and the Gothic (approximately 350 AD) support the Traditional Text. Sir Fredric Kenyon, a noted textual scholar, has stated that the Gothic version represents the type of text found in the majority of Greek manuscripts, supporting the Byzantine textual line.[22]

Variances In Versions

Since there *are* differences in various Greek manuscripts, it is of no surprise that there are differences in various Greek texts and therefore differences in English translations based on those texts. When we compare the Greek Textus Receptus with the Critical Greek Text there are almost six thousand differences. Considering that there are 7,959 verses in the New Testament, we begin to see that the differences have a greater effect than what we might think. In the New Testament of the King James Version we have 181,253 words.[23] When the American Standard Version was translated in 1901, it made 36,191 changes to the King James Version's New

---

[21] Norman Geisler and William Nix, *A General Introduction to the Bible*, rev. ed. (Chicago: Moody Press, 1986), 400.

[22] Kenyon, 240.

[23] Bruce M. Metzger and Michael D. Coogan, eds., *The Oxford Companion To The Bible* (New York: Oxford University Press, 1993), 80.

Testament.[24] This accounts for about one-fourth of the New Testament being changed in one form or another.

The vast majority of these differences, however, are minor. Most deal with spelling or points of grammar. Some are of a more serious nature and cause words, verses, or whole passages to be called into question. Below are a few of the differences that have caused a stir over the past few years. They are divided into several categories so the reader might have a grasp of the situation concerning textual and translational differences.

One notable distinction deals with the number of verses contained in the Textus Receptus that are not contained in the Critical Text, and therefore do not appear in most modern versions based on that text. This, of course, does not prove a certain translation correct and another incorrect. These verses are Matthew 17:21; 18:11; 23:14; Mark 7:16; 9:44, 46; 11:26; 15:28; Luke 17:36; 23:17; John 5:4; Acts 8:37; 15:34; 24:7; 28:29; Romans 16:24; and 1 John 5:7. Additionally, Mark 16:9-20 and John 7:53-8:11 are contained in the majority of Byzantine manuscripts and the Traditional Text. However, most Alexandrian manuscripts do not contain these verses, and therefore are so noted in the Critical Text. This leaves the Christian who believes the commands of Scripture in a dilemma. Three times the Bible warns against adding to or taking from the word of God (Deuteronomy 4:2; Proverbs 30:6; and Revelation 22:18). Either the Greek texts that remove these passages are corrupt or the Greek texts that add them are corrupt; one cannot be biblical and believe that both textual lines are pure.

Here are a few examples of phrases that are contained in the Textus Receptus that are not contained in the Critical Text. "For thine is the kingdom, and the power, and the glory, for ever. Amen" (Matthew 6:13). "To repentance" (Matthew 9:13). "And be baptized with the baptism that

---

[24] Jack P. Lewis, *The English Bible From KJV to NIV: A History and Evaluation* (Grand Rapids: Baker Book House, 1981), 70.

I am baptized with" (Matthew 20:23). "And Joseph" (Luke 2:33). "But by every word of God" (Luke 4:4). "The only begotten Son" (John 1:18). "There is therefore now no condemnation to them which are in Christ Jesus" (Romans 8:1). "Through his blood" (Colossians 1:14). "God was manifest in the flesh" (1 Timothy 3:16). "I am Alpha and Omega, the first and the last: and, What thou seest" (Revelation 1:11).

In addition to the examples above, the following passages demonstrate textual differences. By comparing these passages with translations based on the Traditional Text and those based on the Critical Text, one should be able to note where the textual variant occurs.

Matthew 5:27, 44; 13:51; 15:6, 8; 19:9, 20; 20:7, 16, 22; 22:13; 23:4, 5; 25:13; 26:3, 60; 27:35; 28:2, 9

Mark 1:1, 14, 42; 3:5, 15; 6:11, 33, 36; 7:2, 8; 8:9, 26; 9:38, 45, 49; 10:7, 21, 24; 11:8, 10, 23; 12:23, 29, 30, 33; 13:11, 14; 14:19, 27, 68, 70; 15:3

Luke 1:28, 29; 2:42; 4:5, 8, 18; 5:38; 6:45; 7:31; 8:43, 45, 48, 54; 9:10, 54, 55, 56; 10:38; 11:2, 4, 11, 44, 54; 12:39; 17:9, 24; 18:24; 19:45; 20:13, 23, 30; 22:31, 64, 68; 23:23, 38; 24:1, 36, 42, 46, 51, 52

John 1:27; 3:13, 15; 5:3, 16; 6:11, 22, 47, 51; 7:46; 8:9, 10, 59; 9:6; 10:13, 26; 11:41; 12:1; 13:32; 16:16; 17:12; 19:16

Acts 2:30, 47; 3:11; 7:37; 9:5, 6; 10:6, 12, 21, 32; 13:42; 15:18, 24; 18:21; 20:15; 21:8, 22, 25; 22:9, 20; 23:9; 24:6, 8, 26; 26:30; 28:16

Romans 9:28; 10:15; 11:6; 13:9; 14:6, 21; 15:24, 29

1 Corinthians 6:20; 10:28; 11:24; 15:54

2 Corinthians 5:17; 12:9; 13:2

Galatians 3:1; 4:15; 5:19, 21

Ephesians 1:15; 3:14; 5:30

Philippians 3:16, 21; 4:23

Colossians 1:2; 2:18; 3:6

1 Thessalonians 1:1; 2:15; 3:2

1 Timothy 1:17; 3:3; 5:4, 16; 6:5, 7

Hebrews 2:7; 3:6; 7:21; 8:12; 10:30, 34; 11:11, 13; 12:20

1 Peter 1:22; 4:3, 14; 5:2, 5, 11
2 Peter 1:21; 3:10
1 John 4:3; 5:13
Revelation 1:8; 5:14; 11:1, 17; 14:5; 15:2; 21:24; 22:14, 19

There are also places where names involving deity are either lengthened or shortened, or added or removed. Most on the surface seem minor, though some have enormous significance and may affect biblical doctrine or their historical setting.

Matthew 4:12, 18, 23; 6:33; 8:3, 5, 7, 29; 9:12; 12:25; 13:36, 51; 14:14, 22, 25; 15:16, 30; 16:20; 17:11, 20; 18:2, 11; 19:17; 21:12; 22:30, 32, 37; 23:8; 24:2; 25:13; 28:6

Mark 1:1, 41; 5:13, 19, 6:34; 7:27; 8:1, 17; 9:24; 10:6, 52; 11:10, 11, 14, 15, 26; 12:27, 32, 41; 14:22, 45

Luke 2:40; 4:4, 41; 7:22, 31; 8:38; 9:43, 56, 57, 59, 60; 10:21; 12:31; 13:2, 25; 21:4; 22:31, 63; 23:42, 43; 24:36

John 3:2, 34; 4:16, 42, 46; 5:17, 30; 6:14, 39, 69; 8:1, 4, 6, 9, 10, 11, 16, 20, 21, 29; 9:35; 11:45; 13:3, 32; 16:16; 18:5; 19:38, 39

Acts 2:30; 3:26; 4:24; 7:30, 32, 37, 46; 8:37; 9:5, 6, 29; 15:11, 18; 16:31; 19:4, 10; 20:21, 25; 22:16; 23:9

Romans 1:16; 6:11; 8:1; 14:6; 15:8, 19; 16:18, 20, 24

1 Corinthians 1:14; 5:4, 5; 6:20; 9:1, 18; 10:28; 11:29; 15:47; 16:22, 23

2 Corinthians 4:6, 10; 5:18; 10:7; 11:31

Galatians 1:15; 3:17; 4:7; 6:15, 17

Ephesians 3:9, 14; 5:9

Philippians 4:13

Colossians 1:2, 28; 2:2

1 Thessalonians 1:1; 2:19; 3:11, 13

2 Thessalonians 1:8, 12; 2:4

1 Timothy 1:1; 2:7; 3:16; 5:21

2 Timothy 4:1, 22

Titus 1:4

Philemon 1:6

Hebrews 3:1; 10:9, 30
James 1:12
1 Peter 1:22; 5:10, 14
1 John 1:7; 3:16; 4:3; 5:7, 13
2 John 1:3, 9
Jude 1:4
Revelation 1:8, 9, 11; 12:17; 14:5; 16:5; 19:1; 20:9, 12; 21:3, 4; 22:21

Clearly textual evidence supports the scriptural teaching of biblical preservation. Such evidence plays a vital role in the biblical transmission process, and ultimately, in the culmination of God's preserved word today.

Chapter 2

Tampering With Texts

"I fancy that the poor fellow murmured some incoherent delirious words, and that she twisted them into this meaningless message."

-Sir Arthur Conan Doyle, *The Adventure of the Golden Pince-Nez* (1904)

The Bible warns of those who would "corrupt the word of God" (2 Corinthians 2:17) and handle it "deceitfully" (2 Corinthians 4:2). It refers to false gospels and epistles (2 Thessalonians 2:2), combined with false prophets and teachers who would seek to "make merchandise" of the true believer through "feigned words" (2 Peter 2:1-3). It did not take long for this to occur. In the days of the apostles and shortly afterwards, several doctrinal heresies arose.[25] Their beginnings are referred to in the New Testament (Galatians 1:6-8; 1 John 4:3; 2 John 1:7; and Jude 1:3-4). Such heresies plagued the early church and attempted to influence the transmission of Scripture, changing the text to fit their various doctrines whenever possible.

Gnosticism

Gnosticism was by far the most influential heresy confronting the early church. Historian Will Durant defines Gnosticism as "the quest of godlike knowledge (gnosis) through mystic means."[26] Not only did the Gnostics

---

[25] A standard text on this subject is *Heresies* by Dr. Harold O. J. Brown (New York: Doubleday & Company, Inc., 1984 edition).

[26] Will Durant, *The Story of Civilization*, vol. 3 (New York: Simon and Schuster, 1944), 604.

corrupt many readings found in the New Testament; they offered their own writings as inspired Scriptures such as the *The Gospel of Thomas*,[27] *The Gospel of the Ebionites*, *The Acts of Andrew*, and *The Gospel of Mary (Magdalene)*.[28] Gnosticism assumed a variety of forms and sects that broadened its base and growth.

---

[27] The Gospel of Thomas, perhaps the most famous of the Gnostic writings, has some very interesting teachings. It consists of the sayings of Jesus, some of which are found in the New Testament and others clearly in opposition to New Testament teaching. For example, it concludes with Christ informing Peter that Mary Magdalene (a predominate figure in Gnostic writings) will be changed into a male in order to gain eternal life: "Simon Peter said to them, 'Let Mary leave us, for women are not worthy of life.' Jesus said, 'I myself shall lead her in order to make her male, so that she too may become a living spirit resembling you males. For every woman who will make herself male will enter the kingdom of heaven'" (114). The Gospel of Thomas also has Christ teaching that the resurrection and new world have already occurred: "His disciples said to him, 'When will the repose of the dead come about, and when will the new world come?' He said to them, 'What you look forward to has already come, but you do not recognize it'" (51). The Gnostic teaching regarding the wickedness of all that is physical is also seen: "Jesus said, 'Wretched is the body that is dependent upon a body, and wretched is the soul that is dependent on these two'" (87). Additionally, this Gnostic gospel has Christ advocating slaying another with a sword (98) which is in direct contrast to the Christ of the New Testament (Matthew 26:52). It also enforces the Gnostic teaching of divine aeons in a multiplicity of gods: "Jesus said, 'Where there are three gods, they are gods. Where there are two or one, I am with him'" (30). The passages cited here were translated by Thomas O. Lambdin, *The Nag Hammadi Library In English*, ed. James M. Robinson (San Francisco: Harper San Francisco, 1988), 126-138.

[28] Many of the Gnostic Gospels were known only through second hand accounts in the writings of the church fathers. However, in 1945 an Egyptian named Muhammed Ali and his brother discovered a buried jar in a cave near the village of Nag Hammadi. Inside were old leather bound scraps of papyrus containing Gnostic writings and gospels. This finding would later be known as the Nag Hammadi Library. For the first time in almost two thousand years scholars were able to view for themselves the writings of the Gnostics.

In general, the Gnostics taught that the physical was evil and the spiritual was good. A good god could not have created a physical world because good cannot create evil. So the Gnostic god created a being (or a line of beings called *aeons*) and one of these aeons, or gods, created the world. The so-called *Christian Gnostics* believed that Jesus was one of these aeons who created the world. Some Gnostics taught that Jesus Christ did not have a physical body, and when he walked on the earth he left no footprints because he never really touched the earth (Jesus being spiritual and the world physical). Other Gnostics taught that only our spiritual bodies were important; the physical body could engage in whatever it desired because only the spiritual body would be saved. Still other Gnostics taught that the physical body was so evil, it must be denied in order for the spiritual body to gain salvation, thereby shunning marriage and the eating of meat (1 Timothy 4:1-3).

The influence of Gnosticism may be felt today. For example, the Christian Gnostics taught that Jesus Christ was an aeon, a created god who in turn created the world. To them, Christ was a begotten god from the "Unbegotten Father."[29] The Authorized Version refers to Christ as, "the only begotten Son" (John 1:18). This is a literal translation of the Greek *monogenes huios*. However, some of the Egyptian manuscripts read *monogenes theos* (the only begotten god). The change in the Greek manuscripts reflects a textual variant that also happens to agree with Gnostic

---

[29] Gregory of Nyssa, the fourth century Greek father, confounded the doctrine of the Gnostics in *Dogmatic Treatises*. He compares their teaching regarding Christ as a begotten god to their teaching that God the Father is the Unbegotten God, using the Greek word *agennetos*.

thought. It is possible that *huios* (Son) was changed to *theos* (god) to reflect Gnostic teaching.[30]

Another example of Gnostic teaching concerns the dual sexual nature of God. In her book, *The Gnostic Gospels*, Dr. Elaine Pagels notes that some Gnostics taught that God was both Father and Mother.[31] Pagels states that Clement of Alexandria was influenced by this doctrine of a "masculo-feminine" God and characterized God in both masculine and feminine terms.[32] In today's society the same thought can be found. For example, the politically correct Inclusive Version renders the Lord's Prayer as, "Our Father-Mother in heaven, hallowed be your name."[33] This is not to say that the translators of the Inclusive Version are modern-day Gnostics, nor that they were influenced by Gnostic doctrine. It is to say that the teaching of a masculo-feminine deity propagated by some Gnostics has a contemporary advocate.

Docetism, a form of Gnosticism, taught Christ was a phantom without a physical body in accordance with the sect's teaching that only the spiritual was good and the physical evil. This was the heresy of Simon Magus from the book of Acts. He taught that Jesus Christ was only an appearance

---

[30] Many ancient Christian Gnostics, or those influenced by their teachings, use the textual variant *monogenes theos*. This is the reading used by Tatian, Arius, and the followers of Valentinus, thus agreeing with their teaching that Christ was a created or begotten god. Dr. Allen Wikgren, who served on the committee producing the United Bible Societies Greek text, rejected the reading *monogenes theos* and suggests it was introduced as a primitive transcriptional error (Bruce Metzger, A Textual Commentary *On The Greek New Testament*, 2nd ed., 170). Those who opposed Gnosticism, such as Irenaeus, Tertullian, Chrysostom, and Gregory of Nyssa, cite John 1:18 as *monogenes huios*. This is consistent with other Johannine passages (John 3:16, 18, 1 John 4:9).

[31] Elaine Pagels, *The Gnostic Gospels* (New York: Vintage Books, 1979), 58-59.

[32] Ibid., 81.

[33] *New Testament and Psalms: An Inclusive Version* (New York: Oxford University Press, 1996).

of God, rejecting the orthodox teaching that Christ was God incarnate.[34] Others believed that the nature of Jesus Christ was two-fold, spiritual and physical, with Jesus being physical and "the Christ" spiritual. They believed "the Christ" departed Jesus at the crucifixion and left him on the cross to suffer and die. The *Gospel of Peter* reflects such beliefs. Although cited by Justin Martyr, Origen, and Eusebius, scholars did not discover a manuscript of this Gnostic writing until 1886. While excavating the grave of a monk in Egypt, a French archaeological team discovered a copy of this Gnostic gospel. Only a small portion of it remained, providing a conflicting account of the crucifixion than the four Gospels of the Bible. This separation of Christ from Jesus is seen in the following quotation:

And many went about with lamps, supposing that it was night: and some fell. And the Lord cried out aloud saying: My power, my power, thou hast forsaken me. And when he had so said, he was taken up. And in the same hour was the veil of the temple of Jerusalem rent in two.[35]

These Gnostics believed the power of Jesus, "the Christ," left him while he was on the cross. This may account for variants in Greek manuscripts in places such as 1 John 1:7. Some texts read "the blood of Jesus Christ" while others read "the blood of Jesus." The difference may on the surface seem minor, but when examined in light of such heresy it could reflect a major tampering. These Gnostics would not reject the reading "the blood of Jesus" because they believed Jesus shed his blood and died on the cross when "the Christ" left him. However, the phrase "Jesus Christ," which is the most common phrase used by John in his epistle, would be a direct attack on their dualistic heresy.

---

[34] Chas S. Clifton, *Encyclopedia Of Heresies And Heretics* (New York: Barnes & Noble, 1992), 118-120.

[35] M.R. James (trans.), "Gospel of Peter," *The Apocryphal New Testament* (Oxford: Clarendon Press, 1924), 5:18-20.

The following account of the resurrection in the *Gospel of Peter* is Docetic in nature. The *Gospel of Peter* reads:

> Now in the night whereon the Lord's day dawned, as the soldiers were keeping guard two by two in every watch, there came a great sound in the heaven, and they saw the heavens opened and two men descend thence, shining with a great light, and drawing near unto the sepulchre. And that stone which had been set on the door rolled away of itself and went back to the side, and the sepulchre was opened and both of the young men entered in. When therefore those soldiers saw that, they waked up the centurion and the elders (for they also were there keeping watch); and while they were yet telling them the things which they had seen, they saw again three men come out of the sepulchre, and two of them sustaining the other, and a cross following, after them. And of the two they saw that their heads reached unto heaven, but of him that was led by them that it overpassed the heavens. And they heard a voice out of the heavens saying: Hast thou (or Thou hast) preached unto them that sleep? And an answer was heard from the cross, saying: Yea.[36]

Irenaeus, an early church father who confronted various false doctrines, notes that such Gnostics used and corrected the Gospel of Mark. He wrote, "Those, again, who separate Jesus from Christ, alleging that Christ remained impassible, but that it was Jesus who suffered, preferring the Gospel by Mark, if they read it with a love of truth, may have their errors rectified."[37] The Latin manuscript *k* may reflect such tampering.[38] In Mark 16:4, *k* reads:

---

[36] Ibid., 9:34-10:42.

[37] St. Irenaeus, *Against Heresies* III:11:7.

[38] Edward F. Hills, *The King James Version Defended* (1956; reprint, Des Moines: The Christian Research Press, 1984), 166-167.

Suddenly, moreover, at the third hour of the day, darkness fell upon the whole world, and angels descended from heaven, and as the Son of God was rising in brightness, they ascended at the same time with him, and straightway it was light.[39]

This citation from *k* matches the citation from the *Gospel of Peter* concerning the resurrection.

Gnosticism influenced a second century heretic named Marcion, though he did not fully embrace its teachings. Instead, he developed his own religious following, vowing to complete the work of St. Paul and separate Judaism from Christian teachings. However, he did so in an anti-Semitic fashion. In 140 AD he went to Rome and established his doctrines, teaching that the God of the Old Testament could not have been the Father of Jesus Christ because Christ speaks of his Father as a God of love and the God of the Jews was a God of wrath. Marcion taught that Jehovah, the God of the Old Testament, created the world but that all created flesh was evil. A greater god, claimed Marcion, created the soul. This other god also created the spiritual realm and was the true Father of Jesus Christ. To release man's soul from his flesh, this greater god sent Christ, who appeared as a thirty-year-old male in an unreal-spiritual body and not a physical one. Salvation was gained by renouncing Jehovah and all things physical.

Marcion rejected the Hebrew Scriptures and their quotations in the New Testament. The followers of Marcion issued their own New Testament composed of Luke and Paul's letters. This may account for some of the variations in these books among the manuscripts; followers of Marcion would want these books to reflect their doctrines.[40] Irenaeus

---

[39] The Latin text of *k* reads, "*Subito autem ad horam tertiam tenebrae diei factae sunt per totum orbem terrae, et descenderunt de caelis angeli et surgent in claritate vivi Dei simul ascenderunt cum eo, et continuo lux facta est.*"

[40] Brown, 60-68.

wrote "Marcion cut up that according to [the Gospel of] Luke."[41] This would account for the numerous changes found in varying manuscripts of Luke and the large number of verses omitted. It is, for example, understandable why the sentence "And when he had thus spoken, he shewed them his hands and his feet" (Luke 24:40) would be omitted by Marcion. After all, he did not believe in the physical resurrection of Jesus but only in a spiritual resurrection.[42]

Jesus taught that a corrupt tree will produce corrupt fruit (Matthew 7:17). He was speaking of false prophets and teachers who corrupt the Scriptures (2 Peter 2:1-3). We are told we can recognize them by their fruits. An apple tree produces apples and a fig tree brings forth figs. The fruit of the false prophet is false prophecies and the fruit of the false teacher is false doctrine. If a man's doctrine is suspected of being corrupt, we must conclude that he will corrupt the Scriptures (2 Corinthians 2:17). In the transmission of Scripture, we must understand that there will always be a line of perversion just as there will be of preservation. According to our Lord, we must become "fruit inspectors." The remainder of this chapter and the next will demonstrate both lines in operation.

Tatian (110-180 AD)

Tatian, a disciple of Justin Martyr, was a doctrinal apologist and second century textual scholar. In 170 AD, he produced a harmony of the Gospels called the *Diatessaron* (Gk. *through the four*). It is thought that this harmony was written in Greek and translated into Syriac, but it is possible that it was originally written in Syriac. The Bishop of Syria,

---

[41] Irenaeus, III:11:7. Some translate the phrase as, "But Marcion, mutilating that according to Luke…"

[42] Both Marcion and Codex D05 omit this verse. This verse is also omitted from the text of the New English Bible (NEB) and the Revised Standard Version (RSV). Therefore, we see that Codex D05 and the RSV may reflect some of the tampering done by Marcion and his followers.

Theodoret, thought it so corrupt that he had all two hundred known copies destroyed. Today, we only have a fragment of Tatian's *Diatessaron* along with two Arabic translations and a commentary.

After the death of Justin Martyr, Tatian fell under the influence of Gnosticism.[43] Several details about Tatian's heresy are recorded by the church fathers Irenaeus and Eusebius. Irenaeus testifies that Tatian:

> ...composed his own peculiar type of doctrine. He invented a system of certain invisible Aeons, like the followers of Valentinus; while, like Marcion and Saturninus, he declared that marriage was nothing else than corruption and fornication.[44]

Eusebius quotes Irenaeus' testimony and adds that Tatian:

> ...formed a certain combination and collection of the Gospels, I know not how, to which he gave the title Diatessaron, and which is still in the hands of some. But they say that he ventured to paraphrase certain words of the apostle, in order to improve their style.[45]

Tatian's harmony does not contain verses such as Matthew 21:44; Luke 23:17; 24:12; and John 7:53-8:11. However, since we do not have the original *Diatessaron,* it is hard to say how much influence the *Diatessaron* had on any line of manuscript. Nevertheless, with Tatian and his *Diatessaron* we see the influence of Gnosticism, which may have tainted the transmission of Scripture within the first hundred years of the completion of the New Testament.

---

[43] Norman Geisler and William Nix, *A General Introduction to the Bible,* rev. ed. (Chicago: Moody Press, 1986), 425.

[44] Irenaeus, I:28.

[45] Eusebius, *Ecclesiastical History,* IV:29.

Clement Of Alexandria (150-215 AD)

Titus Flavius Clement was born of pagan parents in Athens, Greece. He was influenced by Christian doctrine, yet held that God inspired the Greek poets in a diminutive sense. He went to Alexandria, Egypt where he became head of the Catechetical School in about 200 AD. A few years later he was forced to leave Egypt under the persecution of the Roman Emperor Septimius Severus. He died in Cappadocia around 215 AD.

There are approximately twenty-four hundred New Testament quotations by Clement in his writings. Dr. Alexander Souter, a textual scholar of the early twentieth century, noted that Clement did not quote Scripture very carefully, and that his Greek text was closely related to Codex D.[46] Dr. Kurt Aland, a prominent textual critic, stated that Clement's citations disagree with the Traditional Text fifty-six percent of the time. Twenty-four percent of the time his citations agree with the Alexandrian line of manuscripts and twenty-nine percent they agree with both. Only fifteen percent of the time does Clement choose the reading of the Traditional Text.[47]

We have already learned that Clement was influenced by the Gnostics in his view of God as both Father and Mother. In *The Instructor (Paedagogus),* written about 202 AD, Clement reveals several other questionable beliefs. He accepted some books from the Old Testament Apocrypha, such as Baruch, as divinely inspired Scripture.[48] He also believed in the divinity of man, agreeing with Heraclitus that men are gods.[49] Protestants would certainly reject the notion of divine inspiration

---

[46] Alexander Souter, *The Text and Canon of the New Testament* (New York: Charles Scribner's Sons, 1917), 81.

[47] Kurt Aland, "The Text of the Church," *Trinity Journal* (Fall, 1987), 139.

[48] St. Clement, *The Instructor*, II:3:2.

[49] Ibid., III:1:4.

attributed to apocryphal books, and both Catholic and Protestant believers would reject the doctrine of the dual sexual nature of God and the mistaken belief that man has the ability to become a god himself.

Origen (185-254 AD)

When Clement left Alexandria because of persecution, Origen succeeded him as headmaster at the Catechetical School. Origen developed the allegorical interpretation of Scripture. He interpreted most of the Bible symbolically. Yet, passages that are clearly symbolic he interpreted literally.[50] As a textual scholar he produced the *Hexapla,* a Bible containing six translations of the Old Testament including the famous Septuagint. He considered the Old Testament Apocrypha inspired Scripture and included it in his *Hexapla*. Additionally, Origen accepted some books from the New Testament Apocrypha as canonical, such as *The Shepherd of Hermas* and *The Epistle of Barnabas.*

Historian Will Durant notes that Origen held to some heresies of his own. Origen rejected the literal interpretation of Scripture, questioned the truthfulness of the book of Genesis, and was skeptical of the fall of man. When the Old Testament depicts certain attributes of God, such as his divine wrath and judgment, Origen explained these away as merely symbolic. Likewise, he did not consider the temptations of Christ as literal temptations, but as symbolic truths.[51] In his work, *De Principiis*, Origen said that he could not determine if the Holy Ghost was born or innate, or if the Holy Spirit is to be considered a Son of God.[52] He believed Christ

---

[50] For example, upon reading Matthew 19:12, it is said he castrated himself. The passage in Matthew reads, "For there are some eunuchs, which were so born from their mother's womb: and there are some eunuchs, which were made eunuchs of men: and there be eunuchs, which have made themselves eunuchs for the kingdom of heaven's sake. He that is able to receive it, let him receive it."

[51] Durant, 614.

[52] St. Origen, *De Principiis*, Preface, 4.

was unable to see the Father.[53] He claimed that those who were in hell could be restored.[54] Origen also suggests that the sun, moon, and stars were living beings.[55] It is clear that he was a man of questionable doctrine, and on three different occasions his orthodoxy was challenged (300 AD, 400 AD, and 550 AD).[56] Ultimately he was considered a heretic, which may explain why so many of his writings have perished.

Someone with the same belief system as Origen would not be our first choice in revising or editing our Bibles for fear that such views may taint the translation. Nevertheless, Origen's position as a textual critic is unquestionable. He was one of the most prolific writers of his day, writing over six thousand letters and books. In his writings he makes almost eighteen thousand quotations and allusions from the New Testament. Dr. Aland showed that Origen's scriptural citations are mostly Alexandrian.[57]

Eusebius (263-340 AD)

Eusebius Pamphili, Bishop of Caesarea, was a church historian and textual critic responsible for writing *The Ecclesiastical History* in 325 AD. His work details what was occurring in the early church, especially during the canonization of Scripture. However, as noted by historian Will Durant, Eusebius sometimes glossed over some facts, a tendency shown in his *Life of Constantine*. Durant calls Eusebius' technique "honest dishonesty" and points out that from reading the biography, one

---

[53] Ibid., 1:1:8.

[54] Ibid., 2:10:3.

[55] Ibid., Preface, 10.

[56] W. A. Jurgens, *The Faith of the Early Fathers* (Collegeville, MN: The Liturgical Press, 1970), 189.

[57] Aland, 139. Further, we can see the influence Origen had on other manuscripts. One of the subscriptions in Codex Sinaiticus states, "Taken and corrected according to the Hexapla of Origen. Antonius collated: I, Pamphilus, corrected." Pamphilus, along with Eusebius, was a disciple of Origen. Therefore, we see the influence Origen had on Codex Sinaiticus as stated in a footnote of that codex.

would never suspect that Constantine had killed his son, his nephew, and his wife.[58] The same sort of exaggerations crept into Eusebius' account of early Christian martyrs.[59]

Eusebius produced a form of the Gospels, dividing them into paragraphs and numbering them for cross-reference (they were not divided as we have chapter and verse divisions today in our Bibles).[60] Concerning the canon of Scripture, Eusebius questioned the authenticity of James, 2 Peter, 2 and 3 John, and the book of Jude.[61]

Emperor Constantine ordered Eusebius to produce fifty copies of the Bible. Constantine stated these copies were to "be written on prepared parchment in a legible manner."[62] Some have suggested that the famous manuscripts Vaticanus and Sinaiticus were two of these fifty copies. These two manuscripts provide the basis of many of the changes in modern translations today. This was the view of Constantin Tischendorf, F. John A. Hort, and Alexander Souter as they commented on the subject.[63] If this is true, Eusebius not only produced the famous Alexandrian manuscripts; he also advocated a text-type that supports this same line of manuscripts. From the many citations of Eusebius, it is certain that he did favor the Alexandrian family.

There should be little doubt that the views and textual changes of Origen found their way into the textual work of Eusebius. Eusebius was the student of Pamphilus (hence the name "Eusebius Pamphili" by which the former was known in ancient times). Together they founded a library at Caesarea consisting of biblical and patristic writings plus Origen's

---

[58] Durant, 663.

[59] Ibid., 649.

[60] Bruce M. Metzger, *The Text Of The New Testament*, 3rd ed. (New York: Oxford University Press, 1992), 24.

[61] Geisler and Nix, 294. Here the authors have provided a chart listing several of the church fathers and books they considered canonical or not.

[62] Ibid., 181.

[63] Souter, 22-23.

works. Pamphilus was the student of Origen while he was in Alexandria. We can see a direct line from Origen to Eusebius and his work in early textual criticism.

Jerome (340-420 AD)

Sophronius Eusebius Hieronymus, known as St. Jerome, was responsible for producing the Latin Vulgate. Pope Damasus requested Jerome to produce a new Latin Version of the Old and New Testaments in 383 AD. Jerome reluctantly agreed, knowing his version would not be welcomed since Christendom had already begun to divide itself as to which line of manuscript and which translation best reflected the original autographs. In 405 AD, Jerome finished the Latin Vulgate and gave the Roman Catholic Church its official Latin Bible.

Most textual scholars believe that Jerome revised the Old Latin manuscripts according to his knowledge of Hebrew and Greek.[64] However, we do not possess many Latin versions which predate the Vulgate of Jerome and what we do have are fragmentary. The vast majority of Old Latin manuscripts we now have were written after the Vulgate and are divided into two groups, *African* and *European*.

Jerome was influenced by the work of Eusebius. Dr. Souter believed that we must look to Egypt for the origin of Codex Sinaiticus, which he claimed was produced by Eusebius. While in Bethlehem, Jerome had a Greek manuscript that was closely related to Sinaiticus.[65] In like manner, Sir Frederic Kenyon noted that the Greek manuscript conspicuously agreeing with Jerome's Latin Vulgate is Sinaiticus,[66] again demonstrating the influence the Alexandrian textual line had on Jerome. However, it

---

[64] Jerome was one of the first scholars to be fluent in both biblical languages.

[65] Ibid., 23.

[66] Frederic Kenyon, *The Story of the Bible* (1936; reprint, Grand Rapids: Eerdmans, 1967), 110.

should be noted that Jerome was willing to reach a compromise and not make as many changes to the text as one finds in the Alexandrian line. Kenyon also notes that Jerome left the Old Latin readings standing whenever possible.[67] The Latin Vulgate produced by Jerome contains several readings that support the Traditional Text because they were originally in the Old Latin manuscripts.[68]

Tischendorf (1815-1874 AD)

Constantin von Tischendorf is responsible for providing the Protestant world with two of the oldest known uncials, Codex Vaticanus (also listed as Codex B) and Codex Sinaiticus (also listed as Codex Aleph). These two manuscripts date between 325 and 350 AD. Codex Vaticanus and Codex Sinaiticus are two of the best examples of the Alexandrian line of manuscripts, and are responsible for numerous changes found in modern Bible versions. These two manuscripts formed the basis for the Greek text later produced by Westcott and Hort, a work that was the foundation for the Critical Greek Text.[69]

Tischendorf edited more New Testament editions and documents than any other scholar of his day.[70] By the age of twenty-nine he had already produced three editions of the Greek New Testament. Believing the Alexandrian line of manuscripts reflected the better readings, Tischendorf set off in search of additional manuscripts.

In 1844, he visited the monastery of St. Catherine located at Mt. Sinai. While there he saw several leaves of a manuscript written on vellum lying in a basket ready to be destroyed. The monks would burn such leaves to warm themselves. Tischendorf, desiring to save the manuscript, was

---

[67] Ibid.

[68] Hills, 187.

[69] Donald Guthrie, "Text and Versions," David Alexander and Pat Alexander, eds., *Eerdmans' Handbook to the Bible*, (Grand Rapids: Eerdmans, 1973), 73.

[70] Souter, 102.

allowed to keep forty-three leaves. The manuscript, which contained the Greek Septuagint, was recognized by Tischendorf to be of the same textual line as Codex Alexandrinus. However, this manuscript was about a hundred years older. A second visit to the monastery occurred in 1853 with nothing found. On his third visit in 1859, Tischendorf was shown the codex that is now known as Sinaiticus. He was denied custody of the manuscript at that time. He went to Cairo to speak to the Superior who granted him the codex. It was not until nine months later, after Tischendorf paid a good sum, that he was given the codex.[71] Codex Sinaiticus contains over half of the Old Testament and almost all of the New Testament except for large passages such as Mark 16:9-20 and John 7:53-8:11, along with several other verses. It has the Old Testament Apocrypha laced within it as Scripture and the New Testament apocryphal books of the *Epistle of Barnabas* and the *Shepherd of Hermas*.

Codex Vaticanus, known to have been in the Vatican Library since 1475, receives its name because it is the property of the Vatican. No Protestant scholars were permitted to view this codex for four hundred years until Rome produced a facsimile in 1890. There were two exceptions to this rule: S. P. Tregelles, who viewed it in 1845 and reproduced a memorized copy of it, and Tischendorf who viewed it between 1843 and 1866. Vaticanus is missing Genesis 1:1-46:28; 2 Kings 2:5-7, 10-13; Psalm 106:27-138:6; Mark 16:9-20; John 7:53-8:11; and everything after Hebrews 9:14.

Westcott & Hort

Brooke Foss Westcott (1825-1901) and Fenton John Anthony Hort (1828-1892) produced a Greek New Testament in 1881 based on the

---

[71] Kenyon, 57-58.

findings of Tischendorf. This Greek New Testament was the basis for the Revised Version (RV) of that same year, and later for the American Standard Version of 1901. They also developed a theory of textual criticism used as a basis for their Greek New Testament and several other Greek New Testaments since (such as the Nestle-Aland and United Bible Societies' texts). Greek New Testaments such as these are the basis for most contemporary English translations of the Bible. Therefore, it is important for us to know the theory of Westcott and Hort as well as something about the two men who have so greatly influenced modern textual criticism.

In short, the Westcott and Hort theory states that the Bible is to be treated as any other book. When textual variants occur, the harder reading is usually considered the correct reading instead of the easier. They also believed the shorter reading among textual variants is most likely the original reading. The Alexandrian textual line tends to contain shorter readings, as well as the more difficult ones. Therefore, they considered this textual line to most likely reflect the original. Using these theories, the Bible is approached as a naturalistic book without divine intervention preserving the text from corruption.[72]

Westcott and Hort believed the Greek text underlining the King James Version was perverse and corrupt. Hort called the Textus Receptus "vile" and "villainous."[73] They believed the Traditional Text did not exist until the fourth century and was created by Lucian of Antioch, under the authority of a church council, to unify the Western and Alexandrian textual lines. This mixing of the two lines, and filling them with additional texts, is called conflation.

---

[72] B. F. Westcott and F. J. A. Hort, *The New Testament in the Original Greek* (2 vols.; London: Macmillan and Co. Ltd., 1881), II, 280-281.

[73] *The Life and Letters of Fenton John Anthony Hort*, vol. 1 (London: Macmillan), 211.

There are several problems with this theory of a Lucian recension (that Lucian conflated the Western and Alexandrian texts to produce the Traditional Text). First, many citations of the early church fathers reflect the Traditional Text with the "fuller readings" long before the fourth century. Second, there is no evidence that there ever was a council or even a conference of scholars in Antioch to produce this *conflated* text.[74] Even Kenyon, who supported the Critical Text, noted that we know the names of several of the revisers of the Septuagint and the Latin Vulgate. It seemed unbelievable to him that such a council could have taken place without *any* historical record whatsoever.[75] Third, God told us not to add to his word. If the Traditional Text has added to God's word, why has it been so greatly used in the history of the church?

As the fathers of modern textual criticism, should we not know something of the beliefs of Westcott and Hort? Westcott denied biblical infallibility.[76] Hort stated that those who believed in biblical authority were perverted.[77] Hort taught that Revelation 3:15 proclaimed Christ was the first thing created, agreeing with the Gnostic teaching that Christ was a begotten god.[78] Westcott denied that Saint John ever claimed Christ to be God.[79] Hort stated that the ransom for our sin was paid to Satan.[80] Both

---

[74] Wilbur N. Pickering, *The Identity of the New Testament Text* (Nashville: Thomas Nelson Publishers, 1977), 37-38.

[75] Frederic Kenyon, *Handbook to the Textual Criticism of the New Testament* (Grand Rapids: Eerdmans, 1912) 302.

[76] Arthur Westcott, *The Life and Letters of Brooke Foss Westcott*, vol. 1 (London: Macmillan, 1903), 207.

[77] Hort, 400.

[78] F. J. A. Hort, *The Apocalypse of St. John 1-3: The Greek Text with Introduction, Commentary, and Additional Notes* (1908; reprint, Minneapolis: James and Klock Publishing, 1976), 36.

[79] B. F. Westcott, *The Gospel According to St. John: The Authorized Version with Introduction and Notes* (1881; reprint, Grand Rapids: Eerdmans, 1975), 297.

[80] F. J. A. Hort, *The First Epistle of St. Peter 1:1-2:17: The Greek Text with Introductory Lecture, Commentary, and Additional Notes* (1898; reprint, Minneapolis: James and Klock Publishing, 1976), 77.

men denied the doctrine of eternal damnation, stating hell is not a place of punishment.[81] These beliefs stand in direct opposition to the teachings of the New Testament and should be carefully considered when those who hold to such beliefs suggest changes in the New Testament. No matter how careful or unbiased a scholar may be, it is the nature of man to slant Scripture towards his understanding.

Since 1881

There have been several findings since the discovery of Vaticanus and Sinaiticus. Perhaps the most famous deals with textual criticism of the Old Testament: the discovery of the Dead Sea Scrolls. Concerning the New Testament, there is the John Rylands fragment known as P52, a Greek manuscript which some date between 117 and 138 AD. It was discovered in Egypt and contains five verses from the gospel of John. It now resides at the John Rylands Library in Manchester, England. There is also some controversy concerning P64 and its redating to before 66 AD. There is even the possibility that New Testament fragments have been discovered among the Dead Sea Scrolls (7Q4 and 7Q5).[82]

Sir Alfred Chester Beatty discovered several papyrus manuscripts known as P45, P46, and P47. They date to the second and third centuries, and demonstrate a mixed text revealing both Alexandrian and Byzantine readings. P46, however, has recently been argued by some to date to the last half of the first century, around 85 AD.[83] The same may be said of the findings of M. Martin Bodmer concerning P66, P72, and P75. These manuscripts traditionally date around the third century. P66, however, has

---

[81] B. F. Westcott, *The Historic Faith* (London: Macmillan, 1885), 77-78. Hort, *Life and Letters*, 149.

[82] Jose O'Callaghan, a noted textual scholar and Qumran authority, maintains that 7Q5 is that of Mark 6:52-53. More information regarding this can be found in *Journal of Biblical Literature* 91 (1972), 1-14.

[83] Young Kyu Kim, "Palaeographical Dating of P46 to the Later First Century," *Biblica*, lxix (1988), 248-257.

been redated by some to the first half of the second century.[84] If the redating of all these texts holds true it lends support to the thought that most textual changes occurred before 200 AD. It also could suggest that the Alexandrian text-type was in an evolutionary stage only to be fully developed by the fourth century. In either case, we see that the earliest manuscripts reveal a mixed text containing both Alexandrian and Byzantine readings.

No one would demand that each and every scholar, theologian, textual critic, and church historian agree on everything as it relates to Bible doctrine. But, when we find early heresies mixed with present day false teachings, it should cause us some concern. The concern should intensify when we discover that many who have influenced biblical transmission held such heresies. At the very least, their influence should be called into question. After all, do we really want to trust the safe keeping of Holy Scripture with those who have proven themselves to be corrupt in regard to biblical doctrine?

---

[84] Herbert Hunger, "Zur Datierung des Papyrus Bodmer II (P66)," *Anzeiger der Osterreichischen Akademie der Wissenschaften*, phil.-hist. Kl., 1960, Nr. 4, 12-33.

Chapter 3

Testimony Through Time

"A word is dead
When it is said,
Some say.
I say it just
Begins to live
That day."

-Emily Dickinson, (1872)

The Church at Antioch has a noteworthy position in Scripture as the first place believers were called Christians (Acts 11:26). It is also interesting that where both Antioch and Alexandria are mentioned in the same passage, Antioch is listed as a place of service and Alexandria as a place of disruption (Acts 6:5-10). Could it be that God, who foreknows all things, provides for us our starting point in searching for the original text? If so, the direction would not be in Alexandria, Egypt. Instead, it would be in the cradle of New Testament Christianity at Antioch of Syria, where the Traditional Text originated.

Ignatius (d. 107 AD)

Ignatius (or Theophorus) was the bishop of Antioch, Syria. Because of his Christian testimony, he was arrested and sent to Rome to be martyred by wild beasts in the imperial games. En route to his martyrdom this saint wrote letters to six different churches (Ephesians, Magnesians,

Trallians, Romans, Philadelphians, and Smyrnaeans), as well as one letter to Polycarp.

Ignatius was sound both in doctrine and spirit. Traditionally it is
claimed that he knew several of the apostles personally and sought to follow their examples. The Apostle Paul wrote, "Wherefore I beseech you, be
ye followers of me" (1 Corinthians 4:16). Ignatius lived this admonition.
He patterned his life after Paul's, and his theology and attitude reflect his
closeness with the Apostle John. Like John, Ignatius proclaimed the
Trinity and deity of Jesus Christ. He states that Christians should be
found "in the Son, and in the Father and in the Holy Ghost" (*Magnesians*
13:1)[85] and refers to Christ as "our God" (*Trallians* 7:1). Concerning biblical atonement, he writes:

> Let no man deceive himself. Both the things which are in heaven,
> and the glorious angels, and rulers, both visible and invisible, if
> they believe not in the blood of Christ, shall, in consequence,
> incur condemnation. (*Smyrnaeans* 6:1).

Ignatius reflects a Christian attitude in regard to others and rejects the
anti-Semitism of Marcion and Origen. Ignatius agrees with Scripture and
crumbles the walls of racism in a day when the Jews were despised by the
Gentile nations.[86]

Sadly, the scriptural citations made by Ignatius are often ignored or
regarded as unimportant in the study of textual criticism. Dr. Alexander

---

[85] Alexander Roberts and James Donaldson, *The Ante-Nicene Fathers* (The Master
Christian Library: Ages Software, Version 7). It should be noted that there are various
editions and translations of the early church fathers. Another source is that of Archbishop
Wake as presented in *The Lost Books of the Bible* (World Publishers). The references substantially differ, but the translation is essentially the same.

[86] This is clearly revealed in *The Epistle of Ignatius to the Smyraeans*: "From whom we
also derive our being, from his divinely-blessed passion, that He might set up a standard
for the ages, through his resurrection, to all his holy and faithful [followers], whether
among Jews or Gentiles, in the one body of his Church" (1:2).

Souter wrote that Ignatius' citations hardly have any bearing in respect to textual variants.[87] With such statements the writings of Ignatius are dismissed. Perhaps this is because the biblical citations used by this early church father support the Traditional Text. When we look at his writings, we find that he made several quotations from and allusions to Scripture.[88] It is true that he does not cite word for word; however, it should be remembered that he was not writing a theological dissertation. He was on his way to be martyred, most likely citing Scriptures from memory. Yet, it is clear from these citations that the text of Ignatius agrees with the Traditional Text.

A textual variant of great importance is found in 1 Timothy 3:16. The King James Version reads, "God was manifest in the flesh." Most contemporary versions, using the Alexandrian Text, read, "He was manifest in the flesh." There is an obvious difference between *He* and *God*. The KJV makes a clear proclamation concerning the deity of Jesus Christ. Ignatius apparently used a text that reflected the reading found in the KJV. He writes, "There is one Physician who is possessed both of flesh and spirit; both made and not made; God existing in flesh" (*Ephesians* 7:1) and "God Himself being manifested in human form" (*Ephesians* 19:1). Ignatius uses the Greek words for *God* (*theos*) and for *flesh* (*sarki*) in the first citation, and a form of the Greek word for *manifest* (*peanerosas*) in the second. This would agree with the Greek found in the Traditional Text.

It is also interesting to read the phraseology of Ignatius in reference to the person of Jesus Christ. Consistently he refers to the Second Person of the Trinity as the "Lord Jesus Christ," or "our God Jesus Christ," or the more often used phrase, "Jesus Christ." Very rarely do we find "Jesus" or

---

[87] Alexander Souter, *The Text And Canon Of The New Testament* (New York: Charles Scribner's Sons, 1917), 76.

[88] Norman Geisler and William Nix, *A General Introduction to the Bible*, rev. ed. (Chicago: Moody Press, 1986), 100.

"Christ" by themselves in his writings. This would demonstrate a *fuller text* concerning divine titles that we also find consistently used in the Traditional Text of the New Testament.

Polycarp (70 to 155 AD)

Polycarp was the Bishop of Smyrna and traditionally is considered a disciple of the Apostle John.[89] In 155 AD Polycarp was martyred for his faith in Jesus Christ. It is said that he was first placed at the stake to be burned, singing hymns while waiting for the fire to devour him. However, the fire burned around him but did not consume him. The order was then given to stab him to death and burn his remains.

The witness of Polycarp is important in the study of textual criticism for the following reasons. First, he makes about sixty New Testament citations in his one letter, *Polycarp to the Philippians*. Over half of these are citations from Paul's epistles, showing his acquaintance with the apostle and the acceptance of Paul's letters as Scripture. Second, he was a contemporary of the apostles and would have had access to either their original writings or copies that were written shortly after the originals. Third, his biblical citations do not differ with the Traditional Text; instead they support it.

Most of what Polycarp writes deals with Christian living. He states his profession of faith early in his letter: "forasmuch as ye know that it is by grace ye are saved, not by works, but by the will of God through Jesus Christ" (*Philippians* 1:3). And, "He that raised Him from the dead will raise us also" (*Philippians* 2:2). Further, he makes a good profession and stands against the dualism of the Gnostics in stating:

---

[89] Earle E. Cairns, *Christianity Through the Centuries* (1954; reprint, Grand Rapids: Zondervan, 1976), 79.

For every one who shall not confess that Jesus Christ is come in the flesh, is antichrist: and whosoever shall not confess the testimony of the Cross, is of the devil; and whosoever shall pervert the oracles of the Lord to his own lusts and says that there is neither resurrection nor judgment, that man is the first-born of Satan. (*Philippians* 7:1).

The biblical quotation Polycarp uses to confront Gnosticism is a citation from the Traditional Text. 1 John 4:3 reads, "And every spirit that confesseth not that Jesus Christ is come in the flesh is not of God." The Alexandrian line does not contain the phrase "is come in the flesh" in verse three. The verse deals with the lack of confession, not the believer's profession found in verse two. As quoted above, Polycarp writes that "every one who shall not confess that Jesus Christ is come in the flesh," agreeing with the Traditional Text.

Some have suggested that Polycarp is really citing 2 John 1:7 and not 1 John 4:3. This does not seem to have been the view of the renowned New Testament and patristic scholar J. B. Lightfoot. In his book, *The Apostolic Fathers*,[90] Lightfoot identifies the quotation as being from 1 John 4:3, as does Archbishop Wake in his translation of Polycarp.[91] Their observations are well taken as the Greek of 1 John 4:3 more closely matches the Greek citation of Polycarp. Note the following comparisons taken from the Greek text of Polycarp and the Greek New Testament:

Reference	Greek	English Translation
1 John 4:3	*en sarki eleluthota*	*in flesh come*
Polycarp	*en sarki elelgthenai*	*in flesh come*
2 John 1:7	*erchomenon en sarki*	*coming* or *is come in flesh*

[90] J. B. Lightfoot, *The Apostolic Fathers*, (London: Macmillan, 1891) 171.

[91] Wake, *The Lost Books of The Bible and the Forgotten Books of Eden* (1927; reprint, Word Bible Publishers), 194.

1 John and Polycarp use the *perfect tense,* 2 John uses the *present tense.* The perfect tense means a present state resulting from a past action (i.e., because Christ came in the flesh, he is now in the flesh). Clearly Polycarp was citing 1 John 4:3, which matches the Traditional Text.

Another example is found in Romans 14:10, "for we shall all stand before the judgment seat of Christ." Polycarp writes "And we must all stand at the judgment-seat of Christ;" (*Philippians* 6:2), agreeing with the Traditional Text. The Alexandrian Text changes "judgment seat of Christ" to "judgment seat of God." Since this passage in Romans is the *only* passage in the New Testament that speaks of the "judgment seat of Christ," Polycarp must have received his reading from the Traditional Text.

The same may be said of the reading in Galatians 4:26, "which is the mother of us all." The Alexandrian Text reads: "and she is our mother." The Greek word *panton* (of us all) is not contained in the Alexandrian manuscripts, while it is in the majority of all Greek manuscripts. Polycarp writes "which is the mother of us all" and uses the Greek word *panton* (*Philippians* 3:3). Where did Polycarp get the phrase if not from the Traditional Text? Plainly the disciple of St. John and friend of the Apostle Paul was using a Greek text very much like the Textus Receptus.

Finally, as with Ignatius, Polycarp uses the fuller text when making reference to the Person of Jesus Christ. In his brief epistle, consisting of only four chapters, Polycarp uses the triune phrase "Lord Jesus Christ" seven times. This seems amazing since the Apostle Paul in his letter to the Philippians used the phrase only three times. However, in his letter to the Ephesians, Paul uses "Lord Jesus Christ" the same number of times as Polycarp. In this light, the thought that the multiple uses of "Lord Jesus Christ" found in the KJV were added to the New Testament text by Byzantine monks long after the apostolic age seems far-fetched. It is obvious from Polycarp that the expanded phrase was in common use at the time of the New Testament and shortly thereafter, again demonstrating a link with the Traditional Text.[92]

Early Translations

In addition to the Greek, we have many early and old translations of the Bible that are classified as Byzantine or have readings that differ from the Alexandrian Text in favor of the Traditional Text. An early translation must have had a source. If an early translation has a certain reading, and a later Greek manuscript has the same reading, we can conclude that the source for the early translation had the reading as well even if we no longer have that original Greek source. The following translations have readings that support the Traditional Text.

The Peshitta

The Peshitta (meaning *clear* or *simple*) is the standard Syrian version and was authorized by two opposing branches of the Syrian Church, the *Nestorians* and the *Jacobites*. Today the Syrian Church still holds this version in a place of special reverence.[93] Their tradition states that the Peshitta was the work of St. Mark or the Apostle Thaddeus (Jude). The Peshitta New Testament resembles the Byzantine text-type and therefore supports the Traditional Text. Alexander Souter noted that "the Peshitta Syriac rarely witnesses to anything different from what we find in the great bulk

---

[92] Dr. James R. White calls this "expansion of piety." He suggests that when these terms are found in the Traditional Text individuals added them over time as a sign of reverence: *The King James Only Controversy: Can You Trust the Modern Translations* (Minneapolis: Bethany House Publishers, 1995), 46. However, the evidence from the early fathers allows us to understand that these extended titles were in common use shortly after the completion of the New Testament and before the establishment of the Alexandrian text-type that generally shortens these titles.

[93] Kurt and Barbara Aland, *The Text Of The New Testament*, 2nd ed., trans. Erroll F. Rhodes (Grand Rapids: Eerdmans, 1989), 194.

of Greek manuscripts."[94] It should be remembered that the "great bulk of Greek manuscripts" are Byzantine.

The Peshitta was considered the oldest of the Syrian versions dating to the second century or perhaps before, although some scholars disagreed and assigned it to the first part of the fifth century.[95] In 1901, textual scholar F. C. Burkitt questioned the early date of the Peshitta and attributed the work to Rabbula, Bishop of Edessa. This soon became the standard position adopted by most textual scholars. Dr. Arthur Voobus attacked Burkitt's view and compared Rabbula's citations with the Peshitta, finding several differences. Likewise, Dr. Edward Hills argued that Rabbula could not have been the translator because the division within the Syrian Church took place during the time of Rabbula, who led one of the divisions. Yet both sides claim the Peshitta as Holy Scripture. Such unanimous acceptance would not have been likely if the leader of one side had translated it.[96] Metzger justly points out that the question as to who really produced the Peshitta will most likely never be answered.[97]

The Old Latin

The Old Latin versions are divided into two types, *African* and *European*.[98] The earliest Old Latin manuscripts in existence today date from the fourth century and onward. However, it is also thought that these later manuscripts strongly reflect the Old Latin New Testament that was in existence in the second and third centuries.

---

[94] Souter, 60.

[95] Bruce M. Metzger, *The Early Versions of the New Testament* (New York: Claredon, 1977), 36.

[96] Edward F. Hills, *The King James Version Defended* (1956; reprint, Des Moines: The Christian Research Press, 1984), 172-174.

[97] Metzger, 59-60.

[98] African manuscripts of the Old Latin include *k, e, h,* and *r*. European manuscripts of the Old Latin include *a, b, d, ff, q, f, g, m, and gig*. Dates of these and other manuscripts are listed in Appendix C.

At the beginning of the twentieth century the majority of textual scholars believed that Antioch of Syria was the birthplace of the Old Latin versions.[99] Today, they are more inclined to look to North Africa. Regardless of where the Old Latin originated, it is clear that it is strongly associated with the Syrian text-type, what we have called the Traditional Text.

An example of this may be found in Mark 1:2. The Traditional Text read, "As it is written in the prophets." The text of Mark then quotes from two prophets, Malachi (3:1) and Isaiah (40:3). The Alexandrian Text reads, "As it is written in the Prophet Isaiah" and then quotes the two prophets. The first reading is found in the King James Verson, the New King James Version and the Traditional Greek Text. It is also found in the Peshitta. Among the Old Latin manuscripts (which are usually classified with small Roman letters in italics), we find the same reading as in the Traditional Text. The reading is in *a* (fourth century), *aur* (seventh century), *b* (fifth century), *c* (twelfth century), *d* (fifth century), *f* (sixth century), *ff2* (fifth century), and *q* (seventh century).

The same is true of the longer ending of Mark and the story of the woman caught in adultery (known as the *pericope de adultera*). The Alexandrian Text does not contain Mark 16:9-20, though it is found in the majority of Greek manuscripts, the Peshitta, and almost all Old Latin manuscripts. The *pericope de adultera*, found in John 7:52-8:11, is also the reading of the Traditional Greek Text and found in the majority of Old Latin witnesses.

Other Early Versions

The Ethiopic Version is thought to have originated at the beginning of the fourth century; however, the existing manuscripts now extant date to

---

[99] Metzger, 288.

the eleventh century. While it does contain a mixed reading, it is classified as basically Byzantine in origin.[100] Likewise, the Armenian Version, Georgian Version, and the Slavonic Version are of the same textual family as the Traditional Text.[101] The Gothic Version dates to the first part of the fourth century, and was translated by Wulfilas who used the Traditional Text.[102] Thus, these early versions are more closely related to the Majority Text and the Textus Receptus than to the Critical Text.

Chrysostom (345-407 AD)

John Chrysostom was both a great biblical expositor and preacher. His parents were Christians and came from Antioch. Chrysostom began his career as a lawyer until his conversion in 368 AD. He then began to preach the gospel of Jesus Christ. He was ordained in 386 AD and preached in Antioch until 398 AD when he became the Bishop of Constantinople. The Greek New Testament he used was of the Traditional Text.

Even though Christian historian Earle Cairns describes Chrysostom as courteous, affectionate, and kindly natured,[103] Chrysostom was not ashamed to boldly proclaim the truth no matter who was offended. While at Constantinople he affronted Empress Eudoxia, the wife of Emperor Arcadius, preaching against her manner of dress and the silver statues of her placed throughout the city. Like the preaching of John the Baptist, his sermon came at a personal cost. He was banished from the city in 404 AD, and died while in exile.

Chrysostom left about six hundred forty sermons that are still in existence. He was so eloquent in his presentation of the gospel that he earned

---

[100] Ibid., 324.
[101] Ibid., 324-327.
[102] Aland, 210-212.
[103] Cairns, 152.

for himself the name Chrysostom meaning *golden mouth*, and is hailed as one of the greatest preachers of the church. Because of the massive amount of homilies left by Chrysostom, and because of his expository style of preaching, it is very easy to determine the text-type he used. Dr. Souter notes that the type of text Chrysostom used is reflected by Codex K, which is of the Byzantine line.[104] However, it should be noted that Codex K dates to the ninth century, several hundred years after Chrysostom. This demonstrates the continued use of the Traditional Text throughout the centuries.

The fact that Chrysostom used the Traditional Text is without question. An example of this may be found in his homilies on the Sermon on the Mount. In Matthew chapter 6:1-15 there are two very notable differences between the major lines of manuscripts. They are found in verses 1 and 13 and can be illustrated by comparing the King James Version with the New International Version:

Matthew 6:1 (KJV)

"Take heed that ye do not your alms before men, to be seen of them: otherwise ye have no reward of your Father which is in heaven."

Matthew 6:1 (NIV)

"Be careful not to do your 'acts of righteousness' before men, to be seen by them. If you do, you will have no reward from your Father in heaven."

The KJV uses the word "alms" (*eleemosunen*), while the NIV uses the phrase "acts of righteousness" (*dikaiosunen*). One can see from the English and the Greek that these are two different words with two different meanings. Chrysostom makes mention of this text and uses the word *alms* (*eleemosunen*). He writes, "Thus, 'take heed' saith he, 'as to your alms'"[105]

Another example may be found in what has been dubbed the Lord's Prayer. Protestants conclude the prayer with the phrase, "for thine is the

---

[104] Souter, 85.

[105] Chrysostom, *Homilies on Matthew*, XIX:5.

kingdom, and the power, and the glory, for ever." Most Roman Catholics end the prayer with the phrase, "but deliver us from evil." The Latin Vulgate of Jerome does not contain the final benediction; however, it is found in the majority of Greek manuscripts and the Traditional Text. Again, the two may be compared in our English versions this way:

Matthew 6:13 (KJV)

"And lead us not into temptation, but deliver us from evil: For thine is the kingdom, and the power, and the glory, for ever. Amen."

Matthew 6:13 (NIV)

"And lead us not into temptation, but deliver us from the evil one."

In this same sermon, Homily XIX, Chrysostom cites the passage as found in the Traditional Text and then expounds on the words *kingdom*, *power*, and *glory*. This would be rather difficult to do if his Bible did not contain them.

The Three Cappadocian Fathers

John Chrysostom was not alone in his use of the Traditional Text. Basil of Caesarea (329-379 AD), Gregory of Nazianzus (330-389 AD), and Gregory of Nyssa (330-395 AD) used the same text. These three saints are known as the *Cappadocian Fathers*. They are noted for their strength in doctrine and opposition to the heresy of Arianism, which denied the Trinity. All three are associated with the Orthodox Church of Constantinople.

The Greek and Old Latin manuscripts used by these men reflect the text of the traditional line. Dr. Souter states that their Greek text most likely originated in Constantinople.[106] Souter also lists the Gospel manuscripts of N, O, S, and F as reflecting the textual line of these three church fathers.[107] These manuscripts (N, O, S, and F) are from the sixth century and represent the Traditional Text.

---

[106] Souter, 9.

[107] Souter, 30.

The following examples help to demonstrate the text-type used by the Cappadocian Fathers. In Matthew 17:21 the Alexandrian Text does not contain the verse. But the verse is found in the Traditional Text and is quoted by the Cappadocian Fathers. In Mark 1:2 we find the reading "Isaiah the prophet" in the Alexandrian Text. The Traditional Text and the Cappadocian Fathers render the passage as "prophets." In Mark 16:9-20, the longer ending is not contained in the Alexandrian Text but found in the Traditional Text and in the Greek of the Cappadocian Fathers. In Luke 2:14 the Alexandrian Text has the phrase "men of goodwill." The Traditional Text and the Cappadocian Fathers render it as "good will toward men." In John 5:4 the Alexandrian Text does not contain the verse. Nevertheless, it is found in the Traditional Text and the Greek text of the Cappadocian Fathers.

The Church Under Fire

Throughout the centuries there have been those strong in the faith that were willing to suffer and die for the cause of Christ. John Foxe, in his *Acts and Monuments* (later called *Foxe's Book of Martyrs*), recorded the bravery and honor with which many of them met death. Those who persecuted them also left written records, often accepted by later historians, which stigmatized the persecuted as "heretics." Among those groups of Christians who suffered were the Paulicians, the Bogomiles, the Anabaptists, the Waldenses, and the Albigenses. They are mentioned here because they used the Traditional Text or a translation that reflected the readings found in the Traditional Text.

Most were labeled as heretics in order to justify their mass murder. A case in point would be the Albigenses, so named because they originated in southern France near the old city of Albiga. To this date, they are listed in most histories of the church as a heretical sect that practiced dualism. It has been claimed that the Albigenses believed in two gods, one good and the other evil. This is not the case. American Baptist historian Dr. Henry

C. Vedder demonstrated that the Albigenses were never dualistic but were Bible-believing Christians. Those who persecuted them did not theologically distinguish between the Albigenses and heretics who were dualists. Actually, the Albigenses opposed the dualists as much as they did the Roman church.[108]

The true "heresy" of these French believers was that they would not conform to Rome. They believed each Christian had the right to read the Bible for himself in his own language. Pope Innocent III declared war on them and began the infamous Inquisition. This cruel war on "heretics" claimed the lives of countless thousands without formal trials or hearings.[109] In this dark period of church history, unnamed thousands died because they wished to place the Bible into the hands of the common man.

Some Catholic historians and theologians today, while opposing the deeds of the Inquisition, argue that there was no need for the Bible to be translated into the language of the common man during this time because most could not read.[110] They further state that since those who could read did so in Latin, there was no need to have any other translation other than Jerome's Latin Vulgate. This by no means justifies the mass torture and murder of thousands of people. Besides, it overlooks several simple truths. First, because someone could not read would not prevent a person from wanting a Bible in his or her own language. It is possible that someone else could have read it to him or her. Second, if there had been only Latin Bibles, those who could not understand Latin would have been without hope of ever hearing the word of God in their own language. Third, history shows that once the Bible is translated into the language of the peo-

---

[108] Henry C. Vedder, *A Short History of the Baptists* (1907; reprint, Valley Forge: The Judson Press, 1969), 103.

[109] Edward Peter, *Inquistion* (The Free Press; 1988), 50.

[110] See Henry G. Graham, *Where We Got the Bible: Our Debt to the Catholic Church*, 22nd ed. (Rockford, IL: Tan Books and Publishers, 1987) or Charles M. Carty and L. Rumble, *Bible Quizzes to a Street Preacher* (Rockford, IL: Tan Books and Publishers, 1976).

ple, the people learn to read. Time and again the Bible has been the basic textbook for individuals to learn their own language in written form.

Another example of persecution concerns the Waldenses, who are often linked in history with the Albigenses. Some have suggested that the name Waldenses came from Peter Waldo, a Bible-believing merchant turned preacher. Others believe the name comes from the Italian or Spanish word for *valley*, implying they originated in the valley region of northern Italy. Regardless of where they derived their name, they strongly stood against many teachings of the Roman Catholic Church of that day.

Catholic and Orthodox historians David Knowles and Dimitri Obolensky call the Waldenses proto-Protestants. This group regarded the Bible as their supreme authority in all matters of practice and faith. They did not believe the Eucharist contained the literal body and blood of Jesus Christ. Instead, they viewed it as a symbolic memorial of Christ's suffering for redemption.[111] They proclaimed salvation was not by works, but was the free gift of God. Baptism for the Waldenses followed conversion and was not administered to infants. The Waldenses copied and translated the Bible in the vernacular and freely published their translation, believing that everyone should have the Bible in their own language.[112] Therefore, their work in using the Traditional Text and providing indigenous translations must not go unnoticed in the biblical study of textual criticism.

Because of the Albigenses, the Waldenses, and others, the Bible was translated into Old French, Old High German, Slavonic, Old and Middle English, and other languages. One such translation that dates from this period is the West Saxon Gospels. This is the oldest version of the Gospels in English. The following example from Luke shows that this version followed the Traditional Text (or a Latin manuscript of the Traditional Text).

---

[111] David Knowles and Dimitri Obolensky, *The Christian Centuries*, vol. 2 (Paulist Press, 1969), 224, 369.

[112] Cairns, 248.

Luke 15:16 (KJV)
"And he would fain have filled his belly with the husks that the swine
did eat: and no man gave unto him."
Luke 15:16 (RSV)
"And he would gladly have fed on the pods that the swine ate, and no
one gave him anything."
Luke 15:16 (West Saxon Version)
"Da gewilnode he his wambe gelyllan of pam beancoddum be oa swyn
aeton: and him man ne sealde."

The subtle difference comes from the variance between the two lines
of manuscripts. The Greek Textus Receptus reads, *gemisai ten koilian
autou apo* (to fill his belly with). The Critical Text reads *chortasthenai ek*
(fed out of). P75, Vaticanus, and Sinaiticus support the reading of the
Critical Text. All the Byzantine manuscripts, most Old Latin manuscripts, the Peshitta, and the Armenian support the Textus Receptus. It
is plain from the reading of the West Saxon Gospels which one they follow. The words "wambe gefyllan" mean "stomach filled" and agrees
with the Traditional Text.

To date we have over five thousand Greek manuscripts of the New
Testament. Eighty to ninety percent of these Greek manuscripts support
the Traditional Text.[113] The agreement within this vast host of manuscripts
is astounding (especially when compared to the tremendous amount of
disagreement found within the few Alexandrian manuscripts). To these
textual witnesses we can add the testimony of history, as we have seen in
this chapter. This wealth of textual evidence is reflected the work of such
men as Desiderius Erasmus (1466-1536), Robert Stephanus (1503-1559),
Theodore Beza (1519-1605), and Bonaventure and Abraham Elzevir

---

[113] Zane Hodges, "The Greek Text of the King James Version," *Bibliotheca Sacra* 124
(1968), 335.

(1624).[114] All of them produced Greek New Testaments supporting the Traditional Text. In turn, their work provided the word of God to the world. The Greek text of Erasmus was the one used by Martin Luther for his eminent and exquisite German Bible. These Greek texts served as the basis for the brilliant and beloved Italian, French, and Spanish Bibles as well. Ultimately the jewel in this textual crown was set in 1611 with the translation of the English Authorized (King James) Version.

These texts and their translations did not go unrewarded by God. The Greek text of the Reformers was that of the Traditional Text. Every Protestant Church formed during this period of church history used the Traditional Text or a translation based on it. The Traditional Text produced reform and revival. It has proven itself to work *effectually* within the community of believers who have received it as the very word of God (1 Thessalonians 2:13). Consequently, it has affected history itself.

---

[114] Bonaventure and Abraham are sometimes falsely called "brothers." In reality, the brother of Bonaventure was Matthew. Abraham was Bonaventure's nephew. Bonaventure and Matthew had worked together as publishers. Later, Abraham worked with Bonaventure and helped with the production of their edition of the Textus Receptus.

Chapter 4

Forging The Metal

"God employs several translators; some pieces are translated by age, some by sickness, some by war, some by justice."

-John Donne, *Devotions Upon Emergent Occasions* (1624)

From the fire of the Reformation the word of God was forged for the laity. No longer did it solely rest in the hands of ecclesiastical orders. Yet the privilege did not come without a price. Many saints sacrificed wealth, reputation, and ultimately their lives, in order to secure a copy of sacred Scripture. It is because of their suffering that we have been granted the franchise to read the Bible for ourselves. For this, we owe them eternal gratitude and the responsibility to recognize their efforts.

The German Bible

Perhaps no other translation of the Bible, apart from the King James Version, has had a greater impact upon its people and their culture than the German Bible of Martin Luther (1483-1546). Not only has this delightful version affected the history and language of Germany, but also the many immigrants and early settlers who carried their copy of Die Heilige Schrift to the United States.

Students of history recognize the great contribution Martin Luther made to the common faith. It was Luther who echoed the cry of justification by faith and brought Reformation to Germany. At first he began a career in law. However, following a narrow escape from a storm, Luther decided to become a Catholic monk. After a study of Scripture on the doctrine of justification through faith, Luther published his *Ninety-Five Theses* and nailed it to the door of the church at Wittenberg in 1517. He spent the next few years defending his charges, only to be excommunicated in 1521. In April of that same year, Luther was summoned before the Holy Roman Emperor at the Diet of Worms. There he refused to recant and was banished from the empire.

Luther fled to Wartburg, and for the next eight months worked on his translation of the New Testament. The Greek text used by Luther was the one produced by Desiderius Erasmus (1466-1536). This text was based on the Traditional Text and later became known as the Textus Receptus. Luther's translation not only provided the German people with the Bible in their own language; it set the standard for the German language for centuries to follow.[115]

The following is taken from Luther's 1545 edition of the New Testament.
Romans 10:9-17

Denn so du mit deinem Munde bekennest JEsum, daß er der HErr sei, und glaubest in deinem Herzen, daß ihn GOtt von den Toten auferweckt hat, so wirst du selig. Denn so man von Herzen glaubet, so wird man gerecht, und so man mit dem Munde bekennet, so wird man selig. Denn die Schrift spricht: Wer an ihn glaubet, wird nicht zuschanden werden. Es ist hier kein Unterschied unter Juden und Griechen; es ist aller zumal ein HErr, reich über alle, die ihn anrufen. Denn wer den Namen des HErrn wird anrufen, soll selig werden. Wie sollen sie aber anrufen, an den sie nicht glauben? Wie sollen sie aber glauben, von dem sie nichts gehöret haben? Wie sollen sie aber hören ohne Prediger? Wie sollen sie aber predigen, wo sie nicht gesandt werden? Wie denn geschrieben stehet: Wie lieblich sind die Füße derer, die den Frieden verkündigen, die das Gute verkündigen!

---

[115] Earle E. Cairns, *Christianity Through The Centuries* (1954; reprint, Grand Rapids: Zondervan, 1967), 318.

Aber sie sind nicht alle dem Evangelium gehorsam. Denn Jesaja spricht: HErr, wer glaubet unserm Predigen? So kommt der Glaube aus der Predigt, das Predigen aber durch das Wort GOttes.

The Spanish Bible

The standard Spanish Bible is the Reina-Valera Version. It has been called the King James Version of the Spanish-speaking world.[116] It is the labor of two men, Casidoro de Reina and Cipriano de Valera, who suffered for the cause of Christ in order to provide their people God's word in their native tongue. As with the German Bible of Luther, this Spanish Bible is based on the Traditional Text.

Casidoro de Reina (1520-1594) was the first to translate the Bible into Spanish. His work took twelve years to complete at the cost of great personal sacrifice. He was born in Seville and became a Catholic monk. While at the San Isidro Monastery of Seville, he heard the lectures of the Superior of the monastery, Dr. Blanco Garcia Arias, who had been influenced by the preaching of the Albigenses. Being exposed to the writings of the Reformers and reading the Old Latin Bible of the Waldenses, Reina was converted to Protestantism.

Upon his conversion, persecution fell upon him. Reina had to flee Spain, never to return, in order to escape the claws of the Inquisition. Along with ten of his friends, Reina arrived in Frankfurt, Germany in 1557. Two years later he moved to London and became the pastor of a group of Spanish Protestants who also had escaped Spain and the Inquisition. Later, because of persecution in England, Reina and his wife fled to Antwerp in the Netherlands. During this time, he worked on his Spanish Bible. In 1569, he published twenty-six hundred copies of the

---

[116] "Remembering Casiodoro De Reina," *Bible Society Record* (1969). Wilton Nelson, "New Light from an Old Lamp," Latin American Evangelist Jan/Feb (1970), 9.

entire Bible in Spanish. It was nicknamed the "Bear Bible" because it featured on its title page an engraving of a bear retrieving honey from a tree.

The Inquisition seized as many copies of this version as possible and had them destroyed, calling it the most dangerous edition of the Bible.[117] The Roman Church had issued a decree stating that the Bible in Spanish or in any other common tongue was prohibited.[118] Consequently, few copies of Reina's Spanish Version ever made it into Spain. Notwithstanding, it was greatly used by Spanish-speaking refugees who fled Spain because of the persecution.

After the publication of his Bible, Reina organized a church that became noted for its zeal and evangelistic outreach in Frankfurt. He remained the pastor of this church until his death on March 16, 1594. To Spanish and Latin-American Christians, Casiodoro de Reina was more than a Bible translator; he was a hero in the faith.

Cipriano de Valera (1531-1602) was one of Reina's friends who fled Spain with him in 1557. Like Reina, Valera had been a monk at the San Isidro Monastery in Seville. It was there he first heard the gospel of redemption and was converted. Soon after he arrived in Frankfurt, Valera moved to Geneva where he became a follower of reformer John Calvin. He became a street preacher and later moved to England to study at the University of Cambridge. Afterwards, he taught at the University of Oxford. While in England, he translated Calvin's *Institutes* into Spanish and wrote a book entitled *El Papa y la Misa* (*The Pope and the Mass*). In it, he condemned the authority of the Pope and the service of the mass, calling it pagan. While in England, he married and began a ministry to seamen as well as a ministry to those imprisoned.

---

[117] S. L. Greenslade, *The Cambridge History of the Bible* (New York: Cambridge University Press, 1983), 126.

[118] Ibid., 125.

In 1582, Valera began to revise the work of Reina. His revision was thorough but conservative in that he made as few changes to Reina's text as possible. At the age of seventy, after twenty long years of working on his revision, Valera published what has become known as the Reina-Valera Version. Valera wrote:

> The reason that motivated me to make this edition was the same that motivated Casidoro de Reina, who was motivated by the pious Person, the Lord himself, and wanted to spread the glory of God and make a clear service to his nation.[119]

Valera believed his Bible was the perfect word of God for the Spanish-speaking people. One authoritative Spanish-language work on Bible translations in that language, *Versiones Castellanas De La Biblia,* states: "The authors [Reina and Valera] claim to have penetrated to the depths of Holy Scriptures and have translated with perfection the Greek and Hebrew languages."[120] Like Reina, Valera is a hero in the faith. Because of his belief in personal salvation by grace alone through faith, and his desire to see the word of God published in Spanish, this same work records that "Valera suffered great misery."[121] It is also noted, "When the Lord rewards his servants, Cipriano de Valera will receive a great prize from the hand of the Saviour."[122]

The following passage is taken from the 1858 edition of the Reina-Valera Version.

1 John 5:1-8

> TODO aquel que cree que Jesus es el Cristo, es nacido de Dios: y cualquiera que ama al que ha engendrado, ama tam-

---

[119] *Versiones Castellanas De La Biblia* (Mexico: Casa De Publicasciones), 38-39. Translation here and afterwards is the present author's.

[120] Ibid., 19.

[121] Ibid., 39. The Spanish reads, "Valera sufiro grande miseria."

[122] Ibid. The Spanish reads, "El Senor recompense a sus siervos, Cipriano de Valera recibira un muy grande galardon de manos de su Salvador."

bien al que es nacido de él. En esto conocemos que amamos á los hijos de Dios, cuando amamos á Dios, y guardamos sus mandamientos. Porque esta es la caridad de Dios, que guardemos sus mandamientos; y sus mandamientos no son graves. Porque todo aquello que es nacido de Dios vence al mundo: y esta es la victoria que vence al mundo, *es á saber*, nuestra fé. ¿Quién es el que vence al mundo, sino el que cree que Jesus es el Hijo de Dios?Este es Jesu Cristo, que vino por agua y sangre: no por agua solamente, sino por agua y sangre. Y el Espíritu es el que da testimonio: porque el Espíritu es la verdad. Porque tres son los que dan testimonio en el cielo, el Padre, la Palabra, y el Espíritu Santo; y estos tres son uno. Tambien son tres los que dan testimonio en la tierra, el Espíritu, el agua, y la sangre, y estos tres son uno.

The Early English Bibles

The history of the English Bible is a rich history. Like the Scriptures themselves, it records the best and worst in man. It shows the beauty of man's expressions, the pureness of his devotion, and the depth of his sacrifice. History also records man's vile thoughts, misguided piety, and the extent of his depravity. The freedom we have to read the word of God in our own language was paid for with the price of sweat and blood.

Before we can understand the labors of English translators, we must understand the times they lived in. Until 1382 there was no English Bible. In fact, to have the Bible in the language of the people was forbidden. The church in power was the Roman Catholic Church, whose Bible was the Latin Vulgate and whose influence spread to the monarchy in England. The Church believed men would misunderstand and mistranslate the Scriptures, and they had the power of the state to enforce this ban. If we are to know the history of the English Bible, we must acquaint ourselves with the history of English monarchs. This is especially true of the years from William Tyndale to the translation of the Authorized Version, for during this time England faced it own Reformation.

The House Of Tudor

To help children remember the kings and queens of England, an unknown poet chronicled their reigns in verse. A great deal of truth concerning the House of Tudor is revealed in this rhyme:

Henry the Seventh was frugal of means;
Henry the Eighth had a great many queens.
Edward the Sixth reformation began;
Cruel Queen Mary prevented the plan.
Wise and profound were Elizabeth's aims.

Henry VIII (reigned 1509-1547):

"Lord! open the King of England's eyes," was the fiery death cry of translator William Tyndale.[123] The king he was praying for was Henry VIII, the second king of the House of Tudor (1485-1603). Tyndale's prayer was answered, for during the time of Henry several major English translations appeared with the king's approval and the Church of England was born.

Henry's elder brother Arthur had been Prince of Wales and heir apparent to their father, Henry VII, but died in 1502 before taking the throne. Arthur was married to Catherine of Aragon in a political alliance between England and Spain. Henry became king upon his father's death and married Catherine to continue the alliance with Spain. All was well for a period of time, but when Catherine did not give Henry any male children he sought to divorce her. As scriptural proof for his divorce the king cited

---

[123] John Foxe, *Foxe's Book Of Christian Martyrs* (Springdale, PA: Whitaker House, 1981), 136.

Leviticus 20:21, "And if a man shall take his brother's wife, it is an unclean thing: he hath uncovered his brother's nakedness; they shall be childless."

Pope Clement VII, however, was unwilling to grant the divorce. This did not stop the king. In 1529 Henry held a trial in London to divorce Catherine. The trial reached no decision, so the king dismissed his chief minister, Cardinal Wolsey, and made Thomas Cromwell his new chief minister. Cromwell proposed to Parliament that England break with Rome and appoint the Archbishop of Canterbury as the highest officer in the English church. Parliament passed legislation to this effect in 1533, and the Archbishop granted the divorce. Immediately afterwards, Henry married Anne Boleyn; however, as is well known to students of history, this was not the end of Henry's marriages. During his reign he married six times: Catherine of Aragon, Anne Boleyn, Jane Seymour, Anne of Cleves, Catherine Howard, and Catherine Parr. Three of Henry's children ruled England: Edward VI, Mary I, and Elizabeth I.

Edward VI (reigned 1547-1553):

Edward was the son of Henry and Jane Seymour, Henry's third wife. He was only nine years old when he became king of England. Educated by Protestant tutors, he favored major reforms in the Church of England. During his reign the Archbishop of Canterbury, Thomas Cranmer, compiled the *Book of Common Prayer*. This prayer book offered an English version of prayers, devotions, and Scripture readings instead of the Latin liturgy used in the Roman Catholic Church. However, the young king became ill in 1552 and died on July 6, 1553.

Mary I (reigned 1553-1558):

"Light came and went and came again." So wrote Thomas Wolfe in his semi-autobiographical story, *The Lost Boy*. The same imagery comes to mind during the reign of Mary Tudor. She brought with her rule days of darkness. Born of Henry and Catherine of Aragon on February 18, 1516, Mary became queen of England upon the death of her half-brother Edward. She was a strong Catholic who sought to bring England back under the Papacy.

Misguided by her zeal, she soon earned for herself the infamous name "Bloody Mary." During the last three years of her reign she executed over three hundred Protestants by burning them at the stake. One of these was the Archbishop himself, Thomas Cranmer. While imprisoned, Cranmer had signed a statement of recantation. Before being burned at the stake it is reported that Cranmer placed the hand he used to sign the statement in the fire first as a sign of his remorse. Many of the great scholars who were not executed fled to Geneva during this period. It was there that they produced the beloved Geneva Bible.[124]

Elizabeth I (reigned 1558-1603):

Light came again with the rule of Elizabeth I. As Mary's reign was noted for its bloodshed, Elizabeth's was noted for its glory. Born on September 7, 1533, Elizabeth was the daughter of Henry and Anne Boleyn. It is during her reign we have what is now referred to as the "Elizabethan Age," considered to be one of England's grandest periods of history.

England's advancements were massive. In literature, great works by Shakespeare, Spenser, and Marlowe were composed and a fine tuning of the English language developed that influenced novelists and playwrights for years to come. In exploration, achievements included the rewards of seamen such as Drake, Hawkins, and Raleigh, the establishment of the East India Company, the first colonies in the New World, and the defeat of the Spanish Armada. Advancements in religion range from the "Elizabethan Settlement" that helped soothe the strong conflict between Catholicism and Calvinism to the reestablishment of the Church of England and the reissuing of the *Book of Common Prayer*. It was also during this time the Bishops' Bible was translated, which helped to guide the translators of the Authorized Version.

---

[124] Bruce M. Metzger and Michael D. Coogan, eds., *The Oxford Companion To The Bible* (New York: Oxford University Press, 1993), 759.

Elizabeth's reign was not without conflict. Mary, Queen of Scots, fled to England in 1568 to escape a rebellion in Scotland. Mary was a strong Roman Catholic and thus became the axis of several English Catholic conspiracies that arose, seeking to reestablish the primacy of the Roman Church. This finally led Elizabeth to have Mary arrested and sentenced to death in 1587. Mary's son, James, was King James VI of Scotland. Upon the death of Elizabeth, he became King James I of England in 1603. As staunch a Protestant as his mother had been a Catholic, James was the monarch who permitted the translators to produce the Bible that now commonly bears his name.

John Wycliffe (1324-1384)

"I believe that in the end the truth will conquer." So wrote John Wycliffe (or Wyclif) to the Duke of Lancaster in 1381. Although Wycliffe's translation was taken from the Latin Vulgate, and was not one of the translations underlying the Authorized Version, his accomplishments demand discussion in any survey of early English versions of the Bible. It was Wycliffe who gave us the first English translation of the whole Bible, and it was his labor that inspired others to follow in his footsteps by translating the word of God in the language of the people.

Wycliffe translated the New Testament by himself, but was most likely aided by Nicholas of Hereford with the Old Testament. His Bible was introduced in 1382 and later was revised by John Pervy. This was a noble task because the printing press had yet to be invented and all copies of the translation were written by hand. Today we have almost two hundred of these handwritten Wycliffe Bibles.[125]

---

[125] The American Bible Society states, "of the nearly 200 existing manuscripts of this translation, only some thirty are copies of the Hereford version; the majority were written within forty years of Purvey's version." *A Ready Reference History of the English Bible* (New York: American Bible Society, 1979), 9. The Catholic view differs: "Cardinal Gasquet has proved that the so-called Wyclifite Bibles in existence today are really the old English Catholic Bibles." Rev. Bertrand Conway, The Question Box (New York: Deus

Though still in the Roman Church, Wycliffe and his followers (a group of poor monks known as Lollards) taught doctrines that differed significantly with the teachings of the Catholic Church of that day. They believed in the authority of the word of God and that it should be translated into English. They believed in a personal salvation based upon divine election. And they rejected the doctrines of transubstantiation and indulgences. Further, they taught that the Church's hierarchy was unscriptural and that the Pope had no more authority then any other priest. Obviously, their doctrines were unpopular with Rome.

Several of the Lollards suffered for their faith. John Purvey and Nicholas of Hereford, who helped with the Wycliffe translation, were arrested and forced to recant their beliefs. In London in 1382, after many of Wycliffe's teachings were condemned as heretical, a great number of his followers in Oxford were also forced to recant. Wycliffe himself, however, was never tried nor martyred. Still his memory and work received the wrath of Rome. Wycliffe was forced into retirement and remained at his rectory at Lutterworth, England until his death in 1384. In 1401 Parliament ordered the penalty of death for those caught teaching and proclaiming the doctrines of John Wycliffe. On May 4, 1415 the Council of Constance ordered Wycliffe's body to be exhumed and burned for heresy.

The following compares the translation of Wycliffe with that of the King James Version in one of the most popular Psalms of Scripture, the *Shepherd's Psalm.*

Book, 1962), 346. However the evidence seems to contradict this position and supports the American Bible Society's claim. The only evidence offered to support the claim that the Wycliffe Bibles we have are not Wycliffe Bibles but early English Catholic Bibles comes from a quote from Sir Thomas More. More was a contemporary of Tyndale and opposed his work. More claimed the Bible had been translated into English long before Wycliffe by "good and godly" scholars who were "devoted" to the Catholic Church. (Ibid).

Psalm 23:1-6 (KJV)

The LORD is my shepherd; I shall not want. He maketh me to lie down in green pastures: he leadeth me beside the still waters. He restoreth my soul: he leadeth me in the paths of righteousness for his name's sake. Yea, though I walk through the valley of the shadow of death, I will fear no evil: for thou art with me; thy rod and thy staff they comfort me. Thou preparest a table before me in the presence of mine enemies: thou anointest my head with oil; my cup runneth over. Surely goodness and mercy shall follow me all the days of my life: and I will dwell in the house of the LORD for ever.

Psalm 23:1-6 (Wycliffe Version)

The lord gouerneth me, and no thing schal fail to me; In the place of pasture there he hath set me. He nourished me on the water of refreshing; He conurtide my soul. He lead me forth on the paths of rightfulness; for his name. For whi though Y shall go in the midest of shadow of death; Y shall not dread evil, for thou art with me. thy yard and thy staff; tho han comforted me. Thou hast made ready a boord in my sight; agens hem that troblen me. Thou hast made fat myn heed with oyle; and my cuppe, fillinge greetli, is ful cleer. And thi merci schal sue me; in alle the daies of my lijf. And that Y dwelle in the hows of the Lord; in to the lengthe of daies.

William Tyndale (1494-1536)

The name of William Tyndale has borne the slander of the Roman Catholic Church. In his own day, Sir Thomas More accused him of "abominable heresies," and twentieth-century Catholic historian Henry

G. Graham refers to Tyndale as an inept rebellious priest.[126] Despite the defamation, God used William Tyndale to provide for us the first English Bible printed on the printing press. Tyndale also set the stage for the English translations that followed.

John Foxe provides us with a contrasting view of this saint of God. Foxe tells us of his early training at the Universities of Oxford and Cambridge, and as a schoolmaster who taught the children of the Knight of Gloucestershire. Foxe also points out it was in this capacity that Tyndale earned himself a reputation for being contentious with local priests who would visit the Knight and his family.[127] Despite his leanings towards biblical debate, Foxe describes Tyndale as a gracious man who opened his heart and home to strangers and offered fellowship to all that wished it.

It was his openness and generosity that led to his demise. While in Antwerp, Tyndale befriended fellow Englishman Henry Philips. Tyndale showed Philips all his works, translations, plans, and personal theology. He trusted Philips as a good man and fellow believer. Philips was neither. Like Judas of old, Philips arranged with officers for the arrest of William Tyndale and then, while in the public street, pointed to Tyndale so the officials knew whom to arrest.

Tyndale's "crime" was the publishing of God's word in the language of the people. He was charged with heresy and sentenced to death by burning. While tied to the stake and awaiting his fiery death, William Tyndale offered his final prayer before being ushered into eternity, beseeching the Lord to "open the King of England's eyes." Once again the English Bible was purchased with the blood of the saints.

Tyndale used the Traditional Text and laid the foundation for the KJV that followed years later. Although Tyndale translated a few Old

---

[126] Henry G. Graham, *Where We Got the Bible: Our Debt to the Catholic Church,* 22nd edition (Rockford: Tan Books and Publishers, 1987), 123.

[127] Foxe, 136.

Testament books, his emphasis was on the New Testament, of which his translation was first published in 1525. However, Cuthbert Tunstall, Bishop of London, seized and burnt most of these editions in London in October of 1526. Only two first editions survive today. Tyndale published revised and corrected editions in 1534 and 1535.

One interesting historical fact concerning Tunstall and his collection and consequent burning of Tyndale's New Testament should be noted. In order to assure that all copies were retrieved, Tunstall arranged to purchase a large quantity of Tyndale's earlier editions. The monies paid by Tunstall for these earlier defective copies were used by Tyndale to finance the revision of his New Testament. Thus, Tunstall unknowingly furthered the translation and publication of the English version he so greatly hated.

The following comparison illustrates the impact Tyndale's New Testament had on the Authorized Version.

Matthew 6:9-13 (KJV)

After this manner therefore pray ye: Our Father which art in heaven, Hallowed be thy name. Thy kingdom come. Thy will be done in earth, as it is in heaven. Give us this day our daily bread. And forgive us our debts, as we forgive our debtors. And lead us not into temptation, but deliver us from evil: For thine is the kingdom, and the power, and the glory, for ever. Amen.

Matthew 6:9-13 (Tyndale)

After thys maner therfore praye ye. O oure father which arte in heven, halowed be thy name. Let thy kyngdome come. Thy will be fulfilled, as well in erth, as it is in heven. Geve us this daye oure dayly breede. And forgeve us oure treaspases, even as we forgeve oure trespacers. And leade us not into temptacion: but delyver us from evyll. For thyne is the kyngedome and the power, and the glorye for ever. Amen.

Miles Coverdale (1488-1569)

Tyndale's final prayer was answered in the work of Miles Coverdale. Coverdale had befriended Anne Boleyn, the second wife of King Henry VIII. In addition, the chief minister to Henry was Thomas Cranmer, the Archbishop of Canterbury who encouraged Coverdale in his translational work. Consequently, the Lord was setting the stage to provide England and the English-speaking world with its first translation approved by a king.

God used Miles Coverdale in a unique way because Coverdale labored on three early English translations: his own Coverdale's Bible (1535), the Great Bible (1539), and the Geneva Bible (1560). Indirectly he helped with the Matthew's Bible (1537) and the Bishops' Bible (1568), as these were revisions of his works. All of these early translations, as well as Tyndale's translations, were based on the Traditional Text and used by the translators of the KJV of 1611. These were the English translations referred to by the KJV translators when they wrote:

> Truly, good Christian Reader, we never thought from the beginning that we should need to make a new translation, nor yet to make of a bad one a good one;…but to make a good one better, or out of many good ones, one principal good one, not justly to be excepted against; that hath been our endeavour, that our mark.[128]

Miles Coverdale was born in Yorkshire, the birthplace of John Wycliffe. He was educated at Cambridge and became an Augustinian friar. In 1528, after embracing the teachings of Martin Luther, Coverdale left the priesthood and was forced to leave England. Coverdale soon became a disciple

---

[128] "The Translators To The Reader," *The Holy Bible: King James Version* (Cambridge: Cambridge University Press), xxii.

of William Tyndale and took up his work of translating the Bible in the English language. His first translation of the Old Testament as it is found in the Coverdale's Bible was not translated from Hebrew, a language he did not know, but from German and Latin. His New Testament was a revision of Tyndale's New Testament. When he published his Bible in October 1535, it became the first complete Bible printed in English.

Matthew's Bible (1537)

Thomas Matthew was the pseudonym of John Rogers (1500-1555). Rogers received his degree from Cambridge in 1525 and became a priest in London. In 1534 he went to Antwerp as chaplain to the Merchant Adventurers. There, he became associated with William Tyndale and was converted to Protestantism. Rogers, with his wife and eight children, went to Wittenberg where he pastored a church. Under the reign of Queen Mary, Rogers was charged with heresy and was burned at the stake for the gospel.

His work is a mixture of Tyndale and Coverdale. The New Testament is William Tyndale's, as are the first five books of the Old Testament. Some also attest that Joshua to 2 Chronicles were likewise the work of Tyndale, which he finished shortly before his death and were first published here by Rogers. The rest of the Old Testament is the work of Coverdale.[129]

The Great Bible (1539)

This was the second major work done by Miles Coverdale, called the Great Bible because of its size.[130] It is a very thick Bible with pages

---

[129] In 1539 an edition of Matthew's Bible was published by Richard Taverner and is sometimes referred to as the Taverner's Bible.

[130] The Great Bible was also known as the Cranmer Bible, because Archbishop Thomas Cranmer wrote the preface to the second edition. It is also called the Whitchurch Bible, so named after Edward Whitchurch who along with Richard Grafton were the appointed printers, and is referred to as such by the translators of the King James Version.

measuring nine inches wide and fifteen inches long. It was produced for English churches with the full approval of the king, Henry VIII. Some consider this the first "authorized" Bible because the king approved it and the Archbishop of Canterbury, Thomas Cranmer, oversaw it.[131]

This version, based on the Traditional Text of the New Testament, was revised and altered in accordance with the Latin Vulgate. It never became "great" with the public and ceased publication within thirty years. The desire for an English Bible still remained. The public longed for a Bible that the average Englishman could hold in his hands and read at home. This need was met with the Geneva Bible that followed.

The following compares the Great Bible with the King James Version. The spelling in the KJV reflects our current editions, while the spelling in the Great Bible remains as it was in 1539.

Mark 1:1-3 (KJV)

The beginning of the gospel of Jesus Christ, the Son of God; As it is written in the prophets, Behold, I send my messenger before thy face, which shall prepare thy way before thee. The voice of one crying in the wilderness, Prepare ye the way of the Lord, make his paths straight.

Mark 1:1-3 (Great Bible)

The begynnynge of the Gospell of Jesu Chryst the sonne of God, As it is written in the Prophetes, behold, I sende my messenger before thy face which shall prepare thy waye before

---

[131] It is interesting to note that Bishop Tunstall, the same Bishop of London who had burnt Tyndale's New Testament, oversaw the third and fifth editions of the Great Bible. Now, because of Henry VIII, the bishop was forced to endorse a translation of the Bible that was essentially the same in the New Testament as the version that he had denounced and burned only a few years earlier.

the. The voyce of a cryer in the wildernes: prepare ye the waye of the Lorde, and make his pathes strayte.

The Geneva Bible (1560)

In 1553, Mary became Queen of England and began a fiery persecution against Protestants. The Great Bible was removed from churches, and many Christians fled the country in order to escape her religious wrath. Many of those who fled persecution found refuge in Geneva. Knowing the need to preserve God's word in English, some who had either suffered persecution under Mary, or had fled because of the persecution she produced, began work on a new translation of the Bible. In 1557 the New Testament was published. It was mostly the work of William Whittingham, brother-in-law of the great reformer John Calvin. With the aid of Anthony Gilby and Thomas Sampson, Whittingham immediately revised his New Testament. For the Old Testament, the 1550 edition of the Great Bible was used and revised. By 1560 the entire Geneva Bible was complete and published.

It was produced in a handy size using Roman type that made it easier to read than the "black letter" used in earlier English Bibles. It also contained several notations that the Catholic Church found offensive. For example, the notation found in Revelation 9:3, which describes the locust coming out of the pit, reads, "Locusts are false teachers, heretics, and worldly, subtle prelates, with monks, friars, cardinals, archbishops, bishops, doctors, bachelors, and masters, which forsake Christ to maintain false doctrine."[132] Unlike previous translations, it was the work of a committee and not the work of one man or a revision of one man's work. Readers of William Shakespeare will undoubtedly recognize many of the citations from the Geneva Bible, for it was the translation from which he quoted in his plays.

---

[132] The spelling here has been modernized.

Colossians 1:12-17 (KJV)

Giving thanks unto the Father, which hath made us meet to be partakers of the inheritance of the saints in light: Who hath delivered us from the power of darkness, and hath translated us into the kingdom of His dear Son: In whom we have redemption through His blood, even the forgiveness of sins: Who is the image of the invisible God, the firstborn of every creature: For by him were all things created, that are in heaven, and that are in earth, visible and invisible, whether they be thrones, or dominions, or principalities, or powers: all things were created by him, and for him: And he is before all things, and by him all things consist.

Colossians 1:12-17 (Geneva Bible)

Gyving thankes unto the Father, whiche hathe made us mete to be partakers of the inheritance of the Saintes in light. Who hathe delivered us from the power of darkenes, and hathe translated us into the kingdome of His deare Sonne. In whom we have redemption through His bloode, (that is,) the forgivenes of sinnes. Who is the image of the invisible God, the first borne of everie creature. For by him were all things created, which are in heaven, and which are in earth, things visible and invisible: whether (they be) Thrones, or Dominions, or Principalities, or Powers, all thynges were created by hym and for hym. And he is before all thynges, and in hym all things consist.

The Bishops' Bible (1568)

Perhaps the loveliest Bible printed at this time was the Bishops' Bible, a large folio with many beautiful engravings throughout. Following the persecutions and the banning of the Scriptures during Queen Mary's reign, Queen Elizabeth, who succeeded Mary to the English throne, ordered the Bible to be restored to the British churches. Archbishop of Canterbury Matthew Parker, desiring a new translation, assigned sections of the Great Bible to a team of bishops for revision. This occurred in 1566, and the new revision was accomplished and published in 1568. It had fewer notes than the Geneva Bible and was designed to give the clergy and congregates of the Church of England one official, standard Bible. However, it was not successful in this task. Because this version was issued under the authority of Queen Elizabeth, it is considered the second "authorized" English Bible.

Revelation 1:1-3 (KJV)

The Revelation of Jesus Christ, which God gave unto him, to shew unto his servants things which must shortly come to pass; and he sent and signified it by his angel unto his servant John: Who bare record of the word of God, and of the testimony of Jesus Christ, and of all things that he saw. Blessed is he that readeth, and they that hear the words of this prophecy, and keep those things which are written therein: for the time is at hand.

Revelation 1:1-3 (Bishops' Bible)

The Revelation of Jesus Christ, which God gave unto him, for to shewe unto his servauntes thinges which must shortly come to passe: and when he had sent, he shewed by his Angel unto his servant John, Which bare record of the word of God, and of the testimonie of Jesus Christ, and of all things that he saw. Happie is he that readeth, and they that heare the wordes of this prophecie, and keepe those things which are written therein: for the time is at hand.

"A Good One Better"

The goal of the translators of the Authorized Version was to make their new translation even better than its predecessors. As we have seen, these translators stated that they did not consider previous translations bad, but wanted to make "out of many good ones, one principal good one, not justly to be excepted against." Their desire was to take God's word in English and provide one principal translation based on these earlier English Protestant versions. Their work was successful. The KJV was not only based on earlier English versions, but also became the standard English Bible for the next four hundred years.

Chapter 5

The English Jewel

"The English Bible—a book which, if everything else in our language should perish, would alone suffice to show the whole extent of its beauty and power."
-Thomas Babington Macaulay, *Edinburgh Review* (1828)

John Rainolds had been addressing the newly crowned king of England, James I. Various concerns among the Puritans had arisen, and now was an opportunity to present them before the king. It was cold and damp that wintry day, much like the coldness that faced this English Church of the Reformation. Elizabeth, the beloved queen, had died and the thick-tongued Scotsman now ruled in her stead. Dr. Rainolds was well aware of the concerns that had risen within the Church and the nation. What would this new king do?

Within the contents of his address, Rainolds raised a proposal: "May your Majesty be pleased to direct that the Bible be now translated, such versions as are extant not answering to the original." With lisping tongue the king answered, stirring the desires of all those who wished to see a new translation that would standardize the word of God among the English-speaking world. "I profess, I could never yet see a Bible well translated in English, but I think that of Geneva is the worst."[133]

---

[133] Gustavus S. Paine, *The Men Behind the King James Version* (1959; reprint, Grand Rapids: Baker Book House, 1982), 1. It is also interesting to note that in the original preface to the Authorized Version the translators made use of the Geneva Bible, the one James labeled as the worst of all. It would appear that the translators did not share the king's assessment.

With these few fateful words, the greatest English translation the world has ever known was born. The place was Hampton Court. The day was Monday, January 16, 1604. By July 22 of the same year, Bishop Richard Bancroft had been notified by the king to appoint certain learned men, numbering fifty-four, for the purpose of newly translating the Scriptures. What they produced John Livingston Lowes called "the noblest monument of English prose." For us, it simply became *the Bible*.

Sadly, of late it has fallen under attack. Not only from skeptics who doubt God's word, but from various theologians and biblical scholars. Many have used faulty forensic reasoning in order to discredit this lovely version. It is, therefore, essential for us to understand the history of the Authorized Version in order to refute the contentions of such individuals, for in disparaging this Bible, they (wittingly or not) imperil the work and word of God among the English-speaking peoples.

James I of England (1566-1625)

Some erroneously believe that the King James Version was the translation of King James I of England (VI of Scotland). Others attempt to discredit the KJV because of the king himself. However, neither of these is a substantive objection to the KJV. James did not translate the Bible, and his character has little to do with the translation that bears his name. He was the King of England in 1611 when the KJV was completed, and it was under his authority that the translators began their endeavor.

James was born in Scotland and was the only son of Mary Queen of Scots. His famous mother was a strict Roman Catholic; however, James was raised a staunch Protestant. He had a love for sports as well as for scholarship. British author Caroline Bingham writes of James that at "seventeen he was a remarkable youth who had already achieved an intellectual and political maturity; already he was recognizable as the canny and learned King who never achieved wisdom, who committed follies but was not a fool."[134] Nevertheless, King Henry IV of France referred to James as the "wisest fool in Christendom."[135] The New Testament reminds us that God is capable of using the foolish to astound the wise of this world (1 Corinthians 1:25-29).

The Translation

On that cold January day when Dr. Rainolds suggested to the king that the English Bible be revised, James reacted with delight and instructed Bishop Bancroft to appoint fifty-four scholars for the purpose of translating the word of God. The actual number of translators who worked on the KJV remains a mystery since some died before the work was completed. Nevertheless, the majority of the translator's names have survived (see Appendix A). These men were divided into three groups located at Westminster, Oxford, and Cambridge. Each group was divided into two sections; one worked on the Old Testament, the other on the New Testament. Only the group at Cambridge had an additional team working on the Apocrypha.

The translators were great scholars. Many laid the foundation for linguistic studies that followed. They spent most of their time in the pursuit of learning and development of their knowledge of biblical languages. Some, while waxing eloquent in Latin or Greek, fared poorly with their native English. Gustavus S. Paine noted that the king's translators were not superb writers doing scholarly work, but were superb scholars doing superb writing.[136] Judged by their other extant works, which are commonplace in style, the writing of what would become the Authorized Version

---

[134] Caroline Bingham, *The Making of a King* (Garden City, NY: Doubleday, 1969), 40.

[135] Lady Antonia Fraser, *King James VI of Scotland: I of England* (New York: Alfred A. Knoph, Inc., 1974), 9.

[136] Ibid., vii.

should have been far beyond their abilities. Yet, they were able to reach beyond themselves. Paine makes the following assessment:

> Though we may challenge the idea of word-by-word inspiration, we surely must conclude that these were men able, in their profound moods, to transcend their human limits. In their own words, they spake as no other men spake because they were filled with the Holy Ghost. Or, in the clumsier language of our time, they so adjusted themselves to each other and to the work as to achieve a unique coordination and balance, functioning thereafter as an organic entity—no mere mechanism equal to the sum of its parts, but a whole greater than all of them.[137]

The translation went through a series of committees, all consisting of various groupings of the translators themselves. Upon finishing the assigned portion given to him, a translator would meet with the first committee and read the work he translated. Those within the committee followed the reading from various sources, such as the original languages, early English translations, and foreign translations including German, French, Italian, and Spanish. If there were no differences of opinion concerning the translation, the reader pressed on. If there were differences, the committee would reach a consensus before proceeding. The findings were then presented to the other two companies for their committees to review in like fashion. If these committees differed at any given point, the differences were compounded and presented to a third committee consisting of twelve members. This committee (known as the *General Meeting*) reviewed what the previous committees had produced and agreed upon the finished translation before presenting the work to two final editors, Bishop Thomas Bilson and Dr. Miles Smith.[138]

---

[137] Ibid., 173.

[138] Ibid., 119-120. Miles Smith is considered the translator who authored the original preface to the 1611 edition: "The Translators To The Reader."

True Rewards

Some writers have asserted that the translators "may have harbored less than perfect motivations" for their efforts, such as seeking royal favor and advancement, or being "far too enamored with the idea of royalty." It has also been charged that the English Crown paid for the translation.[139] None of these accusations are worth serious consideration. There is no hint that any of the translators sought to be on the translational committee to gain favor with the king or promotion. There is some evidence that William Barlow, one of the translators, was a man who was soundly supportive of the British Crown and a man whom King James greatly approved.[140] But many Englishmen of that day held similarly exalted notions of royalty, including James I himself who objected to the Geneva Bible precisely because its marginal notes did not accord with his notions of the obedience due to kings.[141]

As for the matter of who paid for the KJV, the historical truth is that payment did not come from the Crown but from the Church, and Church funds were very limited. Funds were raised and received for the purpose of sustaining the translators during their work on the translation, but they were not given financial reward.[142] It is true that several of the translators did advance within the Church after the translation was complete, but this was due to their ability. Their greatest reward was in the fruit of their labor, the KJV itself. The translators wrote:

---

[139] James R. White, *The King James Only Controversy: Can You Trust the Modern Translations?* (Minneapolis, MN: Bethany House, 1995) 70-71, 88 (note 61).

[140] Paine, 43.

[141] Marvin W. Anderson, "The Geneva (Tonson/Junius) New Testament Among Other English Bibles of the Period," in Gerald T. Sheppard, ed., *The Geneva Bible: The Annotated New Testament*, 1602 Edition. (New York: Pilgrim Press, 1989), 6.

[142] John R. Dore, *Old Bibles: An Account of the Early Versions of the English Bible*, 2nd ed. (London: Eyre and Spottiswoode, 1888), 325.

But amongst all our joys, there was no one that more filled our hearts than the blessed continuance of the preaching of God's sacred Word amongst us; which is that inestimable treasure which excelleth all the riches of the earth; because the fruit thereof extendeth itself, not only to the time spent in this transitory world, but directeth and disposeth men unto that eternal happiness which is above in heaven.[143]

The Cum Privilegio

Another common myth concerning the KJV is that it was under the sole printing authority of the Crown. This is known as the *Cum Privilegio* (i.e., *with privilege*). Some have thought this made it impossible for anyone else to publish the KJV for the first hundred years of its existence.[144] Such a claim is erroneous.

It is true the KJV was under the Cum Privilegio, and that the royal printer was Robert Barker; it is also true that others printed the KJV long before 1711. Royal historian John Dore noted:

> In the year 1642, a folio edition of King James's Version was printed at Amsterdam by "Joost Broersz, dwelling in the Pijlsteegh, in the Druckerije"…The notes of the King James's Bible are omitted, and the arguments and annotations of the "Breeches" Bible are inserted in their place.[145]

Dr. Jack Lewis also notes that the KJV was printed in Geneva, without the Crown's approval, during its first one hundred years. Various editions of the KJV were published outside of England in 1642, 1672, 1683, 1708, and in England itself in 1649.[146]

---

[143] "The Epistle Dedicatory" to the Authorized Version.

[144] White, 244.

[145] Dore, 345.

[146] Jack P. Lewis, *The English Bible From KJV to NIV* (Grand Rapids: Baker Book House, 1982), 29.

Dore points to Scotland as printing the KJV in 1628.[147] He also notes that the KJV was printed in England without the Cum Privilegio. A special dispensation was granted to the University of Cambridge and the University of Oxford so that they could print Bibles without the Cum Privilegio.

> Although the Universities always claimed the right to print the Bible, Cambridge had not exercised that right since the year 1589; but in 1628 a duodecimo Testament was published at Cambridge, by the printers to the University, and the following year Thomas and John Buck issued the first Cambridge Bible…The University of Oxford did not begin to print Bibles until the year 1675, when the first was issued in quarto size; the spelling was revised by Dr. John Fell, Dean of Oxford.[148]

Once again, the evidence shows this assault is unwarranted.

The Apocrypha

Another objection to the KJV concerns the Apocrypha. The KJV translators did not consider the Apocrypha inspired Scripture. They placed it between the Testaments, indicating that they regarded it valuable only as historical record and for edification, not for doctrine. The same is true of other early English versions. For example, on the opening page of the Apocrypha in the Geneva Bible we read:

> These books that follow in order after the prophets unto the New Testament are called Apocrypha—that is, books which were not received by a common consent to be read and expounded publicly in the Church, neither yet served to prove any point of Christian religion, save inasmuch as they had the consent of the other Scriptures called canonical to confirm the

---

[147] Dore, 338-339.
[148] Ibid., 339, 346.

same, or rather whereon they were grounded; but as books pre-ceding from godly men, [which] were received to be read for the advancement and furtherance of the knowledge of the history, and for the instruction of godly manners: which books declare that at all times God had an especial care of his Church, and left them not utterly destitute of teachers and means to confirm them in the hope of the promised Messiah; and also witness that those calamities that God sent to his Church were according to his providence, who had both so threatened by his Prophets, and so brought it to pass for the destruction of their enemies, and for the trial of his children.[149]

Likewise, the translators of the KJV did not give the Apocrypha the respect they had given the Holy Scriptures. Their relative disregard for these books is not expressed in an explicit disclaimer, as in the Geneva Bible, but can be seen in the way they are presented in the first edition of 1611. In addition to placing the Apocrypha between the Testaments (rather than interspersing them with the canon as was Roman Catholic practice), the translators did not mention the Apocrypha at all on the title page, which simply reads, "The Holy Bible, Conteyning the Old Testament, and the New." The listing on the table of contents page refers to them only as "The Bookes called Apocrypha" and segregates them, as in the text, from the Old and New Testaments. Additionally, both the Old and New Testaments have elaborate engravings placed before each Testament; the Apocrypha does not. The running heads that adorn the tops of the pages in the canon with summaries of the contents (e.g., in Genesis, "The creation of man;" "The first Sabbath;" "Marriage insti-tuted") are replaced in the Apocrypha by generic running heads that read only "Apocrypha" throughout and do not summarize. Further, the transla-tors of the KJV did not malign the canonical books of the Bible the way

---

[149] Geneva Bible, Preface

they did the Apocrypha. At 1 Esdras 5:5 the margin states, "This place is corrupt," an allusion found nowhere in either of the Testaments. The additional chapters to the Book of Esther are entitled "The rest of the Chapters of the Booke of Esther, which are found neither in the Hebrew, nor in the Calde."

Revisions And Printing Errors

Another popular argument used to oppose the KJV is to ask which edition of the KJV is being used, implying that the KJV has been substantially changed. If extreme changes in the text have occurred, there would be justification for additional revisions. The truth, however, is that the text has not really been changed. The revisions of the KJV dealt with the correction of early printing errors or the modernization of the text as it regards spelling and punctuation. The verses have remained the same.

There have been four major revisions of the KJV. They took place in 1629, 1638, 1762, and 1769. The 1762 revision was the work of Dr. F. S. Paris of the University at Cambridge. The work of this revision laid the foundation for most modern editions of the text. He greatly enhanced the use of italics (which in the KJV denote supplied words not in the original languages) and modernized most of the spelling. His edition also added several marginal references. The 1769 edition came from Oxford, and was the work of Dr. Benjamin Blayney. In this edition, several additional revisions were made in correcting earlier printing errors, spelling, and expanding marginal and introductory notes. This edition has become the standard by which modern texts are printed.

An example of differences in spelling may be seen in this comparison of Galatians 1:1-5 from a 1612 edition of the KJV and a current one. Note, however, that the text remains the same.

1612 Edition:

1. Paul an Apostle not of men, neither by man, but by Iesus Christ, and God the Father, who reised him from the dead, 2.

And all the brethren which are with me, vnto the Churches of Galatia: 3. Grace be to you and peace, from God the Father, and from our Lord Iesus Christ; 4. Who gaue himself for our sins, that he might deliuer vs from this present euil world, according to the will of God, & our Father. 5. To whom be glory for euer and euer, Amen.

Current Editions:

1. Paul, an apostle, (not of men, neither by man, but by Jesus Christ, and God the Father, who raised him from the dead;) 2. And all the brethren which are with me, unto the churches of Galatia: 3. Grace be to you and peace from God the Father, and from our Lord Jesus Christ, 4. Who gave himself for our sins, that he might deliver us from this present evil world, according to the will of God and our Father: 5. To whom be glory for ever and ever. Amen.

Other revisions sought to correct printing errors. Sometimes the printer omitted a word or words were printed twice. These were corrected in order to produce the text as the translators gave it.[150] The 1632 edition, for example, left out the word "not" in the Commandment "Thou shalt not commit adultery," thus earning it the nickname *The Wicked Bible*. Even today with computerized checking of the text, printing errors can occur. This does not

---

[150] Some examples of textual revisions that corrected obvious errors in printing include the following: Genesis 19:21 "this thing" was corrected to "this thing also." Deuteronomy 4:25 "shalt have remained" was corrected to "ye shall have remained." Nahum 3:17 "The crowned" was corrected to "Thy crowned." Acts 24:24 "which was a Jew" was corrected to "which was a Jewess." Jude 1:25 "now and ever" was corrected to "both now and ever." It is clear that the translators had originally provided the later readings that were corrupted in the process of the original publication of the 1611 edition by the printer. This is clearly seen in 1 Chronicles 5:2 where the 1611 edition mistakenly prints "chief rulers" and subsequent editions read "chief ruler." It is certain that the translators intended the singular and not the plural for the marginal note reads "or, Prince" establishing the reading as singular.

invalidate the preserved word of God or prove the KJV is corrupt. After all, one finds these same errors of transmission within the host of existing Greek manuscripts. Yet, it does not nullify the doctrine of preservation for the original reading still can be found despite copyists' mistakes.[151] It does mean that sometimes printers have made mistakes and the four major revisions of the KJV have sought to correct such errors.

"Printers have persecuted me without cause" (Psalm 119:161). Or so it reads in a 1702 edition of the KJV. One of the great misconceptions about the Authorized Version concerns the diverse errors printers have made throughout its history. Some have concluded that to correct its printing mistakes is to change the text. This, however, is not the case. Others have thought so highly of the King's Bible as to think that the printers were free from error. This, also, is not so. Printers have made quite a few errors in editions of the Authorized Version.

The first edition of the KJV is often called the "He Bible" because of the printing error that occurred at Ruth 3:15. Here, the first edition read "he went into the city" instead of "she went into the city." The corrected edition is sometimes referred to as the "She Bible." The number of printing errors in the first few decades of editions caused William Kilburne to write a treatise in 1659 entitled, *Dangerous Errors in Several Late Printed Bibles to the Great Scandal and Corruption of Sound and True Religion.*

Other misprints in the 1611 edition included Exodus 38:11 where "hoopes" was used for "hooks" and Leviticus 13:56, "the plaine be" for "the plague be." In Ezra 3:5 the printer repeated the word "offered" twice. The running head over the fourth chapter of Micah reads "Joel" instead of its proper name of Micah. "He" is used instead of "ye" in Ezekiel 6:8. In

---

[151] The difference is that there are no uncertain readings in regard to the KJV and errors produced by some printers. They are clearly known and corrected in later editions. This is something that cannot be said of errors produced by copyists in the manuscripts now extant. It is this uncertainty of which reading is original that has produced the science of textual criticism. This uncertainty does not exist regarding printing errors and the KJV.

Ezekiel 24:7, the text was to read, "She poured it not upon the ground"; however, the Royal Printer left out the word "not." In 1 Esdras 4 the running head reads "Anocrynha" instead of "Apocrypha," and several of these headings misnumber chapters immediately afterwards in 2 Esdras.

Between the printing conditions and the style of print, it can be easily understood why such errors occurred. Below are listed five passages where printing errors occurred in the 1611 edition. Even when we make adjustment for the differences in orthography and calligraphy it takes careful reading to locate these printing mistakes.

Genesis 10:15-18

And Canaan begat Sidon his firstborn, and Heth, And the Jebusite, and the Emorite, and the Girgasite, And the Hivite, and the Arkite, and the Sinite, And the Arvadite, and the Zemarite, and the Hamathite: and afterward were the families of the Canaanites spread abroad.

Exodus 14:10

And when Pharaoh drew nigh, the children of Israel lifted up their eyes, and, behold, the Egyptians marched after them; and they were sore afraid: and the children of Israel lifted up their eyes, and, behold, the Egyptians marched after them and they were sore afraid: and the children of Israel cried out unto the LORD.

Leviticus 17:14

For it is the life of all flesh; the blood of it is for the life thereof: therefore I said unto the children of Israel, Ye shall not eat the blood of no manner of flesh: for the life of all flesh is the blood thereof: whosoever eateth it shall be cut off.

Jeremiah 22:3

Thus saith the LORD; Execute ye judgment and righteousness, and deliver the spoiler out of the hand of the oppressor:
and do no wrong, do no violence to the stranger, the father-
less, nor the widow, neither shed innocent blood in this place.

Matthew 16:25
For whosoever will save his life shall lose it: and whosoever will
lose his his life for my sake shall find it.[152]

Other editions contained similar errata. In 1653 one edition read,
"Know ye not that the unrighteous shall inherit the kingdom of God" in 1
Corinthians 6:9. An 1801 edition misreads Jude 16 as, "There are mur-
derers, complainers, walking after their own lusts." The word "murmur-
ers" should have been used. "Discharge" is used instead of "charge" in an
1806 KJV printing at 1 Timothy 5:21, and "wife" was changed to "life" at
Luke 14:26 in an 1810 edition.

Even though errors occur occasionally in print, they are detected and
corrected in later editions. For example, notice how this 1638 edition
changes the text of Acts 6:3, yet it is now corrected to read as the 1611 edition read.

1611 edition:
Wherefore brethren, looke ye out among you seuen men of
honest report, full of the holy Ghost, and wisedome, whom
we may appoint ouer this businesse.

1638 edition:

---

[152] The printing errors are as follows: Genesis 10:16, "Emorite" for "Amorite." Exodus
14:10, three lines repeated. Leviticus 17:14, "ye shall not eat" for "ye shall eat." Jeremiah
22:3, "deliver the spoiler" for "deliver the spoiled." Matthew 16:25, "his" is repeated.

Wherefore, brethren, look ye out among you seven men of honest report, full of the Holy Ghost and wisdom, whom **ye** may appoint over this business.

Current edition:

Wherefore, brethren, look ye out among you seven men of honest report, full of the Holy Ghost and wisdom, whom **we** may appoint over this business.

An example of a printing error found in some current editions is located in Jeremiah 34:16. Here there is a difference in two editions, the one from Cambridge and the one from Oxford.

Cambridge edition:

But ye turned and polluted my name, and caused every man his servant, and every man his handmaid, whom **ye** had set at liberty at their pleasure, to return, and brought them into subjection, to be unto you for servants and for handmaids.

Oxford edition:

But ye turned and polluted my name, and caused every man his servant, and every man his handmaid, whom **he** had set at liberty at their pleasure, to return, and brought them into subjection, to be unto you for servants and for handmaids.

Is the correct reading "whom ye" or "whom he"? After all, both appear in various editions of the King James Version, depending on if they follow the Cambridge edition or the Oxford edition. This problem has nothing to do with preservation or the effectiveness of the KJV as a translation. It has to do with the correction of a printing error still in existence. The original edition of 1611 reads "whome yee had set at libertie at their pleasure." According to John R. Dore, "The University of Oxford did not begin to print Bibles until the year 1675, when the first was issued in quarto size; the spelling was revised by Dr. John Fell, Dean of Oxford."[153] Cambridge, agreeing with the edition of 1611, first began printing KJV Bibles in 1629 by Thomas and John Buck. Although one cannot prove that this error is the fault of Dr. John Fell in his 1675 Oxford edition, we can state that considerable time had passed before the error was introduced, and that the error was limited to the editions published by Oxford or those based on the Oxford edition. This has nothing to do with the issue of biblical preservation, for the correct reading is found in the original edition, the Cambridge edition, and current editions based on either the original 1611 or Cambridge editions.

It must be asserted that the text of the KJV has come to us *unaltered.* What has changed is the correction of printing errors, changes in punctuation and italics, and changes in orthography and calligraphy. This was verified by the American Bible Society in a report published in 1852 (after the fourth major revision of the KJV took place) entitled *Committee on Versions to the Board of Managers.* An additional report was issued in 1858 by the American Bible Society titled, *Report of the Committee on Versions to the Board of Managers of the American Bible Society.* Apart from the changes just listed, the reports stated that the "English Bible as left by the translators has come down to us unaltered in respect to its text."[154] John R. Dore, also attests to this. In a study published by the Royal Printers in 1888, Dore stated, "That pearl of great price, the English Bible of 1611, remained so long without alteration, that many of us had forgotten that it was only one of a series of versions."[155]

---

[153] Dore, 346.

[154] *Committee on Versions to the Board of Managers,* 1852 ed., 7.

[155] Dore, iii.

The Influence And Durability Of The Authorized Version

King James may not have been a great king; he may not have even been a good king. He did something, though, that no other monarch has ever done. He gave us the word of God in such a fashion that it has lasted for four hundred years. In fact, it has affected our very language, culture and history. Many of the common expressions we use have their roots in the Authorized Version. Here are a few examples:

Phrase	Reference
The fat of the land	Genesis 45:18
The skin of my teeth	Job 19:20
At their wit's end	Psalm 107:27
A soft answer	Proverbs 15:1
A thorn in the flesh	2 Corinthians 12:7
Labour of love	1 Thessalonians 1:3; Hebrews 6:10
The root of all evil	1 Timothy 6:10
Clear as crystal	Revelation 21:11; 22:1

Apart from Shakespeare's collected writings, no other body of work has had such influence on English literature. Unlike Shakespeare, who utilized the vast richness of English phraseology, the Authorized Version limited its vocabulary to a mere eight thousand words. Even with such economy of word choice, it has become a valued part of our language and culture. In his book *The Bible: Designed to be Read as Living Literature,* Ernest Sutherland Bates has correctly noted that the King James Version has secured a place for itself in literature along with Shakespeare, Homer, and Dante.[156] However, unlike these great works, it is the only one produced by a committee, and the only translation of Scripture that can make such a claim. Literary scholars have seen its influence on Milton, Pope, Byron,

---

[156] Ernest Sutherland Bates, *The Bible: Designed to be Read as Living Literature* (New York: Simon and Schuster, 1936), 1236.

Keats, Tennyson, Shaw, Whitman, Dickinson, and Twain, to name only a few. The classic Christian masterpiece *Pilgrim's Progress* by John Bunyan made use of this translation above all other early English versions that could have been used. Its rhythm and cadence speaks as no other English version ever has. Without question, the Authorized Version has influenced countless multitudes with its glorious presentation of the truth.

The KJV is not only a literary masterpiece; its representation of the original languages is phenomenal. It is not enough for a proper translation to correctly transmit the words from one language into another; it also must carry the sense of the original. Without question the Authorized Version has successfully accomplished this extremely difficult task. Professor Gerald Hammond of the University of Manchester, England, has correctly noted that the KJV translators "have taken care to reproduce the syntactic details of the originals."[157] He further notes that "At its best, which means often, the Authorized Version has the kind of transparency which makes it possible for the reader to see the original clearly. It lacks the narrow interpretative bias of modern versions, and is the stronger for it."[158] Textual and literary scholar Roland Mushat Frye agrees and writes that the KJV "makes possible translations of Hebrew poetry which are characterized at once by beauty of English form and essential faithfulness to the original."[159] Therefore, the KJV is not only outstanding English, it is outstanding as a representative of biblical languages.[160]

---

[157] Gerald Hammond, "English Translations Of The Bible," *The Literary Guide To The Bible*, eds. Robert Alter and Frank Kermode, (Cambridge, MA: The Belknap Press of Harvard University Press, 1987), 656.

[158] Ibid., 664.

[159] Roland Mushat Frye, "The Bible in English," *The Bible in its Literary Milieu*, eds. John Maier and Vincent Tollers, (Grand Rapids: Eerdmans, 1979), 255.

[160] The following is an example where the KJV provides insight that the Greek reader would also have. In Greek one can tell if the personal pronoun is singular or plural by the ending of the Greek word. The same is true of the English found in the KJV. The words "thou," "thee," "thy," and "thine" are all singular, allowing the reader to understand that personal pronouns beginning with "t" are singular. The words "ye," "you," and "your"

The King James Version has also affected our culture. With the expansion of the British Empire, the English language and culture spread throughout the world, taking with it the English Bible of 1611. In the New World the Authorized Version soon replaced the beloved Geneva Bible, and as early as 1637 it was the preferred translation throughout the Massachusetts Bay Colony.[161] Often the only book carried by pioneers during the western expansion was the King James Version. Likewise, it sometimes served as the sole source in teaching both settler and slave how to read. Historians Will and Ariel Durant credited it for diminishing the anti-Semitism that had run rampant throughout England prior to its translation. They write, "The spread of the Bible, accelerated by the King James Version, modified anti-Semitism by giving England a closer acquaintance with the Old Testament."[162] They may be correct, for the message of the gospel reminds us that "There is neither Jew nor Greek, there is neither bond nor free, there is neither male nor female: for ye are all one in Christ Jesus" (Galatians 3:28). Certainly, the Authorized Version serves as a polished jewel in the crown of English language and culture.

For the past four centuries the Authorized Version has served as the standard English Bible, reaching across denominational lines to reign in

are all plural, allowing the reader to know that personal pronouns beginning with "y" are plural. Luke 22:31-32 provides a good illustration: "And the Lord said, Simon, Simon, behold, Satan hath desired to have you, that he may sift you as wheat: But I have prayed for thee, that thy faith fail not: and when thou art converted, strengthen thy brethren." The Greek reader would understand from the words used that Christ is at first speaking to Peter about the disciples collectively, while in verse thirty-two Christ is speaking to Peter about him singularly. The same is conveyed in English with the words "you," "thy," and "thee." This is lost, however, when all these words are changed to a generic "you." Thus the reader cannot tell if the "you" is singular or plural.

[161] Nathan O. Hatch and Mark A. Noll, eds., *The Bible in America: Essays in Cultural History* (New York: Oxford University Press, 1982), 27-33.

[162] Will and Ariel Durant, *The Age Of Louis XIV* (New York: Simon and Schuster, 1963), 461.

the hearts of the English-speaking people. Even with the plethora of modern versions, the King James remains as the defining emblem of the English Bible. Although the New International Version has replaced the King James Version as the best selling translation among Christian booksellers for the past several years, the King James has remained in a strong second place among these booksellers while seemingly taking a much stronger lead as the version of choice. A 1995 poll concerning Bible translations showed that nearly all Americans own at least one version of the Bible, and that approximately two-thirds of those surveyed claim the Authorized Version as their main translation.[163] Additionally, in 1997 the Barna Research Group established that the King James Version is more likely to be read than the New International Version by a ratio of five to one.[164] Other polling through the Internet has established the King James as the most likely favored English translation.[165] The King James Version has maintained its place as a top selling version, it remains the most reproduced translation for the purpose of evangelism, and is the translation of choice in American households.

For years some have thought that the popularity of the King James Version would soon come to an end. Perhaps a day will come when a new translation of God's word will win the hearts of all English-speaking people as the Authorized Version has done. There may come a day, perhaps, when we will look back at a modern version and see that it has played a major role in the development of our language and literature with the

---

[163] As cited by Jennifer Lowe, "Buy the Book," *Dayton Daily News* (Dayton Ohio, Sept. 16, 1995), 7C.

[164] Barna Research Group, Ltd. (www.barna.org) 1997.

[165] Goshen Net (http://www.goshen.net) has provided an online Bible poll that establishes the KJV as the preferred translation. As of July 18, 2000 over ten thousand Internet users were asked to vote for their favorite English version. Their polling data showed the KJV at 49%, the NIV at 24%, the NKJV at 14%, the NASV at 5%, the ASV at 2% and the RSV and NRSV both at 1%. The category marked "Other" received 4%.

same impact that the version of 1611 has provided for us. Perhaps a day will arise when this new translation will affect our history and our very culture even as the King James Bible has done in the past four hundred years. There very well may come such a day…perhaps…but not today.

Chapter 6

Oracle Of The Jews

"They give us Scriptures, but Thou makest known the sense thereof. They bring us mysteries, but Thou revealest the things which are signified. They utter commandments, but Thou helpest to the fulfilling of them. They show the way, but Thou givest strength for the journey."

-Thomas `a Kempis, *The Imitation of Christ* (1415)

According to Scripture the Hebrews were God's oracles (Romans 3:1-2). It was unto the Jews that the Old Testament revelation and canon were committed. This is why twice in the Old Testament they were instructed not to add to or take from the word of God.

> Ye shall not add unto the word which I command you, neither shall ye diminish ought from it, that ye may keep the commandments of the LORD your God which I command you. (Deuteronomy 4:2).
> Add thou not unto his words, lest he reprove thee, and thou be found a liar. (Proverbs 30:6).

Faithful Hebrew scribes took this task very seriously.[166] Precise steps were taken in preparing the parchment upon which they wrote, and in preparing themselves in order to write on it. According to the Hebrew

---

[166] It is traditionally thought that Rabbi Aqiba (55-137 AD) was responsible either directly or indirectly for the standardization of the Hebrew text and for the strict rules associated with the copying of the text. See Bleddyn J. Roberts, "The Old Testament: Manuscripts, Text and Versions," *The Bible in its Literary Millieu*, eds. John Maier and Vincent Tollers (Grand Rapids: Eerdmans, 1979), 213.

Talmud, a body of civil and religious laws that also provided commentary on the Hebrew Scriptures, the rules for the scribes consisted of the following:

1. The skins of the parchments had to be prepared in a special way and dedicated to God so that they would be clean in order to have God's words written on them.

2. The ink that was used was black and made in accordance to a special recipe used only for writing Scripture.

3. The words written could not be duplicated by memory but must be reproduced from an authentic copy that the scribe had before him. And, the scribe had to say each word aloud as he wrote it.

4. Each time the scribe came across the Hebrew word for God, he had to wipe his pen clean. And when he came across the name of God, Jehovah (YHWH),[167] he had to wash his whole body before he could write it.

5. If a sheet of parchment had one mistake on it, the sheet was condemned. If there were three mistakes found on any page, the whole manuscript was condemned. Each scroll had to be checked within thirty days of its writing, or it was considered unholy.

6. Every word and every letter was counted. If a letter or word was omitted, the manuscript was condemned.

7. There were explicit rules for how many letters and words were allowed on any given parchment. A column must have at least forty-eight lines and no more than sixty. Letters and words had to be spaced at a certain distance and no word could touch another.[168]

---

[167] Or, Yahweh.

[168] There are over twenty rules for scribes to follow when copying the sacred text. These rules are found throughout the Talmud in places such as Tractates Eruvin, Sota, Megillah, Menachot and many more. Because of such strict rules that have been faithfully followed throughout the centuries the textual differences are extremely miniscule. For example, there are 304,805 letters found in the Torah. For hundreds of years, the Yemenite community was not part of the Jewish global checking system. Yet when compared there are only nine letter-differences found in the Yemenite Torah with that of the

In his book, *The Text of the Old Testament*, noted Old Testament textual scholar Dr. Ernst Wurthwein mentions that the scribes counted the verses, words, and letters of each part of the Scriptures they were copying.[169] The Jewish historian Josephus (37-95 AD) comments on the preciseness of the Jewish scribes and their faithfulness in copying the Old Testament Scriptures:

…for during so many ages as have already passed, no one has been so bold as either to add anything to them, to take anything from them, or to make any change in them; but it becomes natural to all Jews, immediately and from their very birth, to esteem those books to contain divine doctrines, and to persist in them, and, if occasion be, willingly to die for them.[170]

Some have taken Josephus' statement to mean *the contents* of the Old Testament. Other have understood it to mean *the canon* of the Old Testament. Either way, his statement affirms the sacredness the Hebrews ascribe to Holy Scripture.

For years it had been thought that the Bible Christ used was the Greek Septuagint (also known as the LXX). The common thought was that the Jews at the time of Christ had all but lost their use of Hebrew since the international language of that day was Greek. However, with the discovery of the Dead Sea Scrolls (which will be discussed in greater detail in the following chapter), it has been established that the Jews did not lose their use of Hebrew. In fact, most of their writings (both sacred and otherwise) were written in Hebrew.

Jewish global community, and these differences deal only with spelling and not word meaning. Certainly this system of copying Scripture has been remarkably successful and helps to illustrate the veracity of biblical preservation.

[169] Ernst Wurthwein, *The Text of the Old Testament* (Grand Rapids: Eerdmans, 1979), 19.

[170] Flavius Josephus, "Flavius Josephus Against Apion," Book 1, *The Works of Josephus*, trans. William Whiston (Peabody, MA: Hendrickson, 1987), 776.

Alan Millard, Professor of Hebrew and Ancient Semitic Languages at the University of Liverpool, England, observed that for years scholars believed that Hebrew was limited to religious usage during the time of Christ. But from the discovery of the Dead Sea Scrolls and books written in common Hebrew among them, it can now be established that a form of Hebrew, like the Hebrew used in the Old Testament yet distinct in form, was in use during the time of Christ and the apostles.[171] This confirms what we find in the Gospels concerning the Hebrew Old Testament used by Christ. Jesus proclaimed; "For verily I say unto you, Till heaven and earth pass, one jot or one tittle shall in no wise pass from the law, till all be fulfilled" (Matthew 5:18). It is interesting that Christ used the words *jot* and *tittle* which are Hebrew letters, not Greek.[172] Additionally, Jesus states in Luke 11:51; "From the blood of Abel unto the blood of Zecharias," attesting to the Hebrew order of Scripture. The placement of Old Testament books are different in the Jewish order, ending with 2 Chronicles and not Malachi. In 2 Chronicles 24:21 we are told of the stoning of faithful Zechariah, and Christ's statement not only spoke of the martyrdom of Old Testament saints, but marks the limits of the Hebrew order: from the beginning (Genesis) to the end (2 Chronicles).[173]

The Masoretic Text

The Masoretic Text is the traditional Hebrew Old Testament text of both Judaism and Protestantism. The Roman Catholic Church historically has used the Latin Vulgate translated by Jerome, though this position has been revised and now the Catholic Church uses the Hebrew text. The

---

[171] Alan Millard, *Discoveries From the Time of Jesus* (Oxford: Lion, 1990), 35.

[172] Homer A. Kent, *The Wycliffe Bible Commentary*, eds. Charles F. Pfeiffer and Everett F. Harrison (Nashville: The Southwestern Company, 1968), 937.

[173] The traditional order of books in Hebrew Scripture are as follows: The Pentateuch (the five books of Moses). The Prophets (major and minor). The Writings (Psalms, Proverbs, Job, Song of Solomon, Ruth, Lamentations, Ecclesiastes, Esther, Daniel, Ezra, Nehemiah, and Chronicles).

Orthodox Church has historically used the Greek Septuagint. *Masoretic*[174] comes from the Hebrew word *masora,* referring to the marginal notes added by Jewish scribes and scholars of the Middle Ages (known as the *Masoretes*).

Until recently, the most ancient manuscripts of the Hebrew Old Testament dated to the ninth century. This has changed with the discovery of the Dead Sea Scrolls, which date from 168 BC to about 68 AD. The Scrolls provide us with Hebrew manuscripts more ancient than the previous manuscripts by one thousand years.[175] What is interesting to the student of textual criticism and the believer in biblical preservation is that the majority of biblical manuscripts among the Dead Sea Scrolls agree with the Masoretic Text.[176] This further provides evidence of the text's credibility and testifies to the accuracy of the Hebrew scribes in their reproduction of biblical manuscripts throughout the ages. Consequently, it establishes the preservation of the Old Testament text in Hebrew by God.

The earliest biblical fragments among the Scrolls come from the book of Leviticus (1QLev.*a*) and add support to the antiquity of the Masoretic Text.[177] These fragments encompass Leviticus 19:31-34 and 20:20-23. There is but one minor variant from the Masoretic Text found in 20:21. The Masoretic Text uses the Hebrew word *hoo* while the Dead Sea Scrolls uses the Hebrew word *he.* It is the same Hebrew word and is a personal pronoun meaning *he, she,* or *it.* The two are used interchangeably throughout the Hebrew Old Testament.

---

[174] Sometimes spelled as *Massoretic.*

[175] Appendix C supplies the reader with a list of biblical texts in the Dead Sea Scrolls, as well as some of the oldest Masoretic manuscripts and Greek manuscripts of the New Testament.

[176] Bruce M. Metzger and Michael D. Coogan, eds., *The Oxford Companion to the Bible* (Oxford: Oxford University Press, 1993), 160.

[177] Wurthwein, 148.

Additional manuscripts have also been found that supports the Masoretic Text. In the early 1960's biblical texts were discovered during the excavation of Masada, the renowned rock fortress where Jewish zealots made a successful last stand against the Roman army after the destruction of Jerusalem in 70 AD. These texts were approximately nineteen hundred years old, dating slightly before 73 AD when Masada finally fell. The manuscripts were exclusively Masoretic.[178] To these we can also add the Geniza Fragments which were discovered in 1890 at Cairo, Egypt. These fragments date to the fifth century AD. They were located in a geniza, a type of storage room for worn or faulty manuscripts. The fragments number around two hundred thousand and reflect biblical texts in Hebrew, Aramaic, and Arabic. The biblical texts discovered support the Masoretic Text.[179]

In one sense, the Masoretic Text may be thought of as the Textus Receptus (Latin for *received text*) of the Old Testament. In fact, some scholars have referred to it as such. Like the Textus Receptus of the New Testament, the Masoretic Text is based on the majority of manuscripts and reflects the Traditional Text used. Although there are differences found in some Masoretic Texts, these differences are minor and usually deal with orthography, vowel points, accents, and divisions of the text. In 1524-25, Daniel Bomberg published an edition of the Masoretic Text based on the tradition of Jacob ben Chayyim,[180] a Jewish refugee who later became a Christian. It was his text that was used by the translators of the King James Version for their work in the Old Testament. Wurthwein notes that the text of ben Chayyim was looked upon as almost canonical, and was considered the authoritative Hebrew text.[181]

For about six generations the ben Asher family reproduced the Masoretic Text. Moses ben Asher produced a text in 895 AD known as

---

[178] Ibid., 31.
[179] Ibid., 12-13.
[180] *Second Rabbinic Bible*
[181] Wurthwein, 37.

Codex Cairensis containing the writings of the Prophets. Codex Leningradensis (cataloged as "Firkovich B 19 A") dates to 1008 AD and was based on the work of Aaron ben Moses ben Asher, the son of Moses ben Asher. This codex is the oldest Masoretic manuscript containing the complete Bible. In 1935 the manuscript was loaned to the University of Leipzig for two years while Rudolf Kittel used it for his *Biblia Hebraica*, third edition. Kittel's *Biblia Hebraica* has since then become the standard Hebrew text used by scholars in producing modern translations of the Old Testament.[182]

Generally scholarship agrees that the Masoretic Text became the standard authorized Hebrew text around 100 AD in connection with the completion of the New Testament. It is obvious the Masoretic Text existed prior to the writings of the New Testament, and it was used as the official Hebrew Old Testament at the time of the establishment of the biblical canon. It has been used since as the official representation of the Hebrew originals.

The Greek Septuagint

The most notable Greek Old Testament, and arguably the most influential early translation of the Hebrew canon, is the Septuagint (LXX). The LXX is believed to have been translated from the Hebrew text by Hellenistic Jews during a period from 275 to 100 BC at Alexandria, Egypt. Scholars such as Ralph W. Klein have noted that the LXX used a different Hebrew text than the one found in the Masoretic Text.[183] Jerome

---

[182] An example of a textual difference between the Masoretic Text and Kittel's *Biblia Hebraica* can be found in Isaiah 9:3. The Masoretic Text reads, "Thou hast multiplied the nation, and not increased the joy" (KJV). Kittel's *Biblia Hebraica* reads, "You have multiplied the nation, you have increased its joy" (NRSV).

[183] Ralph W. Klein, *Textual Criticism of the Old Testament: The Septuagint After Qumran* (Philadelphia: Fortress Press, 1974).

used the LXX extensively as a help in translating his Latin Vulgate, and it remains the official Old Testament of the Greek Orthodox Church.

The association of the Latin numeral LXX (70) with the Septuagint comes from a legend concerning the origin of this Greek translation. According to the *Letter of Aristeas,*[184] Jewish scholars were chosen to translate the Law of Moses into Greek so that it could be added to the great library of Ptolemy Philadelphus in Alexandria, Egypt. The letter states that the High Priest in Jerusalem sent seventy-two scholars to the Egyptian king. According to this document, the High Priest writes to the king as follows:

> In the presence of all the people I selected six elders from each tribe, good men and true, and I have sent them to you with a copy of our law. It will be a kindness, O righteous king, if you will give instruction that as soon as the translation of the law is completed, the men shall be restored again to us in safety.[185]

Six scholars from the twelve tribes of Israel equal a total of seventy-two. It is assumed that the seventy is merely a rounding off of the seventy-two. It is further stated that they accomplished their task in seventy-two days. Even if the story given in the *Letter of Aristeas* could be taken as literally true, it deals only with the translation of the first five books of the Old Testament. Furthermore, most scholars note that there are differences in style and quality of translation within the LXX and assign a much greater time frame than the 72 days allotted in the *Letter of Aristeas.*

The most noted copy of the LXX, produced by Origen, is an Old Testament consisting of six parallel versions of the Scriptures called the

---

[184] *The Letter Of Aristeas* covers events which took place during the lifetime of Queen Arsinoe, who died in 270 BC, and the formation of the LXX. However, the exact date and authorship of this letter is unknown. Both Josephus [Antiq. 12:2] and Philo [On the Life of Moses II, 27-40] record the history of the LXX, most probably based on this epistle.

[185] *The Letter of Aristeas* 2:34-35 as presented in *The Lost Books of the Bible* (World Bible Publishers, Inc.).

Hexapla, meaning *six-fold*. The columns of the Hexapla consisted of: 1. The Hebrew text. 2. The Hebrew transliterated into Greek. 3. The Greek translation of Aquila. 4. The Greek translation of Symmachus. 5. The Septuagint. 6. The Greek translation of Theodotion. With the exception of a few limited fragments, we do not have Origen's Hexapla today. We cannot fully reconstruct Origen's fifth column, let alone a pre-Origenian Septuagint.

Origen's Hexapla was revised and edited by two of his disciples, Pamphilus and Eusebius. As mentioned above, there were other Greek translations of the Old Testament during this time, in addition to the LXX, which were contained in the Hexapla such as the versions of Aquila and Theodotion. Some scholars believe that the translation produced by Theodotion replaced the LXX in the book of Daniel, so that the readings there are really those of Theodotion and not of the LXX. Others have claimed that this is not the case. Concerning Origen's Hexapla and the LXX, the best scholars can say is that what has survived represents Origen's text.[186] Two such manuscripts that represent the text of Origen are Codex Vaticanus and Codex Sinaiticus of the Alexandrian line of manuscripts.

The LXX And The New Testament

There are a number of Old Testament quotations found in the New Testament that are said to be from the LXX. Several of these passages agree because of the limitations of translating Hebrew into Greek. Such would be the case in Genesis 5:24 as compared with Hebrews 11:5. The writer of the book of Hebrews and the LXX both use the phrase "God translated him" in reference to Enoch. The Greek, *metetheken auton o theos*, is the same in both the New Testament and the LXX.

---

[186] Wurthwein, 57.

Genesis 5:24 (KJV)
And Enoch walked with God: and he was not; for God took
him.

Genesis 5:24 (LXX)
And Enoch was well-pleasing to God, and was not found,
because God translated him.

Hebrews 11:5 (KJV)
By faith Enoch was translated that he should not see death;
and was not found because God had translated him: for before
his translation he had this testimony, that he please God.

At first glance it would seem that the passage in Hebrews is closer to the
LXX. However, the Hebrew word for "took" in this passage is *lawkakh,*
which means to take or move from one place to another. The Greek way
of saying the Hebrew *lawkakh* is *metetheken,* which means "translated."
This is not a citation of the LXX, but a Greek translation of the Hebrew
word for *took.*

There are times when the Greek of the LXX and the Greek of the New
Testament match perfectly. There are also places where the two do not
match. To explain this most scholars assume the New Testament writers
were paraphrasing from the LXX. But once we explore the possibility that
the citations are not quotations but paraphrases of the LXX, we can no
longer be certain it was the LXX that was originally used.

Romans 9:17 illustrates this. While part of the passage seems to match
the LXX, part does not at all match. This causes us to wonder why Paul
did not fully quote the LXX if it was his source.

Exodus 9:16 (KJV)
And in very deed for this cause have I raised thee up, for to
shew in thee my power; and that my name may be declared
throughout all the earth.

Exodus 9:16 (LXX)
And for this purpose hast thou been preserved, that I might display in thee my strength, and that my name might be declared throughout all the earth.

Romans 9:17 (KJV)
For the Scripture saith unto Pharaoh, Even for this same purpose have I raised thee up, that I might shew my power in thee, and that my name might be declared throughout all the earth.

The last phrase, "and that my name might be declared throughout all the earth" is a perfect match between the New Testament and the LXX, as is the phrase "that I might shew my power in thee." However, this also matches the Hebrew text as seen in the King James rendering of Exodus 9:16. It is important to note that there are differences between the LXX and the Greek New Testament at the very beginning and in the middle of the verse. The Greek New Testament begins with *Oti eis auto touto exegeira se opos* (For this purpose have I raised out thee, so that). The LXX begins with *Kai eneken toutou dieterethes, ina* (And for this purpose hast thou been preserved, that). These are two differing readings in both Greek and English. Moreover, the New Testament uses the Greek word *dunamin* (power), while the LXX uses the Greek word *ischun* (strength).

Since there are differences between the New Testament citations in both the LXX and the Masoretic Text, the question arises as to what translation the writers of the New Testament used. At times it seems they are using the Traditional Hebrew Text; at other times it seems as if they are taking great liberties with the Hebrew text. Sometimes their quote matches the LXX; other times their citation differs from the LXX. How do we resolve this dilemma?

First, not every passage cited as an Old Testament quotation is actually a quotation. Many times a given passage is simply an allusion or a general reference. Second, just because one quotes from a source does not mean he is fully endorsing that source. We find, for example, Paul citing from the philosophies of the Greeks in order to reach the Greeks (Acts 17:23; Titus 1:12). This did not mean that he accepted their philosophies. Third, we must remember that the writers of the New Testament had a unique position. They wrote under *inspiration*. Both the Old and New Testaments are Holy Scripture inspired by the Holy Spirit. It is God's word and he certainly has the right to make changes as he sees fit, a liberty any author can take when self-quoting.

On the whole, it seems unlikely that the writers of the New Testament favored the Greek LXX over the Hebrew Masoretic Text. Sir Frederic Kenyon brilliantly observed that the biblical guardians of the Old Testament, the Jews, throughout history have not accepted the LXX. Josephus, for example, rejected the LXX because of its addition to the Hebrew canon of Scripture, as did other strict Jewish scribes.[187] Likewise, scholarship recognizes that the enhancement of the LXX in history came not from the Jewish scribes but from sources within Christendom around the third century. Therefore, it does not seem likely that the New Testament writers would have embraced such a translation, at least not to the exclusion of the Hebrew text. Dr. Ernst Wurthwein correctly stated that the LXX does not shed light on the text of the original Hebrew, but only on how *some* interpreted the Hebrew text.[188] Yet, many scholars of the past one hundred years or so have seemed to prefer it over the Masoretic Text, something Wurthwein found to be astounding.[189] When we consider all of this, we understand the wisdom of the KJV translators in preferring the Hebrew Masoretic Text for their translation of the Old Testament.

---

[187] Frederic G. Kenyon, *The Text of the Greek Bible* (London: Gerald Duckworth and Company), 29.

[188] Wurthwein, 63-64.

[189] Ibid.

The LXX And The KJV Translators

It is interesting to note how the translators of the KJV viewed the LXX. They recognized that it was produced by *interpreters* and not by inspired *prophets*. They admitted that although the LXX translates many things well, it also failed many times and departed from the Hebrew causing the New Testament writers to depart from the LXX.

> ...the *Seventy* were interpreters, they were not prophets. They did many things well, as learned men; but yet as men they stumbled and fell, one while through oversight, another while through ignorance; yea, sometimes they may be noted to add to the original, and sometimes to take from it: which made the Apostles to leave them many times, when they left the *Hebrew*, and to deliver the sense thereof according to the truth of the word, as the Spirit gave them utterance. This may suffice touching the *Greek* translations of the Old Testament.[190]

It is also clear that the KJV translators promoted the use of such translations since they recognized the importance of having God's word translated into the language of those who cannot read Hebrew or Greek, despite the lack of quality and accuracy contained in those translations.[191] Their argument with the Catholic Church, which at that time made a practice of burning Bibles that were in any language other than Latin, was that God's word translated poorly was still God's word and must be treated with respect and dignity. They illustrate their point with the Greek translations of Aquila, Theodotion, and the LXX.

---

[190] "The Translators To The Reader," *The Holy Bible: King James Version* (Cambridge: Cambridge University Press), xiv-xv.

[191] This belief conflicts with the modern thought that a plethora of versions in the same language should be made available, even if they differ in wording and meaning.

The Romanists therefore in refusing to hear, and daring to burn the word translated, did no less than despite the Spirit of grace, from whom originally it proceeded, and whose sense and meaning, as well as man's weakness would enable, it did express…The like we are to think of translations. The translation of the *Seventy* dissenteth from the Original in many places, neither doth it come near it for perspicuity, gravity, majesty; yet which of the Apostles did condemn it? Condemn it? Nay, they used it…To be short, Origen, and the whole Church of God for certain hundred years, were of another mind: for they were so far from treading under foot, (much more from burning) the translation of *Aquila* a proselyte, that is, one that had turned Jew; of Symmachus, and Theodotion, both Ebionites, that is, one vile hereticks, that they joined them together with the *Hebrew* original, and the translation of the *Seventy,* (as hath been before signified out of *Epiphanius*) and set them forth openly to be considered of and perused by all.[192]

The demeanor of the New Testament writers, early Christians, and the KJV translators regarding the LXX provide for us a two-fold argument. First, the importance of accuracy and nobility in regard to the translation of God's word. Truth must not be replaced with either ease or simplicity. That which God has given is of utmost importance and should be proclaimed in its unique majesty. After all, one is dealing with the words of the most Sovereign King. Second, the vilest translation of men poorly done should be corrected, not destroyed or defamed. An inferior translation, when that is all one has, is better than

---

[192] Ibid., xix-xx.

no translation. Fortunately for English-speaking people worldwide, the second point has fallen prey to the first. Nevertheless, it is better to promote God's word translated than to disparage it.

Chapter 7

Understanding The Dead Sea Scrolls

"It is concealed and hidden, but God does not forget it. Delayed is not forgotten!"

-Hans Christian Andersen, *Delaying Is Not Forgetting* (1872)

West of the northern half of the Dead Sea lies the ruins of Qumran. A fantastic discovery was made in 1947 in the various caves throughout that region. Scrolls and fragments of scrolls were found. These ancient writings became the center of attention for the media, as well as for students of the Bible and archaeology. Like sheep desiring water, a Bedouin shepherd had led a thirsty world to the most acclaimed find of the twentieth century, the Dead Sea Scrolls.

Many claims have been made regarding the Scrolls. Some, while drinking at this newly found fountain of knowledge, have seen the Scrolls as a pool of Bethesda offering spiritual or academic healing of some sort. Others have seen them as the waters of Marah, bitter and full of corruption. Perhaps the best way to view them is to see them for what they are, scrolls written by scribes. Like the many writings of men, they offer things that are both sweet and bitter.

At least five hundred different scribes were responsible for writing the Dead Sea Scrolls.[193] Most of the Scrolls are dated before the time of Christ,

---

[193] Norman Golb, *Who Wrote The Dead Sea Scrolls?* (New York: Scribner, 1995), 154.

while some are dated during and after Christ. One wonders if any of the writers of the Scrolls heard the message of Jesus Christ and his condemnation for not practicing what they had copied (Matthew 23:13). What is certain, however, is that those scribes who heard the Savior's message had access to what became known as the Dead Sea Scrolls.

Historical Background

The story tells of a shepherd boy, Muhammad adh-Dhib (which means *Muhammad the wolf*), out seeking his lost goat (or sheep according to some accounts). Thinking that the animal had wandered into one of the many nearby caves, Muhammad threw a stone into one of them hoping to hear the sound of his lost goat scurrying off. Instead, he heard the sound of a jar breaking. Calling one of his friends, he entered the cave and found ancient manuscripts lying in the cave, hidden in primitive jars.

There are other versions concerning Muhammad adh-Dhib and his amazing discovery. One account says the fifteen-year-old shepherd was simply herding some goats when he found the cave. Still other accounts say that Muhammad adh-Dhib was seeking shelter from a storm in the cave when he came across the manuscripts. There is also the story of shepherds who were smuggling goods from Jordan to Bethlehem who inadvertently found the Scrolls.

Regardless which account of the story is true, the seven scrolls discovered in this cave are very significant findings. The scrolls found in what was later designated as Cave 1 were the two Isaiah Scrolls (1QIsa.*a* and 1QIsa.*b*), The Habakkuk Commentary, The Manual of Discipline, The Thanksgiving Scroll, The War Scroll, and the Genesis Apocryphon. Later, additional manuscripts were discovered revealing the vast majority of the Old Testament books along with additional religious and secular writings. Scholars consider these scrolls and fragments to be the greatest manuscript discovery of modern times.

Cave 1 is located in the northwest corner of the Dead Sea, about a mile and a half from the shore line in what was then the Wilderness of Jordan. It also stands about a mile from the Khirbet Qumran, the old ruins believed to be the dwelling place of the Essene sect. However, at the time of the discovery, Qumran was thought of as an old fortress.

Dr. Eliezer Sukenik, who purchased some of the shepherd's findings, took three of the scrolls to the Hebrew University in Jerusalem. The other scrolls were sold to St. Mark's, a Syrian Orthodox Church in Jerusalem, where the church's head, Metropolitan Mar Samuel, retained them. Samuel took the scrolls to the American School of Oriental Research, also in Jerusalem, for their examination. It was then that an announcement was made to the world. In the *Times* of London an article dated April 12, 1948, read as follows:

> Yale University announced yesterday the discovery in Palestine of the earliest known manuscript of the Book of Isaiah. It was found in the Syrian monastery of St. Mark in Jerusalem, where it had been preserved in a scroll of parchment dating to about the first century BC. Recently it was identified by scholars of the American School of Oriental Research at Jerusalem.
>
> There were also examined at the school three other ancient Hebrew scrolls. One was part of a commentary on the Book of Habakkuk; another seemed to be a manual of discipline of some comparatively little-known sect or monastic order, possibly the Essenes. The third scroll has not been identified.[194]

---

[194] As cited by James C. VanderKam, *The Dead Sea Scrolls Today* (Grand Rapids: Eerdmans, 1994), 6.

Dr. Sukenik's son, Yigael Yadin (also noted as a Qumran expert), was in the United States in 1954. Mar Samuel was visiting the United States at that same time seeking to sell his scrolls. Yadin purchased the four scrolls from Mar Samuel for $250,000 dollars and gave them to the newly formed state of Israel. The seven scrolls were united and placed in a special museum, shaped like the lid of one of the jars in which the scrolls were kept. The museum is known as the *Shrine of the Book*.

It was difficult to excavate the caves in the late 1940's and early 1950's, an unsettled period in Middle Eastern history. By the time the importance of the scrolls was known, the state of Israel was being formed. War raged in the Middle East. Despite this turbulent interval, the Bedouins continued to search the region and discovered additional scrolls. Eventually, eleven caves were excavated and thousands of fragments were discovered. Through the years these scrolls and scroll fragments have gradually been translated and published. Many of the manuscripts remained unpublished until the early 1990's.[195]

Dating the Scrolls has always been a problem as not all scholars agree in this area. For the most part, the Scrolls are dated from about the third century BC to around 68 AD. The method of dating rests on several factors. Findings among the Scrolls or at Qumran, such as pots and coins, have helped set certain dates. Paleography, the science of dating manuscripts by the shape of letters used in writing, also helps determine the dates of the Scrolls. Carbon-14 dating was used on the cloth that held one of the Isaiah scrolls, but until recently Carbon-14 dating could not be used on the Scrolls themselves because it required a large section of a scroll to be destroyed. Now Carbon-14 dating methods have improved and only a small fragment is needed for this process. George Bonani in the *Biblical Archaeology Review* reports that the dates fixed by paleography have been

---

[195] Robert Eisenman and Michael Wise, *The Dead Sea Scrolls Uncovered* (New York: Barnes & Noble, 1992), 1-16.

confirmed by Carbon-14 dating.[196] It is interesting, however, that the Masada manuscript of Joshua, which is of the Masoretic Text, had been dated by scholars as written somewhere around 30 AD according to pale-ographic studies. Carbon-14 dating on the same manuscript gave it a range of 150 to 75 BC.

Textual Variance Among The Scrolls

Some have mistakenly assumed that the Dead Sea Scrolls contain only biblical writings. Actually the Scrolls reflect a library scattered throughout eleven caves, containing biblical and non-biblical books. Some are still in scroll form, but most are fragmentary after over two thousand years of aging. With the exceptions of Esther and Nehemiah, every book of the Old Testament is represented in the findings at Qumran.[197] It should be noted, however, that *representation* and *full representation* are not the same thing. Some books are represented with only fragmentary evidence in very limited number, while other books are better and more fully represented among the findings.

In the most current published lists of manuscripts among the Dead Sea Scrolls there are thirty-six manuscripts which represent the Book of Psalms, making it the most represented biblical book among the Scrolls. Deuteronomy follows with twenty-nine manuscripts and Isaiah with twenty-one. First and Second Chronicles are represented by only one manuscript, as is Ezra. Most of the others are represented by fewer than ten manuscripts. The exceptions are those previously listed, as well as Genesis (with fifteen manuscripts), Exodus (with seventeen), and

---

[196] George Bonani, "Carbon-14 Tests Substantiate Scroll Dates," *Biblical Archaeology Review*, November/December 1991, 72.

[197] Martin Abegg Jr., Peter Flint, and Eugene Ulrich have recently translated into English the biblical books among the Dead Sea Scrolls. *The Dead Sea Scrolls Bible* (San Francisco: Harper San Francisco, 1999).

Leviticus (with thirteen). There are about eight hundred manuscripts among the Scrolls. Of these, slightly over two hundred represent biblical books, which means only about one-fourth of the Qumran library contained copies of the Scriptures.

It should also be pointed out that not all of these biblical books represent the same textual history. The biblical books found at Qumran are divided into three textual categories:

1. Manuscripts that represent the Masoretic Traditional Text.
2. Manuscripts that represent the text of the Septuagint.
3. Manuscripts that represent the Samaritan text.

However, according to Dr. Emanuel Tov, who became co-editor-in-chief of the Dead Sea Scrolls in 1991, there are two additional groups.

4. Texts that demonstrate a unique style of writing, spelling, and grammar found only at Qumran.
5. Nonaligned texts that do not show any allegiance to the four other groups. About twenty-five percent of the biblical manuscripts found at Qumran fall into the nonaligned category.[198]

The Proto-Masoretic Text

These manuscripts are called Proto-Masoretic because they agree with the Masoretic Text, yet date before the Masoretic Text became the official Hebrew Bible. It should be noted that the Dead Sea Scrolls have greatly enhanced the evidence supporting the authority of the Masoretic Text. Until the findings at Qumran (as well as findings at Wadi Murabbaat), the oldest Masoretic Texts dated to the Middle Ages. With Qumran, we now have manuscripts almost a thousand years older that are Masoretic. Most of the scrolls from Cave 4 are of this text-type and represent biblical books

---

[198] VanderKam, 133-134.

such as Isaiah, Ezekiel, the Minor Prophets, and some fragments of the Law and Historical books.

The most noted group is perhaps the Isaiah Scrolls. Two scrolls containing the book of Isaiah were found in Cave 1. The first is sometimes called the St. Mark's Manuscript (1QIsa.*a*) because it was initially owned by St. Mark's Monastery. The second is sometimes called the Hebrew University manuscript of Isaiah (1QIsa.*b*) because it is owned by that university. Both represent the Masoretic Hebrew Text and are major victories for the Masoretic Text and the Authorized Version.

Textual scholar Dr. James C. VanderKam has pointed out that 1QIsa.*a* is almost identical to the copies of Isaiah dating to the Middle Ages. Any differences are minor and hardly ever affect the meaning of the text.[199] Dr. Menahem Mansoor, another textual scholar, has likewise stated that most of the differences are spelling or grammatical changes. Those that do not fall into this type are minor, such as an omission or addition of a word or two, or the mixing of Hebrew letters.[200] One such minor variant is found in Isaiah 6:3. The Masoretic Text and the King James Bible read, "Holy, holy, holy, is the LORD of hosts." The St. Mark's Isaiah text reads, "Holy, holy is the LORD of hosts." Therefore, while 1QIsa.*a* may be in error in its omission of the third *holy*, the contents of this scroll overwhelmingly support the Masoretic Text.

As close as this scroll is to the Masoretic tradition, the Hebrew University's Isaiah scroll is closer.[201] Textual scholar Dr. Ernst Wurthwein concurred, calling the agreement between 1QIsa.*b* and the Masoretic Text "striking."[202] Considering that a thousand years separate the Isaiah Scrolls from their Masoretic counterparts, the term *striking* may be an

---

[199] Ibid., 126.

[200] Menahem Mansoor, *The Dead Sea Scrolls* (Grand Rapids: Eerdmans, 1964), 74-75.

[201] Ibid., 79.

[202] Ernst Wurthwein, *The Text of the Old Testament* (Grand Rapids: Eerdmans, 1979), 144.

understatement. In either case, the evidence from Qumran demonstrates the Traditional Hebrew Text existed long before the Middle Ages, once again establishing the biblical principle of preservation.

About forty percent of the biblical texts of the Dead Sea Scrolls are Masoretic. Further, the group of manuscripts listed by Dr. Tov as unique to Qumran also resembles the later Masoretic Text.[203] These texts account for twenty-five percent of the Dead Sea Scrolls. Therefore, among the biblical books of Dead Sea Scrolls, sixty-five percent reflect the Traditional Text of the Old Testament.

Providing additional support to the Masoretic readings among the Dead Sea Scrolls are findings at Wadi Murabbaat and Masada. In 1951, caves at Wadi Murabbaat, which is south of Qumran near the Dead Sea, were discovered which contained biblical manuscripts. The major difference here is that these biblical texts *exclusively* reflect the Masoretic Text.[204] These manuscripts, however, are slightly younger and are believed to have been written between 132 and 135 AD. Still, their relationship to the Masoretic Text of the Middle Ages is virtually identical to that of the Proto-Masoretic Qumran group.[205] The findings at Murabbaat include the Pentateuch, Isaiah, the Minor Prophets, and the book of Psalms.

Between 1963 and 1965 manuscripts were discovered while excavating Masada, the famous rock fortress where Jewish nationalists withheld the advances of the Roman army in 73 or 74 AD. Masada is farther south of Qumran than Wadi Murabbaat, along the western coast of the Dead Sea. These manuscripts must date before the fall of the fortress, which place them before 74 AD. Fourteen scrolls containing biblical texts were found that agree extensively with the Masoretic Text. The only possible exception to this amazing agreement is the book of Ezekiel, and even there the textual variants are extremely minor.[206]

---

[203] VanderKam, 143.

[204] Mansoor, 28.

[205] Ibid., 31.

[206] Wurthwein, 31.

The Proto-Septuagint Text

Only five percent of the Dead Sea Scrolls are Proto-Septuagint. These are texts written in Hebrew that reflect a reading closer to the Greek Septuagint than the Traditional Text. For example, the Greek Septuagint and the text of Jeremiah found at Qumran (4QJer.*b*) agree in omitting a healthy portion of the text. The Septuagint and Qumran text (4QExod.*a*) agree in stating the number of descendants from Jacob are seventy-five, instead of the seventy listed in the Masoretic Text. Some have assumed that Stephen was citing either the Septuagint or the Proto-Septuagint text of Qumran in giving the number as seventy-five (Acts 7:14 and Exodus 1:5). Yet, this can also be explained by the way the family was numbered and not the text Stephen was citing.[207]

The Proto-Samaritan Text

As with the Proto-Septuagint textual type of the Dead Sea Scrolls, only five percent of the manuscripts found comprise the Proto-Samaritan textual type. The Samaritan Pentateuch, as indicated by the name, consisted solely of the five books of Moses. The Hebrew text is often the same as the Masoretic Text with differences in spelling rather than textual variants. However, there are nineteen hundred variants that agree with the text of the Septuagint over that of the Masoretic. This text also has some additions to it.

---

[207] In Genesis 46:8-26 we have a total of sixty-six children, grandchildren, and great-grandchildren of Jacob. When we add Jacob to this list along with Joseph and his two sons we have a total of seventy. The number given by Stephen in Acts 7:14 of seventy-five (which does not include Jacob himself) could also be correct if Stephen was counting the wives of Jacob's children, something the New Testament would do since it is much more inclusive regarding gender. Both Judah and Simeon were widowers. Therefore, to the sixty-six persons already mentioned, we add nine wives (not counting Joseph, his wife, and children because they were already in Egypt). Using this method of counting, the number seventy-five is correct.

The information concerning the various textual types found among the Dead Sea Scrolls, along with other findings in that region, should reveal something to the reader. First, as in any library, the one at Qumran demonstrates a diversity of material. Is this not to be expected? If a student were to visit my personal library they would discover a wide variety of texts and general information. Second, considering the extensive use of the Masoretic Text in the Dead Sea Scrolls, and its exclusive use in other manuscript findings near the Dead Sea, the Traditional Hebrew Text must be unquestionably authoritative.

Who Wrote The Scrolls?

The vast majority of scholars answer this question by stating that the Essenes, a strict Jewish sect that lived in piety and isolation, wrote the Dead Sea Scrolls. Like other Jewish groups such as the Pharisees and Sadducees, the Essenes were both a religious group and a political one. Some have suggested the Essenes were a splinter group of the Pharisees.[208]

The Jewish philosopher Philo wrote that a group of Essenes lived west of the Dead Sea in the wilderness.[209] Some assume that the ruins found at Qumran must have been the dwelling place of the Essenes because it fits the general location. Likewise, since John the Baptist dwelt in this same wilderness, some have concluded John was part of the Essenes sect, or else

---

[208] Historian Will Durant writes: "The most extreme of the Jewish sects was that of the Essenes. They derived their piety from the Chasidim, their name probably from the Chaldaic *aschai* (bather), their doctrine and practice from the stream of ascetic theory and regimen circulating through the world of the last century before Christ; possibly they were influenced by Brahmanic, Buddhist, Paress, Pythagorean, and Cynic ideas that came to the crossroads of trade at Jerusalem. Numbering some 4000 in Palestine, they organized themselves into a distinct order, observed both the written and the oral Law with passionate exactitude, and lived together as almost monastic celibates tilling the soil in the oasis of Engadi amid the desert west of the Dead Sea." *The Story of Civilization*, vol. 3 (New York: Simon and Schuster, 1944), 537.

[209] Philo, *Every Good Man is Free*, 12-13 [75-91].

was influenced by the strict teachings of the Essenes. However, such conclusions overstep biblical and historical facts.[210] Josephus provides additional information about the Essenes. In his *Antiquities of the Jews*, he states that the Essenes lived in groups, having all things in common. They "neither marry wives, nor are desirous to keep servants; as thinking the latter tempts men to be unjust, and the former gives the handle to domestic quarrels; but as they live by themselves, they minister one to another" (XVIII. 1:5). They believed in the immortality of the soul and that an eternal reward awaited those who lived a righteous life.

Certainly many of the writings among the Dead Sea Scrolls reflect the views and teachings of the Essenes. The ruins found a mile away from Cave 1 at Qumran most certainly could have been from an Essenes community. Nevertheless, there are those who have come to different conclusions as to who wrote the Dead Sea Scrolls and about the community at Qumran. One such scholar is Dr. Norman Golb, author of *Who Wrote The Dead Sea Scrolls?* Dr. Golb is a recognized authority on Qumran who believes that the Scrolls are the remains of the Jewish library located in Jerusalem. He contends that various scrolls were hidden in the wilderness to protect the Jerusalem Library from the Romans when they destroyed the Second Temple and the city in 70 AD. He also maintains that the city

---

[210] Dr. Barbara Thiering of Sidney, Australia has developed an extreme interpretation concerning the Dead Sea Scrolls. In her book, *Redating the Teacher of Righteousness*, Dr. Thiering believes some of the scrolls speak of Jesus and John the Baptist. In The Manual of Discipline it speaks of the Teacher of Righteousness and the Wicked Priest. Thiering's view is that John was an Essene and the Teacher of Righteousness. This teacher proclaimed the coming doom for that wicked generation if they did not repent and turn again to the God of Israel and a strict interpretation of the Law. His preaching was harsh and judgmental. The one called the Wicked Priest proclaimed a much easier view that differed with the staunch legalistic views of the Teacher of Righteousness. For Thiering, this Wicked Priest was Jesus Christ. Thiering also uses the Dead Sea Scrolls and the teachings of the Essenes to deny the miracles of Christ, his Virgin Birth, his death on the cross, and his physical resurrection.

of Qumran was not the dwelling place of the Essenes, but was a fortress against the Romans. Dr. Golb makes a comparison between the structures at Qumran and the military rock fortress at Masada. He notes that according to Josephus, the Essenes were not limited to a single settlement, but were found in every city of Palestine.[211]

Dr. Golb also points to evidence within the Dead Sea Scrolls themselves. One of the scrolls found was not written on leather, like all the other scrolls, but on flattened copper plates that were riveted together to form a scroll (hence it has been dubbed by scholars *The Copper Scroll*). It tells of treasure from the Temple that was hidden so that the Romans would not pillage it. Part of the Temple treasure includes a library. In accordance with this, Dr. Golb points to the Apocryphal book of 2 Maccabees as evidence that the Jews historically hid their books when enemies approached.

> The same things also were reported in the writings and commentaries of Neemias; and how he founding a library gathered together the acts of the kings, and the prophets, and of David, and the epistles of the kings concerning the holy gifts. In like manner also Judas gathered together all those things that were lost by reason of the war we had, and they remain with us. Wherefore if ye have need thereof, send some to fetch them unto you. (2 Maccabees 2:13-15).

Dr. Golb notes that handwriting experts have detected the Dead Sea Scrolls were written by over five hundred various scribes. He states:

> I began to see that the growing number of scripts was starting to pose still another problem for the sectarian hypothesis [i.e., that the Essenes had lived together and were responsible for writing the scrolls]: How many scribes, after all, could have lived together at Khirbet Qumran at any one time, or even

---

[211] Golb, 5.

over three or four generations?...Had the scrolls been written by fewer than two hundred scribes—a number that one might perhaps live with in defending the notion of a sectarian scriptorium at Qumran—or by a much greater number of copyists as I had begun to suspect? The matter was obviously of crucial importance...I did not know that two more decades would elapse before facsimiles of all the Cave 4 manuscripts would be published in the wake of an acute controversy, and that they would confirm that at least five hundred scribes had copied the scrolls.[212]

Dr. Golb recognizes that his view is strongly rejected by the majority of modern scholars. Yet, he is not alone in his view. In the 1950's, Professor K. H. Rengstorf of the University of Munster in Germany suggested that the Dead Sea Scrolls were the remains of the Jerusalem library. Although Professor Rengstorf had arrived at his conclusion years before Golb, and did so for different reasons, their view still has a common centrality: The Scrolls must have come from Jerusalem and not the sectarian writings of the Essenes. According to Rengstorf and Golb, the Essenes would not have had such a variety of views within their writings since they were sectarian. However, the library at Jerusalem would contain such diverse writings.

Regardless of who wrote the Dead Sea Scrolls, we can safely state that there is little in them that can be used against the Traditional Hebrew Text. In fact, because the evidence from Qumran overwhelming supports the Masoretic Hebrew Text, we must say the findings at Qumran strongly favor the Traditional Text and the Authorized Version. Additionally, as we have seen, findings at Murabbaat and Masada exclusively support the Masoretic Text, proving that the established text accepted as the oracles of

---

[212] Ibid., 151, 153-154.

God (Romans 3:1-2) was the Traditional Hebrew Text. The Scrolls may have been concealed and hidden for thousands of years, but God did not forget them. Today, they bear testimony to the Providential Hand in the keeping of Scripture.

Chapter 8

Textual Considerations

"Sigh no more, ladies, sigh no more!

Men were deceivers ever,

One foot in sea, and one on shore;

To one thing constant never."

-William Shakespeare: *Much Ado About Nothing* (1598)

There are a number of passages found in the Traditional Text that have fallen upon hard times. With the discovery of various manuscripts and advancements in textual criticism, we now have about six thousand places where the Traditional Text differs from the more popular Critical Text. Most of these are minor variants not affecting the gist of the text. Some, however, are of greater significance.

The purpose of this chapter is not to examine all the passages that have textual variations in them. Nor is this chapter designed to condemn the Critical Text simply because it differs from the Traditional Text. It is the focus of this chapter to take a closer look at the textual support of certain passages that are currently considered erroneous. Consequently, the other side of the textual evidence that espouses the Traditional Text and biblical preservation is presented, establishing that what has been handed down to us through the ages has been correct after all.

Despite one's position concerning textual criticism, an additional point needs to be addressed: those who profess to believe its contents should not treat the word of God as they would any other book. Along with sound searching and solid study, we must not forsake our *faith* in biblical principles and promises. William Shakespeare is not the only one to warn us of the folly of man and the ever-changing nature of his comprehension. Scripture itself repeats the charge and informs us that the arm of flesh will fail. Therefore, our confidence must be placed in the Lord and his word (2 Chronicles 32:8; Psalm 118:8).

Matthew 6:13

The passage in question is the conclusion of what is commonly known as the Lord's Prayer. The prayer ends with the doxology, *"For thine is the kingdom, and the power, and the glory, for ever. Amen."* This phrase is found in the majority of Greek manuscripts, the Greek Textus Receptus and Majority Text, and is the reading of early English versions, the KJV, and the NKJV. It is not found in the main body of the Critical Text or most modern versions.

Some have argued that the prayer is the same as the one found in Luke 11:2-4. In that passage the doxology does not appear. It is then suggested that scribes who had a habit of harmonizing various passages in the four Gospels did so with this prayer.[213] While the two passages are similar in content it is doubtful they are the same prayer. The passage in Matthew is given for the multitude when Jesus preached his celebrated *Sermon on the Mount*. The passage in Luke is given specifically for the disciples of the Lord when asked how they should pray. Similarity, it should be remembered, does not mean sameness. It is not a surprise to find this prayer, or at least a form of it, appearing on more than one occasion.

The question then arises: "Did the prayer in Matthew originally contain the concluding phrase as found in the Traditional Text?" Among the Greek uncials it is found in W (fifth century), L (eighth century), 0233

---

[213] Bruce M. Metzger, *The Text Of The New Testament*, 3rd ed. (Oxford: The Clarendon Press, 1992), 197.

(eighth century), K (ninth century), Δ (ninth century), Θ (ninth century), and Π (tenth century). It is found in the majority of all Greek minuscules such as: 28, 33, 565, 700, 892, 1009, 1010, 1071, 1079, 1195, 1216, 1230, 1241, 1242, 1365, 1546, 1646, 2174 (dating from the ninth century to the twelfth century). It is also found in the majority of all existing Greek lectionaries. Therefore, the weight of the Greek witnesses argues for its inclusion and validity.

It is likewise found in several ancient translations such as some Old Latin manuscripts, the Old Syrian, and some Coptic versions. The Syriac Peshitta (second/third century)[214] reads, "And bring us not into temptation, but deliver us from evil: For thine is the kingdom, and the power, and the glory, for ever and ever: Amen."[215] Therefore, the reading embraces antiquity as well as geographical support.

The passage also has patristic support. The distinguished orthodox father of the fourth century, John Chrysostom, cites this passage. He writes, "by bringing to our remembrance the King under whom we are arrayed, and signifying him to be more powerful than all. 'For thine,' saith he, 'is the kingdom, and the power, and the glory'."[216] The oldest witness, which outdates all Greek manuscripts containing Matthew chapter six, is the *Didache* (otherwise known as the *Teaching of the Twelve Apostles*). This ancient catechism dates to the early second century, shortly after 100 AD, and contains a form of the Lord's Prayer:

> But let not your fasts be with the hypocrites; for they fast on
> the second and fifth day of the week; but do ye fast on the
> fourth day and the Preparation (Friday). Neither pray as the

---

[214] Textual scholar F. C. Burkitt argued that the Peshitta did not exist before the fifth century. Although most scholars no longer hold to Burkitt's theory, most date the Peshitta to this time period. Others, such as E. Hills and A. Voobus have placed the origin of the Peshitta in the second century.

[215] James Murdock, *The Syriac New Testament* (Boston: H. L. Hastings, 1896), 9.

[216] John Chrysostom, "Homily XIX," *The Preaching of Chrysostom*, ed. Joroslav Pelikan, (Philadelphia: Fortress Press), 145.

hypocrites; but as the Lord commanded in his Gospel, thus pray: Our Father who art in heaven, hallowed be Thy name. Thy kingdom come. Thy will be done, as in heaven, so on earth. Give us today our daily (needful) bread, and forgive us our debt as we also forgive our debtors. And bring us not into temptation, but deliver us from evil; for Thine is the power and the glory for ever. Thrice in the day thus pray.[217]

Finally, in his studies on old papyri, Dr. George Milligan includes a sixth century prayer that incorporates the prayer of Matthew 6:13. Despite the fact that this papyrus is badly worn, it clearly contains the phrase in question.[218] The textual evidence for the traditional reading is both ancient and massive, and should be retained in our English translations.

Mark 1:2

The Traditional Text reads, *"As it is written in the prophets,"* and then cites from Malachi 3:1 and Isaiah 40:3. Other texts read, *"As it is written in the Prophet Isaiah,"* before quoting Malachi and Isaiah. The reading of the Traditional Text has considerable support. It is found in many of the Greek uncials (A, K, P, W, Π), the majority of Greek minuscules (28, 1009, 1010, 1079, 1195, 1216, 1230, 1242, 1252, 1344, 1365, 1546, 1646, 2148) and the majority of Greek lectionaries. Thus the Greek support dates from the fourth century onward. Additionally we also find the same reading in the Syriac Harclean version (616 AD), the Armenian version (fourth/fifth century) and the Ethiopic versions of the sixth century. It also receives patristic citations from many of the church fathers such as

---

[217] *Teaching of the Twelve Apostles*, 8:1

[218] George Milligan, *Sections From The Greek Papyri* (Cambridge: University Press, 1912), 132-134. Interestingly, Dr. Milligan notes of this papyri that it contains, "a passage which some may be tempted to quote in support of the A.V. rendering of Mt. VI.13." Since the phrase is included in this personal prayer, Dr. Milligan is correct in both his understanding of the origin of the quote and in its support for the Authorized Version.

the Latin version of Irenaeus (202 AD), Photius (895 AD), and Theophylact (1077 AD).

Contextually there arises a problem with the reading as found in the Critical Text. The passage cites both the Prophet Malachi (3:1) and the Prophet Isaiah (40:3). The reading, "As it is written in Isaiah the Prophet," seems inconsistent. Nevertheless, it has been noted that Isaiah was the major prophet and therefore he takes preeminence over Malachi. To illustrate this point, scholars often refer to Matthew 27:9. They claim this passage is not really a citation of Jeremiah but instead a quotation of Zechariah 11:12. Jeremiah receives the preeminence as the major prophet.

However, this point can be argued. The text in Matthew does not say it was *written* as the passage in Mark does. Instead, the text in Matthew states, "Then was fulfilled that which was *spoken* by Jeremy." God, the Author of Scripture, is aware of who writes what and who speaks what. Simply because Zechariah writes the passage does not mean Jeremiah did not speak it. Also, Zechariah warned Israel to pay attention to what the former prophets had spoken (Zechariah 7:7). The ancient Jews had a saying that, "the spirit of Jeremiah was in Zechariah."[219] Much of what Zechariah received, he did so from both the Lord and the former prophet, Jeremiah.

The position presented by many that some copyist made the change from "Isaiah the Prophet" to "the prophets" in Mark 1:2 in order to correct what was perceived as a possible error is conjecture.[220] One can just as easily speculate that an Egyptian copyist not overly familiar with Jewish Old Testament prophets recognized the Isaiah quote and made the change for what he considered to be better clarity. The point still remains that

---

[219] In his Bible commentary regarding Matthew 27:9, Matthew Henry notes this saying of the Jews concerning the spirit of Jeremiah being in Zechariah.

[220] Bruce Metzger, *A Textual Commentary On The Greek New Testament* (New York: United Bible Societies, 2nd ed., 1994), 62.

both sides have textual support for their respective positions. It also is understood, as Dr. George Kilpatrick has noted, that most of these types of textual variants were introduced into the manuscripts by the second century.[221] Therefore, one reading is as likely (textually speaking) as the other. The difference is contextually. It is more truthful to say "the prophets" when citing two prophets. Accordingly, the reading in the Traditional Text is both textually substantial and contextually correct.

Mark 16:9-20

This passage is referred to as the *longer ending* of Mark.[222] Many textual critics doubt its authenticity, believing it was an addition made in the second century. It often appears in modern versions in brackets with footnotes questioning its authenticity.[223] Most textual scholars believe that the text abruptly ends after verse eight. Even the so-called *shorter ending* that is added after verse eight is considered to have originated in the second century. The shorter ending reads:

> But they reported briefly to Peter and those with him all that they had been bold. And after this, Jesus himself sent out by means of them, from east to west, the sacred and imperishable proclamation of eternal salvation.[224]

---

[221] George D. Kilpatrick, *The Principles And Practice Of New Testament Textual Criticism* (Belgium: Leuven University Press, 1990), 34.

[222] The manuscripts reveal four endings to Mark's Gospel. 1. The longer ending, which is the reading of almost all existing Greek manuscripts, and is in line with the Traditional Text. 2. The shorter ending, sometimes referred to as the intermedate ending. This ending is found in Λ, Ψ, 099, 0112, 274, and 579. 3. The expanded ending, which is found in Codex W. This ending is widely rejected. 4. No ending after verse eight. This is the view held by most textual scholars and agrees with Codex Sinaiticus and Codex Vaticanus.

[223] Kurt and Barbara Aland, *The Text Of The New Testament*, 2nd ed., trans. Erroll F. Rhodes (Grand Rapids: Eerdmans, 1989), 232.

[224] Revised Standard Version, footnote

Most scholars believe the original ending to Mark's Gospel has been lost.[225] If this is true, the concept of preserving the words of Scripture is forever annihilated. The words cannot be preserved and lost at the same time. However, textual scholars usually call for its inclusion even if they question its originality. Dr. Bruce Metzger departs from the maxim of modern textual critics, *Brevior lectio potior* (the shorter reading is preferable), and supports the longer ending even though admittedly he does not regard the passage as genuine. He considers it to be a legitimate part of the New Testament because of its traditional significance to the body of Christendom.[226] The passage is not contained in the Alexandrian texts, minuscule 2386, the Syrian Sinaitic Version, and a few other translations.

However, it is in most of the Greek uncials (A, C, D05, K, Ξ, Δ, Θ, and Π) dating between the fifth and ninth centuries. It is also contained in the later dated Greek minuscules (such as 137, 138, 1110, 1210, 1215, 1216, 1217, 1221, and 1582). It is the reading found in the majority of Old Latin texts as well as the Coptic versions and other early translations. Finally, it is cited (at least in part) by many of the early church fathers such as Justin (165 AD), Tertullian (220 AD), Hippolytus (235 AD), Ambrose (397 AD) and Augustine (430 AD).[227]

In 177 AD Irenaeus wrote *Against Heresies*. In it he cites from Mark 16:19, establishing that the longer reading was in existence at this time and was considered canonical, at least by Irenaeus:

---

[225] Metzger, 105. Dr. Metzger footnotes the following regarding the ending of Mark. "Three possibilities are open: (a) the evangelist intended to close his Gospel at this place; or (b) the Gospel was never finished; or, as seems most probable, (c) the Gospel accidentally lost its last leaf before it was multiplied by transcription."

[226] Bruce Metzger, *Christian History* (interview with Dr. Metzger downloaded from Christian History Magazine, America Online, 9/17/96).

[227] John William Burgon, *The Revision Revised* (Paradise, PA: Conservative Classics, 1883), 422-423. Burgon also supplies additional names of church fathers who support the reading.

Also, towards the conclusion of his Gospel, Mark says: "So then, after the Lord Jesus had spoken to them, He was received up into heaven, and sitteth on the right hand of God;" confirming what had been spoken by the prophet: "The LORD said to my Lord, Sit Thou on My right hand, until I make Thy foes Thy footstool." Thus God and the Father are truly one and the same; He who was announced by the prophets, and handed down by the true Gospel; whom we Christians worship and love with the whole heart, as the Maker of heaven and earth, and of all things therein. (3:10:5).

The difference here is extremely important. If we conclude that this passage is not authentic, then we must question what happened to the original ending of Mark. It is not logical that the Gospel would end at this place so abruptly. Nor is it likely, as some scholars have suggested, that the Gospel was never finished, calling biblical inspiration into question. The conclusion held by most textual scholars, whether liberal or conservative, that the original ending has been lost over the passage of time certainly denies the doctrine of biblical preservation. If we allow that a passage of inspired Scripture has been lost from this section of the Bible, what stops us from making the same application to other passages? It is certainly within the realm of scholastic studies to note any and all textual differences. But once we open the possibility that this or that passage has been lost, we are now trusting in the understanding of men over the biblical promises of God. Certainly it is better to embrace the textual evidence and hold to the promise of preservation.[228]

Luke 2:22

Here the variant is small but the difference is profound. The Authorized Version and Textus Receptus (Beza's edition and Elzevir's edition) use the phrase, *"of her purification"* (*katharismou autes*). Modern versions and the

---

[228] The internal evidence supporting Mark 16:9-20 is examined in Appendix B.

Critical Text read, *"of their purification"* (*katharismou auton*). Contextually, the reading must stand as reflected in the KJV. Under the Levitical Law a woman was considered unclean after giving birth and needed purification. The passage in Leviticus 12: 2-4 reads,

> Speak unto the children of Israel, saying, If a woman have conceived seed, and born a man child: then she shall be unclean seven days; according to the days of the separation for her infirmity shall she be unclean. And in the eighth day the flesh of his foreskin shall be circumcised. And she shall then continue in the blood of her purifying three and thirty days; she shall touch no hallowed thing, nor come into the sanctuary, until the days of her purifying be fulfilled.

The citation is quite clear: this was *"her purifying"* and not the purifying of both mother and child. Therefore, the Authorized Version and the Greek Textus Receptus agree with the Levitical Law.

To offset this point, some have suggested that the word *them* is a reference to Mary and Joseph. The argument is that since Joseph and Mary are mentioned in verse 16 and referred to in the second half of verse 22, the word *them* referred to the married couple. The obvious doctrinal problem with this is that under the Law of Moses, as set forth in Leviticus 12, the woman and not the husband needed purification after giving birth. The best contextual reading agrees with the Authorized Version, as it would support both the Old Testament Law and the actions presented in Luke's Gospel.[229]

---

[229] As one can see, the internal evidence would support the reading *of her purification* in Luke 2:22. There is a debate among textual critics regarding eclecticism. Most support what is commonly called "reasoned eclecticism" which tends to focus on the age and number of existing Greek manuscripts. However, scholars such as G. D. Kilpatrick and J. K. Elliot promote *"rigorous eclecticism"* which focuses on the internal evidence above the external textual evidence. Therefore, according to this type of eclecticism, any textual variant regardless of age or number could conceivably be the correct reading if the internal evidence is sufficient. See Kilpatrick, 33-52.

Admittedly, the Greek support now known for the reading as found in the Textus Receptus is extremely poor. It is found in a few Greek minuscules such as 76 and a few others.[230] There is an additional textual variant within the Greek manuscripts. Codex D05 (sixth century), which is highly acclaimed among textual scholars, has the reading *autou* (of it). While the reading *autns* (of her) is preferred, both readings stand in the genitive singular and not the plural as *auton* (of them). Additionally, we find the Sinaitic Syriac and the Sahidic Coptic versions supporting 2174 and D05.

The reading *her purification* has a great deal of textual support among the Latin witnesses. The majority of all Latin manuscripts read, *et postquam impleti sunt dies purgationis eius secundum legem mosi* (And after the days of her purification, according to the law of Moses). The Latin word *eius* (or *ejus*) means *her* and stands in the feminine genitive singular, thus *of her*. In order to have the translation *of them*, the Latin texts would have to use the word *eorum*. When we consider the age and the number of extant Latin manuscripts, we find the reading is both ancient and well substantiated. It is also interesting to note that the reading has some support in the forged *Gospel of Pseudo-Matthew* (possible third century). Written in Latin, it allows us to see that the purification spoken of in Luke 2:22 was a reference to Mary. *Pseudo-Matthew* reads: "Now, after the days of the purification of Mary were fulfilled according to the law of Moses, then Joseph took the infant to the temple of the Lord" (15:1).

The translators of the Authorized Version were well aware of the textual difference concerning this verse. The Geneva Bible and Bishops' Bible read, "the days of her purification." However, Tyndale's New Testament

---

[230] Edward F. Hills, *The King James Version Defended* (1956; reprint, Des Moines: The Christian Research Press, 1984), 221.

and the Great Bible read, "the time of their purification." It should be remembered that the KJV was mainly based on the 1589 and 1598 editions of the Greek New Testament by Theodore Beza. In his annotations Beza writes:

> Most of the [Greek] Codices read "of them" and likewise so does Origen, and unfortunately so does Erasmus. However, they have not considered what the actual Law says about the purification of the mother. And so consequently the old editions [of the Greek] are unfavorable…because they have distorted the truth of Scripture and in some degree have lessened the image of Mary's purity.[231]

A careful reading of Beza's note reveals that he had some textual evidence, based on his study of the then-existing Greek manuscripts, for the reading *her*. Additionally, he recognized that this was the reading that agrees with the Mosaic Law. In his Latin translation, which was placed between the Greek and the Vulgate, Beza renders the phrase as "*dies purationis Mariae*" (days of Mary's purification). This would agree with Pseudo-Matthew in substituting the word *her* with the name of *Mary*.

John 5:4

This verse is usually consigned to footnotes in most modern English versions, and is generally considered an addition by some scribe in order to convey a traditional story regarding the healing pool at Bethesda. Yet, to consider this text as a figment of tradition is conjecture. The passage should be considered genuine. It appears in the Greek Textus Receptus, the majority of all existing Greek manuscripts, all of the early English versions, the Authorized Version, and the New King James Version.

---

231 Theodore Beza, *Nouum Sive Mouum Foedus Iesu Christi*, 1589. Personal translation from the Latin text.

If we are to accept a reading based on its wide geographical distribution, we should accept this reading because it has old textual support with the greatest amount of geographical distribution. It is found in codices A, E, F, G, H, I, K, L, Δ, Θ, Π and the third corrector of C. The Greek minuscules overwhelming support the verse and is contained in 28, 565, 700, 892, 1009, 1010, 1071, 1195, 1216, 1230, 1241, 1242, 1253, 1344, 1365, 1546, 1646, and 2148. It is also included in the majority of Old Latin manuscripts and early translations.

The verse is found in the Old Coptic Version as edited from the Coptic manuscript Huntington 17 and is translated into English as follows:

> There was an angel (who) came down every hour in the pool, and moved the water. And any one (who) shall come down first after the moving of the water shall be healed of every sickness which (may) be his.[232]

The same is true of the Old Syriac. James Murdock's translation of this passage from the Peshitta reads:

> For an angel, from time to time, descended into the baptistery, and moved the waters; and he who first went in, after the moving of the waters, was cured of whatever disease he had.[233]

The passage also has patristic citations. It is found in the *Diatessaron* of the second century. Tertullian (200 AD) notes that an "angel, by his intervention, was wont to stir the pool at Bethsaida."[234] The passage is also cited by Ambrose (397 AD), Didymus (398 AD), Chrysostom (407 AD) and Cyril (444 AD), demonstrating that both Greek and Latin fathers accepted the reading as genuine.

---

[232] *The Coptic Version Of The New Testament: In The Northern Dialect*, vol. 2 (Oxford: Clarendon Press, 1898), 377-379.

[233] Murdock, 172.

[234] *The Writings Of Tertullian* 3:2:5.

John 7:53-8:11

This passage is designated as the *Pericope De Adultera,* referring to the woman caught in the act of adultery. The passage is included in numerous uncials such as D05, G, H, K, M, U, and Γ. Among the minuscule or cursive manuscripts it is in 28, 700, 892, 1009, 1010, 1071, 1079, 1195, 1216, 1344, 1365, 1546, 1646, 2148, and 2174. Most Greek manuscripts contain this passage. It also is in early translations such as the Bohairic Coptic Version, the Syriac Palestinian Version and the Ethiopic Version, all of which date from the second to the sixth centuries. It is clearly the reading of the majority of the Old Latin manuscripts and Jerome's Latin Vulgate. The passage has patristic support: Didascalia (third century), Ambrosiaster (fourth century), Ambrose (fourth century), the Apostolic Constitutions (which are the largest liturgical collections of writings from Antioch Syria in about 380 AD), Jerome (420 AD), and Augustine (430 AD).

Most textual scholars consider the evidence against it to be overwhelming and reject the reading as original.[235] Yet, the passage still finds its way into the text of the majority of contemporary translations. Unlike John 5:4, which is confined to a footnote, this passage is retained in the text but usually separated with brackets (as with Mark 16:9-20). If the evidence against it is so convincing and the text is not considered genuine, should not this entire passage be removed from the text itself as other shorter passages are? If one is to remove smaller sections, would not consistency demand the same be done with larger sections if the amount of textual evidence is either the same or greater? Perhaps it is a matter of acceptance. Since this passage is beloved by the majority of the Bible reading public, to remove it from the text would be unthinkable.

---

[235] Metzger, *A Textual Commentary On The Greek New Testament*, 187.

Supporters of the Textus Receptus and the Majority Text, on the other hand, have soundly defended the authenticity of this passage.[236] The vast majority of all known Greek manuscripts contain this section. It is clearly part of the Traditional Text. Additionally, the internal evidence demonstrates that this passage is original. If we remove it we have a very erratic jump in textual thought.

The question arises as to why this passage was ever omitted. We find the answer in church history. Augustine makes an astounding statement concerning the authenticity of the passage. After citing the forgiving phrase of Christ, "Neither do I condemn thee: go, and sin no more," Augustine writes:

> This proceeding, however, shocks the minds of some weak believers, or rather unbelievers and enemies of the Christian faith: inasmuch that, after (I suppose) of its giving their wives impunity of sinning, they struck out from their copies of the Gospel this that our Lord did in pardoning the woman taken in adultery: as if He granted leave of sinning, Who said, Go and sin no more![237]

Augustine implies some fearful scribes who thought the inclusion might lead to adultery omitted this passage. This argument not only seems logical, but also consistent with human nature. It is, at least, as good as modern scholarship's view that the passage was added as a piece of oral tradition apart from inspiration.[238]

---

[236] See Hills, 150-159. John W. Burgon "Pericope De Adultera," *Counterfeit Or Genuine*, ed. David Otis Fuller, (Grand Rapids: Grand Rapids International Publications, 1975) 133-158. Arthur L. Farstad, *The New King James Version In The Great Tradition* (Nashville: Thomas Nelson Publishers, 1989) 113-114.

[237] Augustine, *De Conjug. Adult.*, II:6.

[238] Metzger, 188.

Acts 8:37

Here the testimony of this faithful and beloved African, the Ethiopian eunuch, does not appear in the Critical Text. Some have argued that the verse is not genuine because it is found in only a few late manuscripts and was inserted into the Greek text by Erasmus from the Latin Vulgate. It is true that the passage appears in the Latin Vulgate of Jerome. However, the passage also appears in a vast number of other Old Latin manuscripts (such as *l, m, e, r, ar, ph,* and *gig*). It also is found in the Greek Codex E (eighth century) and several Greek manuscripts (36, 88, 97, 103, 104, 242, 257, 307, 322, 323, 385, 429, 453, 464, 467, 610, 629, 630, 913, 945, 1522, 1678, 1739, 1765, 1877, 1891, and others). While there are differences even among these texts as to precise wording, the essence of the testimony still remains where it has been removed from other manuscripts.[239] Additionally, Irenaeus (202 AD), Cyprian (258 AD), Ambrosiaster (fourth century), Pacian (392 AD), Ambrose (397 AD), Augustine (430 AD), and Theophylact (1077 AD) all cite Acts 8:37.

The natural question posed by textual scholars is this: if the text were genuine, why would any scribe wish to delete it?[240] In his commentary on the book of Acts, Dr. J. A. Alexander provides a possible answer. By the end of the third century it had become common practice to delay the baptism of Christian converts to assure that they had truly understood their commitment to Christ and were not holding to one of the

---

[239] The variants within the manuscripts that maintain this passage are minor. For example, 88 omits *o Philippos* (Phillip) and adds o eunouchos (the eunuch) and *auto* (very). Thus the verse reads in 88, "And he said, If thou believest with all thine heart, thou mayest. And the eunuch answered and said, I believe that Jesus Christ is the very Son of God." Such variants are common among the vast host of Greek manuscripts. It should be noted, nevertheless, that such variants do not constitute the removal of the passage from the text. Nor, are such variants of like significance as those that would remove the passage from the text.

[240] Metzger, 315-316.

various heretical beliefs prevalent at that time.[241] It is possible that a scribe, believing that baptism should not immediately follow conversion, omitted this passage from the text, which would explain its absence in many of the Greek manuscripts that followed. Certainly this conjecture is as possible as the various explanations offered by those who reject the reading.

Nevertheless, because of biblical preservation, the reading remains in some Greek manuscripts as well as in the Old Latin manuscripts. Clearly the reading is far more ancient than the sixth century, as some scholars have suggested. Irenaeus noted that "the believing eunuch himself:…immediately requesting to be baptized, he said, 'I believe Jesus Christ to be the Son of God'."[242] Likewise, Cyprian quotes the first half of the verse in writing, "In the Acts of the Apostles: 'Lo, here is water; what is there which hinders me from being baptized? Then said Philip, If thou believest with all thine heart, thou mayest'."[243] These statements, clearly quotations of Acts 8:37, appear by the end of the second century and at the first half of the third. We see that the passage was in common use long before the existing Greek manuscripts were ever copied. This in itself testifies to its authenticity and to the assurance of biblical preservation.

Acts 9:5-6

The phrase from verse five, *"it is hard for thee to kick against the pricks,"* is in the Old Latin and some Vulgate manuscripts. It is also in the Peshitta and the Greek of Codex E and 431, but in verse four instead of verse five.

---

[241] J. A. Alexander, *The Acts Of The Apostle* (New York: Scribner, 1967), vol. 1, 349-350.

[242] *Against Heresies*: I 1:433.

[243] *Treatise* 12:3:43.

The passage from verse six that reads, *"And he trembling and astonished said, Lord, what wilt thou have me to do? And the Lord said unto him"* is in the Old Latin, the Latin Vulgate, and some of the Old Syrian and Coptic versions. These phrases, however, are not found in the vast majority of Greek manuscripts and therefore do not appear in either the Critical Text or the Majority Text. Yet, they are included in the Textus Receptus. On the surface the textual evidence looks weak. Why, then, should the Textus Receptus be accepted over the majority of Greek witnesses at this point? Because the phrases are preserved in other languages, and the internal evidence establishes that Christ in fact spoke these words at the time of Paul's conversion and are therefore authentic.

Acts chapter nine is not the only place in Scripture where the conversion of Paul is established. In Acts 22:10 and 26:14 we have the testimony of the Apostle himself. There, in all Greek texts, the phrases in question appear.

Acts 22:10
And I said, What shall I do, Lord? And the Lord said unto me, Arise, and go into Damascus; and there it shall be told thee of all things which are appointed for thee to do.

Acts 26:14
And when we were all fallen to the earth, I heard a voice speaking unto me, and saying in the Hebrew tongue, Saul, Saul, why persecutest thou me? it is hard for thee to kick against the pricks.

When the apostle Paul recounts his conversion he cites the words in question. It is certain that the Holy Spirit inspired these words which should be included at Acts 9:5-6. We must conclude that these words were spoken when the event originally occurred. Although they have not been preserved in the Greek manuscripts at Acts 9:6, they have been preserved in the Latin manuscripts (*ar, c, h, l, p, ph, t*) as well as other translations

(Georgian, Slavonic, Ethiopic). The greatest textual critic of all, the Holy Spirit, bears witness to their authenticity by including them in Acts 22:10 and 26:14.

A similar example may be noted in Matthew 19:17, although the textual evidence is much stronger there. The King James Version reads, "And he said unto him, Why callest thou me good? there is none good but one, that is, God: but if thou wilt enter into life, keep the commandments." Modern texts render "why callest thou me good" to "why do you ask me about what is good." Also, the reply of Christ, "there is none good but one, that is, God" is rendered "there is only one who is good."

This verse, as it stands in the King James, wonderfully establishes the deity of Jesus Christ. If only God is good and Christ is called good, he must be God. The Greek support for the reading of the KJV, as presented in the Traditional Text, is substantial. Among the uncials it is found in C and W (fifth century), K and Δ (ninth century) and a few others. It is the reading of the majority of Greek cursives and lectionaries. It is also the reading of the Old Latin, the Old Syriac, the Coptic, and other early translations. The textual evidence is much stronger than that of Acts 9:5-6. Similarly, this passage has additional references to determine what the original reading must be. Again the Holy Spirit comes to the aid of this textual problem by providing for us two other places where this event is cited. In both cases there is no textual variant in the places supporting the disputed passage.

Mark 10:18
And Jesus said unto him, Why callest thou me good? there is none good but one, that is, God.

Luke 18:19
And Jesus said unto him, Why callest thou me good? none is good, save one, that is, God.

In neither passage does the Lord say anything like, "Why do you ask me about what is good?" And, in both passages we find the noun "God." Therefore, we do not have to ask ourselves which reading in Matthew 19:17 is correct because the Holy Spirit has made it clear in additional passages which one is the correct reading. The same principle may be applied to Acts 9:5-6. Once again God bears testimony to his word.

Romans 8:1

The phrase *"who walk not after the flesh, but after the Spirit"* appears in verses one and four. Most scholars consider this a special type of scribal error called *dittography*, which is the repetition of a letter, syllable, word, or phrase. The thought is that a scribe accidentally copied the phrase from verse four in verse one, and that the textual error repeated itself in later manuscripts. Scribal errors do occur as is testified in the large amount of variants within the textual witnesses. However, just because a word or phrase is repeated does not mean that a scribal error has occurred.

The Greek phrase *me kata sarka peripatousin alla kata penuma* (who walk not after the flesh but after the Spirit) is supported by the vast majority of Greek manuscripts. Among them are 33, 88, 104, 181, 326, 330, 451, 614, 630, 1241, 1877, 1962, 1984, 1985, 2492, and 2495. These date from the eleventh to the fifteenth century. The phrase is also included in Codex K (ninth century), Codex P (ninth century), and stands in the margin of Codex Sinaiticus. This is also the reading of the majority of Greek lectionaries. Early versions that contain the phrase include some Old Latin manuscripts (such as *ar* and *o*), the Harclean version, and the Georgian version. Another textual variant that contains part of the phrase reads *me kata sarka peripatousin* (who walk not after the flesh). This is the reading found in A, D06, Ψ, and several minuscules (such as 81, 256, 263, 365, 629, 1319, 1573, 1852, and 2127). It is also the reading of the

Latin Vulgate (fourth century),[244] and the Peshitta. The reading in part or in whole has massive and ancient textual support.

The whole verse is cited, with the phrase in question, by Theodoret (466 AD), Ps-Oecumenius (tenth century), and Theophylact (1077 AD). We also have partial citation of the verse by Basil (379 AD). He writes:

> And after he has developed more fully the idea that it is impossible for one who is in the power of sin to serve the Lord, he plainly states who it is that redeems us from such a tyrannical dominion in the words: "Unhappy man that I am, who shall deliver me from the body of this death? I give thanks to God through Jesus Christ, our Lord." Further on, he adds: "There is now, therefore, no condemnation to them that are in Christ Jesus, who walk not according to the flesh."[245]

When the phrase is not included it creates a possible doctrinal problem. To say there is no condemnation of any kind to all who are in Christ Jesus is to overlook the whole of Scripture. We are told that it is very possible for those who are in Christ to suffer some condemnation, albeit not eternal condemnation. The Christian who walks after the flesh instead of the leading of the Spirit produces works of wood, hay and stubble (1 Corinthians 3:12). Everyone's works will be tried so as by fire. Fleshly works will be burned and spiritual works will endure. We are told, "If any man's work shall be burned, he shall suffer loss: but he himself shall be saved, yet so as by fire" (1 Corinthians 3:15). Therefore, worldly Christians face a certain amount of condemnation.

---

[244] The Latin Vulgate was produced in the fourth century; however the earliest extant Vulgate manuscript dates from the fifth century.

[245] Basil, "Concerning Baptism," *The Fathers Of The Church: Saint Basil Ascetical Works*, trans. M. Monica Wagner, vol. 9 (New York: Fathers Of The Church, Inc., 1950), 343.

We must remember that the word *condemnation* not only carries the meaning of judgment, but also of disapproval.[246] John informs his "little children" that the heart of the believer is able to pass such condemnation or disapproval on our Christian living (1 John 3:20-21). Not only is there a judgment for believers who stand before the Judgment Seat of Christ (1 Corinthians 3:12-15; 2 Corinthians 5:9-10), but there can also be a judgment on believers that may cost them their lives if they continue in sin (Acts 5:1-10; 1 John 5:16). Biblically speaking, there is condemnation for believers who walk after the flesh and not after the Spirit. Consequently, the phrase at the end of Romans 8:1 is theologically sound.

1 John 5:7

The passage is called the *Johannine Comma* and is not found in the majority of Greek manuscripts.[247] However, the verse is a wonderful testimony to the Heavenly Trinity and should be maintained in our English versions, not only because of its doctrinal significance but because of the external and internal evidence that testify to its authenticity.

---

[246] The context of Romans 8 teaches that faithful Christians are to walk after the Spirit and not after the flesh. The Christian is in a constant battle between the Spirit and the flesh (Galatians 5:16-18). There is no condemnation for the Believer who is following the Holy Spirit. However, there is condemnation for those who do not follow the leading of the Spirit, but seek to follow their own flesh.

[247] The first and second editions of Erasmus' Greek text did not contain the Comma. It is generally reported that Erasmus promised to include the Comma in his third edition if a single manuscript containing the Comma could be produced. A Franciscan friar named Froy (or Roy) forged a Greek text containing it by translating the Comma from the Latin into Greek. Erasmus was then presented with this falsified manuscript and, being faithful to his word, reluctantly included the Comma in the 1522 edition. However, as has now been admitted by Dr. Bruce Metzger, this story is apocryphal (*The Text Of The New Testament*, 291). Metzger notes that H. J. de Jonge, a respected specialist on Erasmus, has established that there is no evidence of such events occurring. Therefore, opponents of the Comma in light of the historical facts should no longer affirm this report.

The External Evidence: Although not found in most Greek manuscripts, the Johannine Comma is found in several. It is contained in 629 (fourteenth century), 61 (sixteenth century), 918 (sixteenth century), 2473 (seventeenth century), and 2318 (eighteenth century). It is also in the margins of 221 (tenth century), 635 (eleventh century), 88 (twelfth century), 429 (fourteenth century), and 636 (fifteenth century). There are about five hundred existing manuscripts of 1 John chapter five that do not contain the *Comma*.[248] It is clear that the reading found in the Textus Receptus is the minority reading with later textual support from the Greek witnesses. Nevertheless, being a minority reading does not eliminate it as genuine. The Critical Text considers the reading *Iesou* (of Jesus) to be the genuine reading instead of *Iesou Christou* (of Jesus Christ) in 1 John 1:7. Yet *Iesou* is the minority reading with only twenty-four manuscripts supporting it, while four hundred seventy-seven manuscripts support the reading *Iesou Christou* found in the Textus Receptus. Likewise, in 1 John 2:20 the minority reading *pantes* (all) has only twelve manuscripts supporting it, while the majority reading *panta* (all things) has four hundred ninety-one manuscripts. Still, the Critical Text favors the minority reading over the majority in that passage. This is common place throughout the First Epistle of John, and the New Testament as a whole. Therefore, simply because a reading is in the minority does not eliminate it as being considered original.

While the Greek textual evidence is weak, the Latin textual evidence for the Comma is extremely strong. It is in the vast majority of the Latin manuscripts, which outnumber the Greek manuscripts. Although some doubt if the Comma was a part of Jerome's original Vulgate, the evidence suggests that it was. Jerome states:

---

[248] Kurt Aland, in connection with Annette Benduhn-Mertz and Gerd Mink, *Text und Textwert der Griechischen Handschriften des Neuen Testaments: I. Die Katholischen Briefe Band 1: Das Material (Berlin:* Walter De Gruyter, 1987), 163-166.

In that place particularly where we read about the unity of the Trinity which is placed in the First Epistle of John, in which also the names of three, i.e., of water, of blood, and of spirit, do they place in their edition and omitting the testimony of the Father; and the Word, and the Spirit in which the catholic faith is especially confirmed and the single substance of the Father, the Son and the Holy Spirit is confirmed.[249]

Other church fathers are also known to have quoted the Comma. Although some have questioned if Cyprian (258 AD) knew of the Comma, his citation certainly suggests that he did. He writes: "The Lord says, 'I and the Father are one' and likewise it is written of the Father and the Son and the Holy Spirit, 'And these three are one'."[250] Also, there is no doubt that Priscillian (385 AD) cites the Comma:

As John says "and there are three which give testimony on earth, the water, the flesh, the blood, and these three are in one, and there are three which give testimony in heaven, the Father, the Word, and the Spirit, and these three are one in Christ Jesus."[251]

Likewise, the anti-Arian work compiled by an unknown writer, the *Varimadum* (380 AD) states: "And John the Evangelist says,…'And there are three who give testimony in heaven, the Father, the Word, and the Spirit, and these three are one'."[252] Additionally, Cassian (435 AD),

---

[249] *Prologue To The Canonical Epistles. The Latin text reads, "si ab interpretibus fideliter in latinum eloquium verterentur nec ambiguitatem legentibus facerent nec trinitatis unitate in prima joannis epistola positum legimus, in qua etiam, trium tantummodo vocabula hoc est aquae, sanguinis et spiritus in ipsa sua editione ponentes et patris verbique ac aspiritus testimoninum omittentes, in quo maxime et fides catholica roboratur, et patris et filii et spirtus sancti una divinitatis substantia comprobatur."*

[250] *Treatises* 1 5:423.

[251] *Liber Apologeticus.*

[252] *Varimadum* 90:20-21.

Cassiodorus (580 AD), and a host of other African and Western bishops in subsequent centuries have cited the Comma.[253] Therefore, we see that the reading has massive and ancient textual support apart from the Greek witnesses.

Internal Evidence: The structure of the Comma is certainly Johannine in style. John is noted for referring to Christ as "the Word." If 1 John 5:7 were an interpretation of verse eight, as some have suggested, than we would expect the verse to use "Son" instead of "Word." However, the verse uses the Greek word *logos*, which is uniquely in the style of John and provides evidence of its genuineness. Also, we find John drawing parallels between the Trinity and what they testify (1 John 4:13-14). Therefore, it comes as no surprise to find a parallel of witnesses containing groups of three, one heavenly and one earthly.

The strongest evidence, however, is found in the Greek text itself. Looking at 1 John 5:8, there are three nouns which, in Greek, stand in the neuter (Spirit, water, and blood). However, they are followed by a participle that is masculine. The Greek phrase here is *oi marturountes* (who bare witness). Those who know the Greek language understand this to be poor grammar if left to stand on its own. Even more noticeably, verse six has the same participle but stands in the neuter (Gk.: *to marturoun*). Why are three neuter nouns supported with a masculine participle? The answer is found if we include verse seven. There we have two masculine nouns (Father and Son) followed by a neuter noun (Spirit). The verse also has the Greek masculine participle *oi marturountes*. With this clause introducing verse eight, it is very proper for the participle in verse eight to be mascu-

---

[253] Some other sources include the *Speculum* (or *m* of 450 AD), Victor of Vita (489 AD), Victor Vitensis (485 AD), Codex Freisingensis (of 500 AD), Fulgentius (533 AD), Isidore of Seville (636 AD), Codex Pal Legionensis (650 AD), and Jaqub of Edessa (700 AD). Interestingly, it is also found in the edition of the Apostle's Creed used by the Waldenses and Albigenses of the twelfth century.

line because of the masculine nouns in verse seven. But if verse seven were not there it would become improper Greek grammar.

Even though Gregory of Nazianzus (390 AD) does not testify to the authenticity of the Comma, he makes mention of the flawed grammar resulting from its absence. In his *Theological Orientations* he writes referring to John:

> ...(he has not been consistent) in the way he has happened upon his terms; for after using Three in the masculine gender he adds three words which are neuter, contrary to the definitions and laws which you and your grammarians have laid down. For what is the difference between putting a masculine Three first, and then adding One and One and One in the neuter, or after a masculine One and One and One to use the Three not in the masculine but in the neuter, which you yourselves disclaim in the case of deity?[254]

It is clear that Gregory recognized the inconsistency with Greek grammar if all we have are verses six and eight without verse seven. Other scholars have recognized the same thing. This was the argument of Robert Dabney of Union Theological Seminary in his book, *The Doctrinal Various Readings of the New Testament Greek* (1891). Bishop Middleton in his book, *Doctrine of the Greek Article,* argues that verse seven must be a part of the text according to the Greek structure of the passage. Even in the famous commentary by Matthew Henry, there is a note stating that we must have verse seven if we are to have proper Greek in verse eight.[255]

While the external evidence makes the originality of the Comma possible, the internal evidence makes it very probable. When we consider the

---

[254] *Fifth Orientation: The Holy Spirit.*

[255] Actually the 1 John commentary is the work of "Mr. John Reynolds of Shrewsbury," one of the ministers who completed Matthew Henry's commentary, which was left incomplete [only up to the end of Acts] at Henry's death in 1714.

providential hand of God and his use of the Traditional Text in the Reformation it is clear that the Comma is authentic.

Revelation 22:19

While the focus of this verse deals with the phrase *"book of life,"* as opposed to *"tree of life,"* the issue is deeper. The manuscript Codex 1r used by Desiderius Erasmus in the production of his Greek New Testament is missing the last six verses of Revelation chapter twenty-two. It is thought that Erasmus took the Latin Vulgate and retranslated these verses back into Greek.[256] Assuming this hypothesis is true we must ask ourselves the following questions. First, if Erasmus did make use of the Latin Vulgate to supply these last six verses, has the usage of the Latin corrupted the text? Second, was Codex 1r really the only Greek manuscript used by Erasmus for this passage?

Certainly the Latin Vulgate and the Greek Textus Receptus are similar in these last six verses. This, of course, would be natural if the Latin was based on early Greek manuscripts that correspond with the Textus Receptus. We must remember that most of the Greek manuscripts of the second, third, and fourth centuries have not survived the passage of time. However, the Vulgate and the Textus Receptus are not identical either. For example, the conclusion of Revelation 22:20 reads in the Receptus, *Amen. Nai, erchou, kurie Iesou* (Amen. Even so, come Lord Jesus). The Latin reads, *amen veni Domine Iesu* (Amen come Lord Jesus). The Textus

---

[256] Erika Rummel, Erasmus' Annotations on the New Testament: From Philologist to Theologian (Toronto: University of Toronto Press, 1986), 93. It is claimed that Erasmus openly declares in the Annotations of his 1516 edition (page 675) that he "ex nostris Latinis supplevimus Graeca" (supplied the Greek from the Latin). Thus the claim that the last six verses of Revelation chapter twenty-two were retranslated from the Vulgate into Greek. However, the reprint of the 1516 edition of Erasmus does not contain this phrase on page 675 of his Annotations, which is the conclusion of his notes on the book of Revelation, nor is such a phrase found elsewhere in that edition.

Receptus includes an additional affirmation *nai* (even so), an addition not found in either the Greek Critical Text or the Latin Vulgate.

If Erasmus did translate back into Greek from the Latin text, he did an astounding job. These six verses consist of one hundred thirty-six Greek words in the Textus Receptus, and one hundred thirty-two Greek words in the Critical Text. There are only eighteen textual variants found within these verses when the two texts are compared.[257] Such textual variants,

---

[257] The following are the eighteen textual differences found in these six verses. Because of the nature of this footnote, I have not transliterated these Greek words.

Reference	Textus Receptus	Critical Text
22:16	του δαβιδ *(the David)*	δαυιδ *(David)*
22:16	και ορθρινος (and morning)	ο πρωινος (the morning)
22:17	ελθε (come)	ερχου (come)
22:17	ελθε (come)	ερχου (come)
22:17	ελθετω και (let him come and)	ερχεσθω (let him come)
22:17	λαμβανετω το (let him take the)	λαβετω (let him take)
22:18	συμμαρτυρουμαι γαρ (for I testify to everyone)	μαρτυρω εγω (I testify to everyone)
22:18	επιτιθη προς ταυτα (should add to these things)	επιθη επ αυτα (adds to them)
22:18	βιβλιω (book)	τω βιβλιω (the book)
22:19	αφαιρη (should take)	αφελη (takes away)
22:19	βιβλου (book)	του βιβλιου (the book)
22:19	αφαιρησει (shall take away)	αφελει (shall take away)
22:19	βιβλου (book)	του ξυλου (the tree)
22:19	και των (and the)	των (the)
22:19	εν βιβλιω (in book)	εν τω βιβλιω (in the book)
22:20	αμην ναι ερχου (Amen; even so, come)	αμην ερχου (Amen, come)
22:21	κυπιου ημων ιησου χριστου (our Lord Jesus Christ)	ιησου χριστου (Lord Jesus)
22:21	μετα παντων υμων αμην (with all you Amen)	μετα των αγιων (with all)

both in number and nature, are common throughout the New Testament between these two Greek texts. For example, the preceding six verses, Revelation 22:10-15, have fourteen textual variants which are of the same nature, and in Revelation 21:3-8 we find no fewer than twenty textual variants. One would expect, therefore, a greater number of textual variants if Erasmus was translating from the Latin back into Greek, and yet the two texts are extremely close. Even if he did translate from the Latin into Greek it would have no bearing on the doctrine of biblical preservation. Preservation simply demands that God has kept and preserved the words throughout the generations from the time of their inception until this present day and even beyond. It does not demand that these words be preserved in the original languages only.

However, this brings us to our second question. Did Erasmus really translate the Latin back into Greek? Textual scholar Herman C. Hoskier argued that Erasmus did not do this. Instead, he suggests that Erasmus used other Greek manuscripts such as 2049 (which Hoskier calls 141), and the evidence seems to support this position.[258] Manuscript 2049 contains the reading found in the Textus Receptus including the textual variant of Revelation 22:19. To this we can also add the Greek manuscript evidence of 296, and the margin of 2067.

Additionally, the Greek text copied by Erasmus in Revelation 22:16-21 reflects a consistency that is found elsewhere in the Textus Receptus, suggesting that it was copied from other Greek manuscripts and not translated from the Latin back into Greek. In Revelation 22:16 we find the phrase *tou dabid* (the David) in the Textus Receptus as opposed to the Critical Text's *dauid* (David). While the English would translate the two identically, it is interesting to note that in Revelation 3:7 we find

---

[258] H. C. Hoskier, *Concerning the Text of the Apocalypse*, vol. 2 (London: Bernard Quaritch, Ltd., 1929), 644.

the same thing. In that passage the Textus Receptus places the definite article before the name of David just as it does in Revelation 22:16, while the Critical Text does not use the definite article before David's name in either passage.

To counter this, it has been noted that within the text of Erasmus at Revelation 22:16-21 there are a few unusual spellings; for example, *elthe* (come) instead of the normal *erchou* (come). This suggests that Erasmus was copying from a Greek manuscript and not translating from the Latin. Erasmus, it should be remembered, was one of the greatest scholars and thinkers of his day. He was fluent in Greek and several other languages. He would have known that the normal New Testament word for *come* is not *elthe* but is instead *erchou*. In fact, Erasmus used *erchou* in Revelation 22:7; 22:12; and even in 22:20. There must have been a reason for Erasmus to depart from the normal form of the word and write *elthe* in 22:17. Moreover, the Latin for *come* in 22:17 is the same Latin word in 22:20, *veni*. This further suggests that Erasmus was not really translating from the Latin, but was using an additional Greek manuscript other than Codex 1r.

Likewise, there is textual evidence for the reading *book of life* instead of *tree of life*. As noted above, the reading is found in a few Greek manuscripts. It is the main reading among the Latin witnesses. The phrase *book of life* is also the reading of the Old Bohairic version. Finally, it is the reading found in the writings of Ambrose (397 AD), Bachiarius (late fourth century), Primasius (552 AD) and Haymo (ninth century).

One must also consider the internal evidence. The phrase *tree of life* appears seven times in the Old Testament and three times in the New Testament. In these verses we are told we will be able to eat of this tree, and that this tree of Eden will reappear in Eternity. The idea that one can have their share taken away from the tree of life seems abnormal to Scripture. However, the phrase *book of life* appears seven other times in the New Testament (Philippians 4:3; Revelation 3:5; 13:8; 17:8; 20:12, 15; and 21:27). In each case we find the book of life either contains or does not contain names, or names are blotted out of it. Therefore, the phrase, "And if any man shall take away from the words of the book of this prophecy, God shall take away his part out of the book of life," is extremely consistent with the biblical texts.

As can be seen from this text, the warning is ominous. While one may understand this passage to apply only to the book of Revelation, it is clear from other passages that the same is true of the whole of Scripture (Deuteronomy 4:2; Proverbs 30:6). When applied to the verses discussed in this chapter we must conclude that somewhere in the process of transmission someone either added to the text or omitted from it. *There's the rub*, and it should be taken seriously. Scholarship is a noble and honorable profession. However, it ceases to be both if it seeks to usurp the authority of the Lord God. After all, our commitment does not so much rest with our scholarship as it does with the ultimate Scholar.

Chapter 9

Translational Considerations

"'Tis written: 'In the beginning was the Word!'
Here now I'm balked! Who'll put me in accord?
It is impossible, the Word so high to prize,
I must translate it otherwise"

-Johann Wolfgang von Goethe: *Faust* (1808)

Shortly after the Authorized Version was first published in 1611 it came under fire. In 1612 Hebrew scholar Hugh Broughton wrote a thesis entitled, *A Censure of the Late Translation for Our Churches*, in which he expostulated the new translation. Broughton had been considered for a position as one of the translators but was overlooked. Therefore, his reproach for the King James Version may have been a result of not being placed on the committee. Nevertheless, it does establish that very early this beloved version was condemned by some. Time has not changed such condemnation. In fact, there has been a revival of criticism as contemporary versions have found their way into the mainstream of the Bible reading public.

Such criticism is usually unwarranted and frequently demonstrates the lack of perspective offered by the one who is disparaging the translation. An anecdote involving one of the KJV translators, Dr. Richard Kilby, provides for us a wonderful example of this very thing. Kilby, who had headed the Old Testament group at Oxford, was in the congregation of a young minister who found fault with a certain way a phrase was translated in the KJV. The minister, who did not realize that Kilby was in his congregation, offered his own translation as the correct one and questioned why it had not been considered. After the service, Kilby took the parson aside and addressed the issue noting that the translators had indeed considered the parson's reading as well as thirteen other readings. However, because of the Hebrew syntax, they had settled on the reading found in the KJV.[259]

Hebrew and Greek words can be translated in more than one way. Those familiar with Biblical languages know that many phrases have several meanings. Therefore, it is a risky thing to suggest the translators have erred. In most cases such objections reflect the shortsightedness of the critic, or else his or her lack of understanding either the original or host languages. It is one thing to offer another possible translation and another to state that a translation is in error. More times than not, the one who is mistaken is the critic.

Mark 6:20

"For Herod feared John, knowing that he was a just man and an holy, and **observed him***; and when he heard him, he did many things, and heard him gladly."*

It is suggested that the phrase *observed him* is incorrect and should be translated *kept him safe.*[260] The problem is not with the translation, but with the lack of comprehending the English language. According to *Webster's Third New International Dictionary*, the word *observe* comes from the Latin word *observare*, which means to *watch, guard,* and *observe.*[261] This agrees with Dr. John C. Traupman's *Latin Dictionary* which defines *observare* as "to watch, watch out for, take careful note of; to guard; to observe,

---

[259] Gustavus S. Paine, *The Men Behind the King James Version* (1959; reprint, Grand Rapids: Baker Book House, 1982), 137-138. David Otis Fuller, *Which Bible?* (Grand Rapids: International Publications, 1975), 17.

[260] James R. White, *The King James Only Controversy: Can You Trust the Modern Translations?* (Minneapolis: Bethany House, 1995), 224-225.

[261] *Webster's Third New International Dictionary*, ed. Philip Babcock Gove (Springfield, Massachusetts: Merriam-Webster Inc., 1981), 1558.

keep, obey, comply with; to pay attention to, pay respect to."[262] Further, the *Oxford English Dictionary* offers the definition of *observe* as, "To regard with attention; to watch; to watch over, look after."[263]

For the most part, we think of the word *observe* as meaning to *watch, study,* or *take notice of.* However, it also means *to keep, protect,* or *preserve.* For example, we speak of *observing the speed limit.* We do not mean that we are watching how fast we travel down the road; we mean we are obeying or keeping the law of the land. Some *observe* the Sabbath or a religious holiday. Again, this means they keep or respect the day. When the Coast Guard speaks of *observing our shores,* they are protecting them. So it is with forest rangers who set up *observation posts* for the purpose of watching and protecting the wilderness. Both *observe* and *preserve* mean *to keep something.* This is why the same Greek word is used in Luke 2:19 and is translated as *kept*: "Mary kept all these things, and pondered them in her heart."

The Greek word is *suntereo.* In *The Analytical Greek Lexicon* this word is defined as "to observe strictly, or to secure from harm, protect."[264] James H. Moulton and George Milligan note that one of the uses of this word in ancient non-literary writings was when "a veteran claims that in view of his long military service, exemption from public burdens ought to be 'strictly observed' in his case."[265] Clearly either *observe* or *kept safe* are proper translations.

Luke 20:26

> *"And they could not take hold of his **words** before the people: and they marvelled at his answer, and held their peace."*

---

[262] John C. Traupman, *Latin Dictionary* (New York: Amsco School Publications, 1966), 200.

[263] *The Oxford English Dictionary*, 2nd edition, eds. J.A. Simpson and E.S.C. Weiner (Oxford: Clarendon Press, 1989), 1196 (compact edition).

[264] Harold K. Moulton, *The Analytical Greek Lexicon* (Grand Rapids: Zondervan), 392.

[265] James H. Moulton and George Milligan, *The Vocabulary Of The Greek Testament* (Grand Rapids: Eerdmans, 1949), 614.

This passage, along with some others, is considered an error by some because the Greek word *rhematos* (word) is translated in the plural instead of the singular. On the surface, and to those who only have a general understanding of the Greek language, the complaint seems legitimate. The Greek word does stand in the singular and most certainly can be translated as *a word*. Most modern versions translate it as *saying*, thus using the singular instead of the plural. The KJV and NKJV translate it as *words*.

Both renderings are correct. The Greek word *rhematos* (or *rhema*) can refer to a word. It also can refer to a group of words gathered together in a single discourse, speech, or clause. That is how it is used in this verse. The *saying* (*rhematos*) that proceeds this verse is the famous phrase from Christ regarding our duty to both God and government. Christ states, "Render therefore unto Caesar the things which be Caesar's, and unto God the things which be God's" (Luke 20:25). This was the saying at which they marveled. As with all sayings, it does not consist of a single word but exists as several words. A *saying, speech,* or *discourse* contains *words*. Therefore, it is proper to translate the singular (which is in reference to the clause) in the plural (which is likewise in reference to the clause). As with idioms, they can be translated literally but are better translated colloquially. Consider the following example: "I would like to have a word with you." While the singular is used in this idiom it is not to be understood literally. Instead, it is understood in the plural. Likewise is the use of *rhematos* in Luke 20:26. While the singular is used, referring to a clause, the plural is understood.

Still, this verse serves to illustrate a point regarding translations. A literal translation need not be strictly word-for-word in every instance. To do so would render a translation that would be wooden and extremely difficult to read. When we have idioms and expressions used in the original languages that would allow the reader to take the words in a less than literal fashion, it is proper to render them in like manner in the translation. The Greek reader of Luke 20:26 would never understand this to mean that Christ only spoke one singular word. The reader would understand that several words were spoken and that the reference concerns the discourse itself. This is something we find throughout the New Testament with other Greek words and phrases. To think of these as translational errors reveals the quality of comprehension lacking in the denouncement.

John 1:18

> *"No man hath seen God at any time; the **only begotten Son**, which is in the bosom of the Father, he hath declared him."*

There are really two problems here, although only one appears on the surface. Should the proper translation be "only begotten Son" or should it be as the New American Standard Version renders it, "only begotten God"? This particular problem is not translational but textual because there is a difference in the Greek texts underlining these two translations. However, there is another problem that has to do with the Greek word *monogenes*. Both the King James and the New American Standard correctly translate it as *only begotten*. There is a growing movement to understand this word as *unique*, *one of a kind*, or simply *only*. We will deal with this difference first.

Many of the current handbooks on Greek syntax state that *monogenes* should **not** be translated as *only begotten*.[266] Instead, they take the word to mean *only* or *unique*. If this were true, the translation of the KJV would not be alone in its "error" for this is the translation of the New American

---

[266] See Newman and Nida, *A Translator's Handbook on the Gospel of John* (New York: United Bible Societies, 1980), 24. Also, Moulton and Milligan, *The Vocabulary of the Greek Testament* (Grand Rapids: Eerdmans, 1930), 416-417. However, others recognize that *monogenes* means *only begotten*. See Thayer, *Greek-English Lexicon of the New Testament* (Milford, MI: Mott Media, 1977 ed.), 417-418. Moulton, *The Analytical Greek Lexicon Revised* (Grand Rapids: Zondervan, 1978 ed.), 272. And, Prestige, *God in Patristic Thought* (London: SPCK, 1952) 37-51, 135-141, 151-156.

Standard Version, the New King James Version, and several other translations of the twentieth century.

The problem here is a misunderstanding of the Greek language (both Koine and Modern). The word *monogenes* does means *one* or *unique* in the sense that an only child is the only one of his parents. It does not mean unique, as in *special*, such as in the phrase, "his work is very unique." Here the Greek would be *monadikos*, not *monogenes*. As we examine the New Testament we find the word *monogenes* used eight times (not counting its usage here in John 1:18). In every case it is used to describe a relationship between a parent and child (Luke 7:12; 8:42; 9:38; John 1:14; 3:16, 18; Hebrews 11:17; 1 John 4:9). Since this is how the Holy Spirit uses the word in the New Testament, we must accept this definition when reading John 1:18.[267]

The evidence establishes that Jesus Christ, although God (John 1:1), is also the only begotten Son of God. No other can claim hold to this title. Those who accept Christ as their personal Savior are spiritually born of God and are called his sons (John 1:12). But no human can lay claim to the title of *only begotten Son*. This phrase has not only to do with Christ's virgin birth, but also his eternal place within the Trinity.

Having established this point, we are now faced with the question of the word following *monogenes*. Should it be *heios* (Son) or *theos* (God)? The oldest known Greek manuscripts that contain John 1:18, P66 and P75, read *only begotten God.* However, these manuscripts all come from the Alexandrian line and smack of ancient Gnosticism. The Gnostics

---

[267] It has further been established that the word *monogenes* has as its root word *genos*. Again, some have suggested that this root word means *kind or type*. This is true, but in the sense that those who are born of a given parentage are a certain type or kind. The Greek word *genos* appears twenty-one times in the New Testament. It is translated as kind, nation, stock (of Abraham), *nation, offspring, kindred, generation*, and *country* in the KJV, demonstrating the word has to do with descendents. The New International Version translates it as *born* in Mark 7:26, and the New American Standard Version translates it as *birth* in Acts 4:36.

taught that Christ was a begotten god, created by God the Father, whom they called the unbegotten God.[268]

When those who had been tainted with Gnosticism cite John 1:18, they cite it as *only begotten God*. Such is true of Tatian (second century), Valentinus (second century), Clement of Alexandria (215 AD), and Arius (336 AD). On the other hand, we find many of the orthodox fathers who opposed Gnosticism quoting John 1:18 as *only begotten Son* (Irenaeus, Tertullian, Basil, Gregory Nazianzus, and Chrysostom).[269]

Even some that served on the textual committee for the UBS-4 recognized that the proper reading of John 1:18 is *only begotten Son*. Dr. Allen Wilkgren, who served on the committee, writes, "It is doubtful that the author [i.e., John] would have written *monogenes theos*, which may be a primitive, transcriptional error in the Alexandrian tradition."[270] Additionally, Professor Bart Ehrman of the University of North Carolina at Chapel Hill has noted that he believes the original reading is *monogenes heios* and not *monogenes theos*.[271] Although Professor Ehrman did not serve

---

[268] The phrase "unbegotten" as applied to God the Father does not appear in the Gnostic writings of the Nag Hammadi Library. Nevertheless, it is found throughout the writings of Gregory of Nyssa in his defense against Gnosticism and Arianism. Therefore, we can conclude that it was a phrase used by Gnostics in their understanding and comparison of the Father with Jesus Christ. Gregory makes the following comment regarding this heresy: "As they [i.e., Gnoticis] say that the Only-begotten God [the Gnostic term for Christ] came into existence 'later,' after the Father, this 'unbegotten' of theirs, whatever they imagine it to be, is discovered of necessity to exhibit with itself the idea of evil." (*Against Eunomius*, Book 9:4)

[269] It is also interesting to note that the *New World Translation* of the Jehovah's Witnesses uses the phrase *only begotten god*. This is, of course, in line with their teaching that Christ is a created god. Once we accept the reading only begotten god, we have opened the door to reinterpret all other verses concerning the deity of Jesus Christ.

[270] Bruce Metzger, A Textual Commentary On The Greek New Testament (New York: United Bible Societies, 2nd ed.), 170.

[271] Bart D. Ehrman, *The Orthodox Corruption Of Scripture* (New York: Oxford University Press, 1993), 78-82.

on the UBS-4 committee, he is a recognized scholar in the field of Biblical textual criticism.[272] Thus, not all scholars agree as to the original reading in this regard.

The majority of orthodox church fathers support the reading *monogenes heios*, as do the majority of existing Greek cursive manuscripts. The reading contained in the majority of uncials (such as A, C3, K, W, Θ, Ψ, Δ, Π, Ξ, and 063), Old Latin, Latin Vulgate, and the Old Syrian also support the reading *monogenes heios*.

Since we know the Greek word *monogenes* concerns the parent/child relationship, and that God is never called *monogenes* (except for Christ in his relationship to the Father), it is clear that *monogenes heios* is the correct reading.

---

[272] In fairness to Professor Ehrman's position he does not support the Traditional Text, and his support for the traditional reading here should not be taken as an endorsement of that text. Ehrman believes that many of the textual variants are a result of scribes seeking to establish orthodox Christianity by altering the text in favor of orthodoxy. It is his hypothesis that John 1:18 in the Critical Text is an orthodox corruption, stating that Christ was the *unique God*, thereby supporting the orthodox view regarding the deity of Jesus Christ.

My hypothesis is that many of the textual variants were caused by scribal corruption. However, not by orthodox scribes seeking to establish orthodoxy, but by heretical scribes seeking to corrupt Scripture to support their false doctrines. Once we understand that *monogenes theos* does not mean that Christ is *uniquely God*, but instead would be understood as a *begotten god*, we have a reading that would support the Gnostic teaching which proclaimed this very heresy. When we consider those in the second, third, and fourth centuries who support this false reading and the doctrine they held in this regard, it is not far fetched to draw such conclusions. If one accepts Ehrman's position as feasible than they should also be willing to accept the possibility of the opposite being true. Namely, that the corruption of the text may be afforded to various heretical groups who sought to move the text of Scripture away from Biblical orthodoxy and toward their heretical position.

Acts 5:30

*"The God of our fathers raised up Jesus, whom ye **slew and hanged** on a tree."*

Some scholars object to the phrase, "whom ye slew and hanged on a tree." They argue that the correct rendering is "whom you killed by hanging on a tree" and that the conjunctive *and* in the KJV misleadingly suggests that the Jews first killed Christ and then hanged his body on the cross.[273] This suggestion is faulty in that it misconstrues the text of the Authorized Version, making the text say "whom ye slew and **THEN** hanged on a tree."

In English, the word *and* does not usually mean a period of time, as is suggested with the addition of the word *then*. The text is not saying that the Jews murdered Christ *and then* placed him on the cross. The word *and* is a conjunction which simply links two thoughts together. As such, it is used as the word *further*. We understand the text to mean that the Jews were responsible for killing their Messiah. *Further*, they were responsible for having him placed on the cross. This is a proper use of English. When one assumes that the text is stating that the Jews murdered the Lord *and then* crucified him, they are reading their own thoughts into the text. The translation "whom ye slew and hanged on a tree" is just as correct as the translation "whom you killed by hanging on the tree."

Acts 12:4

*"And when he had apprehended him, he put him in prison, and delivered him to four quaternions of soldiers to keep him; intending **after Easter** to bring him forth to the people."*

The Greek word *pascha* is translated as *Passover* in the KJV with this one exception where it is translated as *Easter*. Therefore, some point to this

---

[273] White, 225-226.

passage as a translation error on the KJV's part. However, earlier English translations such as Tyndale's NT, the Great Bible, and the Bishops' Bible also translated *pascha* as Easter in this verse, showing that the understanding here dealt with something other than the Jewish Passover. Also, the translation of *pascha* as Passover in Acts 12:4 was known to the king's translators since this is the reading of the Geneva Bible.

The use of the word *pascha* in early Christian writings dealt with the celebration of Easter, and not just the Jewish Passover.[274] Dr. G. W. H. Lampe has correctly stated that *pascha* came to mean *Easter* in the early Church. The ancient Christians did not keep the Jewish Passover. Instead they kept as holy a day to celebrate the resurrection of Christ near the time of both Passover and the pagan festival celebrating the goddess Ostara. Dr. Lampe lists several rules and observances by Christians in celebration of their *pascha* or *Easter*. Lampe also points to various Greek words such as *paschazo* and *paschalua* that came to mean *celebrate Easter* and *Eastertide*.[275] Likewise, Dr. Gerhard Kittel notes that *pascha* came to be called *Easter* in the celebration of the resurrection within the primitive Church.[276]

It should be noted that the English word *Easter* originally carried a meaning that would encompass the Jewish Passover. The *Oxford English Dictionary* states that Easter also means "the Jewish passover" and cites examples dating to 971 A.D. Likewise, the Coverdale Bible often used the word *Easter* instead of *Passover* in its translation because the two had the same meaning to the English mind. Further, the *Homilies* of the Church of England (1563) refers to "Easter, a great, and solemn feast among the

---

[274] Walter Bauer, *A Greek-English Lexicon Of The New Testament And Other Early Christian Literature* (Chicago: The University of Chicago Press, 1957), 633.

[275] G. W. H. Lampe, *A Patristic Greek Lexicon* (Oxford: Clarendon Press, 1961), 1048-1049.

[276] Gerhard Kittel, *Theological Dictionary Of The New Testament*, vol. 2 (Grand Rapids: Eerdmans, 1965), 901-904.

Jewes."[277] Therefore, we see by definition, that the word *Easter* is correct in the understanding of the English language.

There is also a connection between the Christian Easter as we have it and the pagan celebration of Ostara. Early Christians in Rome could not openly celebrate the resurrection of Christ, so they held their celebration at the same time as the pagans. Dr. William C. Martin writes:

> Modern observance of Easter represents a convergence of three traditions: (1) The Hebrew Passover, celebrated during Nisan, the first month of the Hebrew lunar calendar; (2) The Christian commemoration of the crucifixion and resurrection of Jesus, which took place at the feast of the Passover; and (3) the Norse *Ostara* or *Eostra* (from which the name "Easter" is derived), a pagan festival of spring which fell at the vernal equinox, March 21. Prominent symbols in this celebration of the resurrection of nature after the winter were rabbits, signifying fecundity, and eggs, colored like the ray of the returning sun and the northern lights, or aurora borealis.[278]

It seems that *pascha* can mean more than the Jewish holy day of Passover. In fact, Greeks today who wish to send the greeting *Happy Easter* say, *kalee pascha*. Literally it means *good Passover*. However it has come to mean *good* or *happy Easter*.

Additionally, there is a possible problem if we understand this verse to mean the Jewish Passover. Verse three of this chapter states that Peter was taken during, "the days of unleavened bread." The next verse then speaks of *Easter* in the KJV. If the word is translated as *Passover* we have the Days of Unleavened Bread coming before the Passover. In the Biblical use of the

---

[277] *Oxford English Dictionary*, 492.

[278] William C. Martin, The Layman's *Bible Encyclopedia* (Nashville: The Southwestern Company, 1964), 209.

term, Passover came before the Days of Unleavened Bread (Exodus 12:1-8, 15, 19; 13:7; Leviticus 2:11; and Deuteronomy 16:4). Contextually, it would seem that this *pascha* that followed the Days of Unleavened Bread was not the *pascha* that preceded the capture of Peter. Instead, it is likely to refer to the Roman celebration of Ostara, hence called *Easter*.

Acts 19:2

"*He said unto them, Have ye received the Holy Ghost **since** ye believed? And they said unto him, We have not so much as heard whether there be any Holy Ghost.*"

Some have claimed the KJV is in error in its use of the word *since* and suggest the passage should be rendered "Did you receive the Holy Spirit when you believed." The Greek phrase *Ei pneuma agion elabete pisteusantes* is literally translated as, "[The] Spirit/Ghost Holy did ye receive having believed?"

This phrase stands in the Greek aorist and refers to past time; thus, we have the past tense with the words *received* and *believed*. This would establish the translation *when you believed* as correct as it relates to the Greek itself. However, the English word *since* also reflects past tense and is correct as it relates to the Greek text. H. E. Dana and Julius R. Mantey, noted Greek grammarians, address the use of the aorist. They write, "The fundamental significance of the aorist is to denote action simply as occurring, without reference to its progress."[279] Therefore, the words *since* or *when* both reflect the proper use of the aorist. In reference to what is called the *Culminative Aorist*, Dana and Mantey add:

The aorist is employed in this meaning when it is wished to view an event in its entirety, but to regard it from the viewpoint of its existing

---

[279] H. E. Dana and Julius R. Mantey, *A Manual Grammar of the Greek New Testament* (Toronto: Macmillan, 1927), 193.

results. Here we usually find verbs which signify effort or process, the aorist denoting the attainment of the end of such effort or process.[280]

In this regard, the word *since* is proper as it relates to the aorist tense. It can indicate a past action, but one that was attained through a process. Dr. George Ladd recognized this and stated of this passage, "The Greek participle is having believed, and it is capable of being translated either since ye believed (Authorized Version) or when you believed (Revised Standard Version)."[281] Therefore, both translations are correct and neither are in error.

2 Corinthians 2:17

*"For we are not as many, **which corrupt the word of God**: but as of sincerity, but as of God, in the sight of God speak we in Christ."*

The majority of modern versions render this as "peddle" or "sell the word of God for profit" instead of "corrupt the word of God." The Greek word *kapeleuontes* does carry the meaning of a *peddler* or *retailer*. However, it connotes one who sells with *deceit*, a *corrupter*. Dr. Walter Bauer states that the word came to mean "to adulterate."[282] Dr. Joseph Thayer agrees, noting, "But as peddlers were in the habit of adulterating their commodities for the sake of gain…[the word] was also used as synonymous with *to corrupt, to adulterate*."[283] Likewise, Dr. Gerhard Kittel states that *kapeleuontes*, "also means 2. to falsify the word (as the *kapelos* purchases pure wine and then adulterates it with water) by making additions…This refers to the false Gospel of the Judaizers."[284]

---

[280] Ibid., 196-197.

[281] George Ladd, *The Wycliffe Bible Commentary* (Nashville: The Southwest Company, 1962), 1160.

[282] Walter Bauer, *A Greek-English Lexicon Of The New Testament And Other Early Christian Literature*, 403.

[283] Joseph Thayer, *A Greek-English Lexicon Of The New Testament* (Grand Rapids: Baker Book, 1977 edition), 324-325.

[284] Kittel, vol. 3., 605.

The early church fathers understood the verse to refer to those who corrupt God's word. Athanasius (373 AD) wrote, "Let them therefore be anathema to you, because they have 'corrupted the word of truth'."[285] Gregory of Nazianzus (390 AD) alludes to 2 Corinthians 2:17, Isaiah 1:22 and Psalm 54:15, using the word "corrupt":

And who is sufficient for these things? For we are not as the many, able to corrupt the word of truth, and mix the wine, which maketh glad the heart of man, with water, mix, that is, our doctrine with what is common and cheap, and debased, and stale, and tasteless, in order to turn the adulteration to our profit...[286]

Both translations are possible. But in light of its historical and contextual usage, the word *corrupt* is much more likely. Regardless, it is clearly not a translational error. Dr. James R. White, noted Christian apologist and author, makes an interesting claim concerning this verse. He writes, "Surely if the KJV translators were alive today they would gladly admit that 'peddle' is a better translation than 'corrupt, ' and would adopt it themselves."[287] If this is true, how would one explain the notes of Dr. John Bois, one of the translators of the KJV? In his notes on 2 Corinthians 2:17, Dr. Bois writes, "Ibid. v. 17. *kapeleuontes*] [being a retail dealer, playing tricks, corrupting] i.e., *notheuonetes* [adultering]. kapelos is derived *apo tou kallunein ton pelon* [from glossing over lees] by corrupting and adultering wine."[288] Apparently, the translators of the KJV were aware of the meaning of this word.

Titus 2:13

*"Looking for that blessed hope, and the glorious appearing of **the great God and our Saviour Jesus Christ;**"*

---

[285] Athanasius, *Apologia Contra Arianos (Defence Against The Arians)*, III:49.

[286] Gregory Nazianzus, *Oratition 2* ("In Defence Of His Flight To Pontus"), 46.

[287] White, 114.

[288] John Bois, *Translating For King James*, trans. Ward Allen (Vanderbilt University Press, 1969), 51.

Modern versions such as the NIV render this as, "While we wait for the blessed hope—the glorious appearing of our great God and Savior, Jesus Christ." It is argued that the KJV incorrectly translated this passage and violated the *Granville Sharpe Rule* of Greek grammar.[289] Basically this rule states that the two nouns (*God* and *Savior*) refer to the same Person, Jesus Christ. They are correct in their understanding of this grammatical rule. They are incorrect in stating the Authorized Version has violated it.

The problem is not with the KJV, but rather a lack of understanding English grammar. In English, when two nouns are separated by the phrase *and our*, the context determines if the nouns refer to two persons or to two aspects of the same person. Consider the following sentence, "He was a great hero and our first president, General George Washington." This statement is not referring to two persons but two aspects of the same person. Washington was a great hero by anyone's standards, but he was not everyone's president. He was *our president*.

The same is true of the phrase in Titus 2:13. When Christ returns he is coming as King of kings and Lord of lords (Revelation 19:16). He is returning as *the great God* (Titus 2:13; Revelation 19:17). Therefore, he will return as everyone's King, everyone's Lord, as the great God over all. But he is not everyone's Savior. He is only the Savior of those who have placed faith in Him. When he returns he is coming as *the great God* but he is also returning as *our Savior*, two aspects of the same Person.

This is illustrated elsewhere in Scripture. Consider the following two passages in the New Testament. In both cases two nouns are separated by the phrase *and our*. However, it is also clear that the two nouns refer to the same Person: God, who is our Father. In Galatians 1:4 we read, "Who gave himself for our sins, that he might deliver us from this present evil world, according to the will of God and our Father." Likewise, in 1

---

[289] White, 267-270.

Thessalonians 1:3 we read, "Remembering without ceasing your work of faith, and labour of love, and patience of hope in our Lord Jesus Christ, in the sight of God and our Father." In both passages we know that *God* and *Father* are the same Person. They are separated by *and our* to convey the truth that the Eternal God over all is also our Father, thereby personalizing our relationship with Him.

The King James translation of Titus 2:13 is also consistent. In the Book of Titus we find the Greek phrase *soteros emon* (Savior of us) used six times (1:3, 4; 2:10, 13; 3:4, 6). Each time the Authorized Version consistently translates it as *our Saviour*. In the final analysis, we see that the KJV is harmonious in its use of Greek as well as in its proclamation of the deity of Christ.

Hebrews 10:23

*"Let us hold fast the profession of our **faith** without wavering; (for he is faithful that promised;)"*

The common word for *faith* is the Greek word *pistis*. However, the word used here is *elpidos* (a form of the word *elpis*), usually translated as *hope*. This does not mean the translation of *elpidos* or *elpis* as *faith* is a mistranslation. In fact, the King James translators stated that they were not bound by strict word counts, and that sometimes the context demands that the same Greek word be translated differently.

The English words *faith* and *hope* carry the idea of trust, assurance that what has been told will occur. The word *hope* means *confidence, faith, reliance, trust, belief,* and *assurance*. There is within Scripture a clear connection between faith and hope. "Faith is the substance of things hoped for" (Hebrews 11:1). The Scriptures state, "By whom also we have access by faith into this grace wherein we stand, and rejoice in hope of the glory of God" (Romans 5:2). And in reference to Abraham, the word of God says, "Who against hope believed in hope, that he might become the father of many nations, according to that which was spoken, So shall thy seed be. And being not weak in faith, he considered not his own body now dead, when he was about an hundred years old, neither yet the deadness of Sara's womb" (Romans 4:18-19). We are saved by hope (Romans 8:24) and yet we are saved by grace through faith (Ephesians 2:8). We are told to place our faith and hope in God (1 Peter 1:21).

The context of Hebrews chapter ten informs us that we are to have full assurance of faith (verse twenty-two) and the One we are trusting is "faithful" (verse twenty-three). The context of the Greek word *elpis* in this verse can be expressed by the English words *faith, hope,* or *trust.* Dr. Gerhard Kittel notes the comparison of faith and hope when defining the Greek word *elpis* (hope). He even notes that in the Greek Septuagint (LXX) there is an "interrelating" of the two Greek words for faith and hope. [290]

Faith, trust, and hope are used interchangeably. A related word to *elpis* (hope) is *elpizo.* It is translated as *hope* in places such as Luke 6:34 and Romans 8:25. However, it is mostly translated as *trust* in places such as Matthew 12:21 and Romans 15:24. A related word to *pistis* (faith) is *pistio.* It is translated as *believe* in places such as Matthew 8:13 and John 3:16. However, it is also translated as *trust* in 1 Timothy 1:11 (as is another form of it in 1 Thessalonians 2:4 which is translated as *trust*). The context of Hebrews chapter ten and eleven permits this type of *trust* be translated as *faith* instead of its normal translation *hope.*

1 Peter 3:1

*"Likewise, ye wives, be in subjection to your own husbands; that, if any obey not the word, they also may without the word be won by **the conversation** of the wives;"*

This verse, along with a handful of others, is questioned because of the word *conversation.* The objection is that today *conversation* means *talk,* but the verses in question refer to *lifestyle* or *behavior.* The Authorized Version

---

[290] Kittel, vol. 2, 531.

translates the Greek word *anastrephw* (or *anastrophe*) as *conversation* fifteen times in the New Testament (2 Corinthians 1:12; Galatians 1:13; Ephesians 2:3; 4:22; 1 Timothy 4:12; Hebrews 13:7; James 3:13; 1 Peter 1:15, 18; 2:12; 3:1, 2, 16; 2 Peter 2:7; 3:11).

The majority of good quality English dictionaries will note that the word *conversation* means the life style or character of an individual in addition to its common context of conversing. The English word *conversation* comes from the Latin *conversatio* which concerns social conduct in public life, which is exactly how the word is used in the context of the Authorized Version. The Greek word *anastrephw* is also translated as "behave" (1 Timothy 3:15) and "live" (Hebrews 10:33; 2 Peter 2:18) within the text of the KJV, revealing that the word has to do with how one behaves or lives their life before others. Even today we speak of those who have been changed in both word and deed (Romans 15:17-19) as *converts*. One may accuse the word of being somewhat antiquated, but to call it a mistranslation only reveals the limited awareness of the accuser.

2 Peter 1:1

"Simon Peter, a servant and an apostle of Jesus Christ, to them that have obtained like precious faith with us through the righteousness of God and our Saviour Jesus Christ:"

The Authorized Version has been accused of inconsistency in its translation of 2 Peter 1:1 when compared with its translation of 2 Peter 1:11. In the later passage we read, "For so an entrance shall be ministered unto you abundantly into the everlasting kingdom of **our Lord and Saviour Jesus Christ.**" In making such an accusation, some have provided the following comparison between 2 Peter 1:1 and 2 Peter 1:11.

1:1:   *tou theou emon kai soteros Iesou Christou*

1:11:   *tou kuriou emon kai soteros Iesou Christou*

It is then noted that the only difference between the two verses is the substitution of *kuriou* (Lord) in verse eleven instead of *theou* (God) as found in verse one. Therefore, according to the Greek, verse one must be translated as "our God and Savior" in order to be consistent.[291] Since the KJV does not do this, it is looked upon as mistranslating this passage.

The point is well taken, and would be correct if the Greek text that underlies the KJV read as presented. However, it does not. The Greek text used by the King James translators was Beza's text of 1589 and 1598. There we find an additional *emon* (our) at 2 Peter 1:1 that is not provided by those who call this a mistranslation. The two are compared below with Beza's text presented first.

Tou theou emon kai soteros emon Iesou Christou
Tou theou emon kai soteros Iesou Christou

The translation of Beza's text is correct in the Authorized Version, and is consistent since the additional *emon* appears in 2 Peter 1:1 and not 2 Peter 1:11.

The question exists why Beza provided the additional *emon* at 2 Peter 1:1 that is not found in other Greek texts. Dr. Bruce Metzger may supply the answer. Although not discussing this passage, Dr. Metzger does note the following concerning Beza:

> Accompanied by annotations and his own Latin version, as well as Jerome's Latin Vulgate, these editions [of Beza's text from 1565, 1582, 1589, and 1598] contained a certain amount of textual information drawn from several Greek manuscripts which Beza had collated himself, as well as the Greek manuscripts collated by Henry Stephanus, son of Robert Stephanus.[292]

Since the Greek text of Robert Stephanus did not contain the addition, and the Greek text of Beza does, it is logical to assume that Beza added the

---

[291] White, 268.

[292] Bruce M. Metzger, *The Text Of The New Testament*, 3rd ed. (Oxford: Oxford University Press, 1992), 105.

emon at 2 Peter 1:1 based on the various manuscripts that he possessed (or the ones possessed by Henry Stephanus). We would be mistaken to presume that all existing manuscripts used in the sixteenth century are still in existence today. Some have undoubtedly passed away over time. Regardless, the inclusion of the extra *emon* in this passage provides evidence of its preservation. It is certainly not a mistranslation on the part of the KJV.

We have seen in these few examples how some express a certain amount of disdain for the Authorized Version with meaningless objections. They do not like this or that reading and therefore seek to find a flaw in this literary masterpiece. It is easy to find fault, especially if one does not like a certain rendering. However, upon closer examination it usually can be shown that the difference has more to do with the manner of how words or phrases are understood and not the correctness of the translation itself. To disparage the word translated is to disparage the word. We would do well to take note and exercise caution when seeking to correct what we *perceive* is a mistranslation. It just may be that the one in error is the one passing judgment.

Chapter 10

Deliberating The Arguments

"Except the Word of God beareth witness in this matter,
other testimony is of no value."

-John Bunyan: *Pilgrim's Progress* (1678)

When there are differences in the Greek manuscripts, textual scholars usually depend on two basic principles to determine the perceived original reading. First, they consider the *external evidence*. This means they regard the age of a manuscript, its geographical distribution, and its relationship with other textual families. Second, they will observe the *internal evidence*. This means they consider the textual variant in light of what the original writer would most likely have written. It takes into account style and vocabulary, the context, and how the variant harmonizes with other passages written by the same writer. These evidences are logical and certainly are of great value. Nevertheless, we should also embrace the biblical promises from God concerning preservation, thereby approaching the issue both scripturally and scholastically.[293]

---

[293] There has been a growing movement among some evangelical and conservative scholars to promote biblical preservation. This is especially true among supporters of the Majority Text and the Textus Receptus. The position is that "God has Divinely preserved His text in a continuous, uninterrupted tradition." Donald L. Brake, "The Preservation Of The Scriptures," *Counterfeit Or Genuine?*, ed. David Otis Fuller (Grand Rapids: Grand Rapids International Publications, 1975), 179. Other scholars reject a theological basis stating that "a theological a priori has no place in textual criticism." Daniel B. Wallace, "The Majority Text Theory: History, Methods, And Critique," *The Text Of The New Testament In Contemporary Research*, eds. Bart D. Ehrman and Michael W. Holmes (Grand Rapids: Eerdmans, 1995), 309.

There are basically two arguments against the Traditional Text, with an additional one as it concerns the Authorized Version. First, there are those who reject the Traditional Text at a certain reading based on manuscripts that are considered *older*. Second, the Critical Text is embraced because the manuscripts it is based on are characterized as *better*. One does not have to look long to find this older/better argument employed. Both arguments sound authoritative and certainly deserve our consideration. To this a third argument is added to support modern versions of the Bible. It concerns the need for *simplicity*.

Older Manuscripts

Textual scholars will point to the age of a manuscript, as in the case of very old papyri, as supporting their argument for a given reading. On the surface such patronage seems sound. After all, the older manuscript would be closer in age to the original autographs. It is therefore assumed, quite logically, that this manuscript would most likely contain the original reading. The earliest Greek manuscripts are the papyri discovered in Egypt, south of the Delta region. They were unearthed in the "rubbish heaps" of such places as Oxyrhynchos, Atfih (Aphroditopolis), and Heracleopolis.[294]

Although most of these papyri are fragmentary, others contain large sections of Scripture and have been given very early dates by paleographers. P75 (containing part of Luke and John) dates from 175 to 225 AD. P66 (containing part of John) and P46 (containing part of Romans and the Pauline epistles) dates to about 200 AD or before. P52, a small fragment containing only John 18:31-33 and 37-38, had been considered the oldest manuscript, dating to 125 AD. However, papyrologist and textual scholar Dr. Carsten Peter Thiede has redated P64 (the Magdalen papyrus)

---

[294] Eldon Jay Epp and Gordon D. Fee, *Studies in the Theory and Method of New Testament Textual Criticism* (Grand Rapids: Eerdmans, 1993), 279.

from the early third century to 66 AD.[295] P64 consists of three small fragments containing Matthew 26:7-8, 10, 14-15, 22-23 and 31. Thiede has likewise redated P67 from the third century to around 70 AD. This manuscript contains Matthew 3:9, 15; 5:20-22, 25-28. If his position is correct, these would be the oldest existing manuscripts.

The papyri manuscripts mentioned above are very old indeed. The fact that these manuscripts seem to have originated in Egypt, or at least survived there, and were not used by the majority of believers throughout the existence of the church does not carry much weight with textual scholars. But it is something we should consider. After all, why should we think that the majority of believers in church history were deprived of God's pure word? And, if we make such limitations, what does this say about preservation at any given time in history?

It does not seem to bother most textual critics that these manuscripts do not generally agree with later Alexandrian texts. The early papyri, although considered Alexandrian in nature, reflect a mixed text with many Byzantine readings in them. Consequently, Kurt Aland has labeled P46 and P66 as "free"[296] while Bruce Metzger simply calls P66 "mixed."[297] In his introduction to the Chester Beatty Papryi, Sir Frederic Kenyon likewise observes the mixed nature of these early manuscripts.[298]

There are many places where the oldest manuscripts support the readings of the Traditional Text. Yet, these readings are mostly rejected in light of the later Alexandrian readings. For example, in John 4:1 Codex Sinaiticus (fourth century), Codex D05 (sixth century) and Codex Θ

---

[295] Carsten Peter Thiede and Matthew D'Ancona, *Eyewitness To Jesus* (New York: Doubleday, 1996), 124-125.

[296] Kurt and Barbara Aland, *The Text Of The New Testament*, 2nd ed., trans. Erroll F. Rhodes (Grand Rapids: Eerdmans, 1989), 99-100.

[297] Bruce M. Metzger, *The Text Of The New Testament*, 2nd ed. (Oxford: Oxford University Press, 1992), 40.

[298] Sir Frederic G. Kenyon, *The Chester Beatty Biblical Papyri: Fasciculus I* (London: Emory Walker, 1933), 16.

(ninth century) have the reading *Iesous* (Jesus). The Traditional Text reads *kurios* (Lord). This is also the reading in Codex Vaticanus (fourth century), Alexandrinus (fifth century), Codex C (fifth century), and the majority of uncial manuscripts and cursive manuscripts. Both P66 and P75 have the reading *kurios*, agreeing with the Traditional Text. Nevertheless, this reading is rejected by the Critical Text in favor of the reading found in Sinaiticus. Consequently, modern translations such as the NIV and NRSV forsake the early manuscripts in favor of Sinaiticus. There are many other examples of this sort. There are also many places where P66 and P75 differ with each other. In such cases, P66 is sometimes chosen, while at other times P75 is cited.

Dr. Gordon D. Fee, a noted and respected textual scholar, produced a comparison study of early manuscripts with various text types.[299] It yielded some very interesting results. In his study, Dr. Fee notes several passages in the Gospel of John where Codex Sinaiticus agrees or disagrees with P66, P75, the Texus Receptus, and some other witnesses. In John chapter four, Fee notes that out of sixty-one possible textual variations P66 produced the following statistics:

Texus Receptus=thirty-seven times or 60.6% in agreement with P66.

Sinaiticus=twenty-one times or 34.4% in agreement with P66.

Likewise, P75 showed a stronger relationship with the Traditional Text than it did with Codex Sinaiticus; however, its strongest relationship is clearly with Codex Vaticanus. The agreement with P75 among these texts is as follows:

Texus Receptus=thirty-two times or 52.5% in agreement with P75.

Sinaiticus=nineteen times or 31.5% in agreement with P75.

Vaticanus=fifty-two times or 85.2% in agreement with P75.[300]

---

[299] Epp and Fee, 221-243.

[300] Ibid., 228.

Dr. Fee then broadened the study to cover John 1-8, with a total of three hundred twenty possible textual variations. The statistics show a strong relation between the Traditional Text and P66, agreeing 50.9% of the time when there are textual variations. P66 and Sinaiticus agreed only 43.7% of the time.[301] Although Dr. Fee maintains that the pro-Traditional Text readings are "of little consequence," he does concede that the early papyrus have produced evidence away from the Alexandrian textual line.[302] Further, the point is not that the earliest existing manuscripts are Byzantine in nature, just that they are mixed and are not pure Alexandrian. Therefore, the modern Critical Text does not always follow the oldest existing manuscripts.

We should also consider the recent evidence produced by Dr. Carsten Thiede regarding P64. If he is correct in redating this manuscript to 66 AD, we not only have the earliest known manuscript of the New Testament, we have one that supports the textual reading found in the Traditional Text. In Matthew 26:22 the Critical Text reads, *legein auto eis ekastos* while the Traditional Text reads, *legein auto ekastos auton*. The difference is reflected in the Revised Standard Version when compared with the King James Version. "And they were very sorrowful, and began to say to him one after another, 'Is it I, Lord?'" (RSV). "And they were exceeding sorrowful, and began every one of them to say unto him, Lord, is it I?" (KJV). While the difference is minor and does not affect doctrine, this is still a reflection of the type of textual variants common between the Alexandrian and Byzantine textual lines. If the oldest manuscript is to be considered more original, a change must occur in the Critical Text because P64 has the same reading found in the Traditional Text and the King James Version. Although the papyrus fragment is worn, Dr. Thiede was able to determine the original reading using an extremely powerful device

---

301 Ibid., 233.
302 Ibid., 201.

known as an *epifluorescent confocal laser scanning microscope.*[303] Here is another example where the oldest reading that agrees with the Traditional Text is rejected in favor of the later Alexandrian reading.

However, the argument over the oldest manuscripts and their textual variants with later manuscripts may be moot. According to textual scholars such as George D. Kilpatrick and H. Vogels, the great majority of textual variants in the New Testament text occurred before the start of the third century.[304] If this is true the debate over the age of a manuscript is not as important as the age of the textual variant. Additionally, Dr. Kurt Aland has noted the *tenacity* of a textual variant in that once injected into the text it can reappear centuries later in later manuscripts without any subsequent existing manuscripts between.[305] If this is true of textual variants, it is likewise true of the original reading. Therefore, the original reading may just as likely be found in later manuscripts as it is in the older ones. This being the case, more is needed than the age of a manuscript when making a textual decision.

Better Manuscripts

Dr. Frederik Wisse has correctly noted that the majority of all existing manuscripts have a striking bias against them as far as modern textual scholarship is concerned. In an attempt to provide a working profile of the majority of Greek manuscripts, Wisse has observed that scholars such as Kurt Aland are not interested in the Byzantine text, but only in texts that "significantly diverge from the Byzantine text."[306] The majority of textual scholars today consider the Alexandrian family of manuscripts closer to

---

[303] Thiede and D'Ancona, 60.

[304] G. D. Kilpatrick, *The Principles And Practice Of New Testament Textual Criticism* (Leuven: University Press, 1990), 34.

[305] Aland, 56.

[306] Frederik Wisse, *The Profile Method For Classifying And Evaluating Manuscript Evidence* (Grand Rapids: Eerdmans, 1982), 21.

the original and therefore better. The Byzantine or Traditional Text has been considered a *conflation* (a mixing or joining) of the Alexandrian and Western texts in the fourth century by Lucian at Antioch in Syria. Therefore, the latter text is considered inferior.

Some nineteenth century scholars strongly promoted the *Lucian Recension* theory. This particular theory stated that Lucian of Antioch, Syria, who died in 311 AD, was the leader of a group of scholars who edited and conflated the various existing texts to produce what became the Traditional Text. Since Lucian was from Syria, and the work was said to have occurred there, this text is sometimes called the Syrian Text. The basic problem with this theory, established by Fenton John Anthony Hort, is that there is no evidence of any such event ever having occurred. Sir Frederic Kenyon correctly noted that we have the names of several of the revisers of both the Greek Septuagint and the Latin Vulgate and it would be notably unusual for history and church authorities to have omitted any record of such a major revision of the New Testament.[307] Further, as has been noted, the majority of all textual variants had already come into existence before the third century. Therefore, the Byzantine Text is more than likely to have been established long before the existing manuscripts that reflect it.

Apart from the promise of Scripture, we simply do not know which text is original and which one is corrupt. It is valid to argue that despite the absence of early Byzantine manuscripts, the traditional textual line reflects the original autographs better than the Alexandrian line. Since the Scriptures are to be used and read we would expect these texts to wear sooner than texts that were considered corrupt and therefore not used by the majority of Christians during the first three hundred years of the

---

307 Sir Frederic G. Kenyon, *Handbook To The Textual Criticism Of The New Testament* (London: Macmillan and Co., 1926), 302.

church. This would explain the absence of Byzantine manuscripts until later in the church's history. However, the Byzantine textual line has early witnesses. We have Byzantine readings in the oldest existing manuscripts; we also have Byzantine readings in ancient versions and the citations of the church fathers. What scholars classify as better manuscripts may therefore rest more on subjectivity than is usually admitted.

The Need For Simplicity

The argument against the King James Version now turns from one of textual criticism to one of translation. Apart from the textual issues, the most common plea for contemporary revisions of Scripture is that of simplicity. Time and again we are informed that the King James Version is too difficult to read and should be simplified. This objection is so well established that it is hardly even questioned.

To illustrate the need for simplicity, several examples of difficult readings are sometimes offered.[308] The following are a few instances. "And Mt. Sinai was altogether on a smoke" (Exodus 19:18). "Thou shalt destroy them that speak leasing" (Psalm 5:6). "Nevertheless even him did outlandish women cause to sin" (Nehemiah 13:26). "Solomon loved many strange women" (1 Kings 11:1). "The ships of Tarshish did sing of thee in thy market" (Ezekiel 27:25). "We do you to wit of the grace of God" (2 Corinthians 8:1).

These are good examples and do illustrate changes and difficulties in our English language. Each case could easily be resolved with footnotes or an English dictionary. Regardless, one can make similar arguments against many modern versions. Consider the following from the New International Version. "Waheb in Suphah and the ravines" (Numbers 21:14). "The

---

[308] Jack P. Lewis, *The English Bible From KJV to NIV: A History and Evaluation* (Grand Rapids: Baker Book House, 1981), 53-54.

Nephilim were on the earth in those days" (Genesis 6:4). "Fearing that they would run aground on the sandbars of Syrtis" (Acts 27:17). "The meeting of the Areopagus" (Acts 17:22). "Then the governor's soldiers took Jesus into the Praetorium" (Matthew 27:27). "He agreed to pay them a denarius" (Matthew 20:2).

It is also popular to compile lists of difficult words contained in the KJV as reason for simplicity. However, just because something is difficult does not mean it should be abolished. The following examples are words that may be considered difficult for the average reader:

> Soliloquized, onslaught, ferule, cruelly, gesticulation, filial, geniality, titter, garret, haunches, forlorn, fetched, dismalest, well-nigh, reckon, unkempt, serape, palpable, gunwale, auspicious, procured, oaken, labyrinth, tallow, and stalwart.

The above list did not come from the Elizabethan English of the Authorized Version, but from four chapters of the narrative of Mark Twain's children's classic, *The Adventures of Tom Sawyer*. One can point to difficulties in anything, but our growth as humans is to seek to understand what we do not know. Some words that are difficult in the KJV include the following:

> Amiable, anon, begat, centurion, chode, churlish, corban, espied, fain, forthwith, fray, gat, hardness, knob, ligure, leasing, mammon, pate, perdition, pityful, sod, suffer, trode, verily, wanton, waxed, wench, wot, wont.

These words, standing on their own, may be difficult or misunderstood. Yet, each of these words have found their way into contemporary literature. The word *wont* is a wonderful example of this. It means *customary* and is used nine times in the King James Version. A recent *Star Trek* novel reads: "The next morning, Commander Riker arrived at the ready room fifteen minutes early, as was his wont; he was surprised to see Wesley

Crusher already waiting."[309] The need for a comprehensive vocabulary may be an argument favoring the Authorized Version.

In his booklet, *All About Bibles*, Dr. John R. Kohlenberger III has listed the reading level of several English translations as provided by Dr. Linda H. Parrish and Dr. Donna Norton of Texas A & M University. They list Today's English Version (TEV) with a 7.29 reading grade level. The NIV received a 7.80 reading grade level, while the New American Standard Version (NASV) received an 11.55 reading grade level. The highest reading grade level was 12.00 and given to the KJV.[310] This would mean that anyone who graduated from high school should be able to read this "outdated" version. Additionally, its reading level is not that much higher than the NASV.

Once we begin an argument against any translation that is based on simplicity, where do we stop? Do we reject the readability of the KJV and embrace the NASV as easier to read because it is a half-grade lower? Should we reject the NASV and accept the NIV because it is even easier to read? Do we then stop with the NIV? What if someone cannot read at the seventh grade level? Do we lower the standard even more? Do we take the approach that some modern educators have and "dumb-down" our language? Or do we seek to raise the standard higher and educate our people? These are important questions when it comes to readability. After all, historically the church has always sought to raise the educational level of the masses, not lower it.

There is also a scriptural principle here. We must consider that it is not so much the words as the concepts of Scripture that are difficult to understand. As Isaiah 55:8-9 reminds us, our thoughts are not God's thoughts;

---

[309] Dafydd Ab Huge, Star Trek: *The Next Generation: Balance Of Power* (New York: Simon and Schuster, Peter David, 1995), 261.

[310] John R. Kohlenberger III, *All About Bibles* (New York: Oxford University Press, 1985), 12.

the same passage admonishes us that our ways are different than those of the Lord. When Christ came and preached He spoke in parables, not to make the message easier to understand but to make it harder (Matthew 13:10-16). We are under the command to search the Scriptures daily and to study to show ourselves approved (Acts 17:11; 2 Timothy 2:15). This is not to say that simplicity does not have its place; that is an individual choice. We should not disparage something because it is more difficult. We may end up finding that the more difficult is the more profitable. Since we are to love the Lord with all our heart, soul, strength, and mind (Mark 12:30), it may be that God wishes to enrich more than just our spirits.

These three arguments, therefore, are not as weighty as some would have us believe. Older manuscripts are not always better, nor are they always used. When older manuscripts support the Byzantine reading, that reading is usually rejected. What scholars may consider the better manuscript is really a matter of opinion that usually omits the providential hand of God. There are usually at least two sides to most textual arguments and we would do well to view things from alternate perspectives. Ultimately, our final conclusions must be biblical. Finally, what is considered difficult may be for our own good and edification. After all, the wisest man who ever lived, King Solomon, reminds us, *"It is the glory of God to conceal a thing: but the honour of kings is to search out a matter"* (Proverbs 25:2).

A Plea For Preservation

There are several verses that furnish the basis for biblical preservation (1 Samuel 3:19; Psalm 12:6-7; 105:8; 119:89, 160; 138:2; Ecclesiastes 3:14; Isaiah 40:8; Matthew 4:4; 5:17-18; 24:35; John 10:35; 2 Timothy 3:15-16; 1 Peter 1:23-25). Of these, perhaps the most cited and questioned is Psalm 12:6-7: "The words of the LORD are pure words: as silver tried in a furnace of earth, purified seven times. Thou shalt keep them, O LORD, thou shalt preserve them from this generation for ever." This is also the reading of the American Standard Version and the New King James Version. The passage provides a scriptural basis for the belief that God keeps and preserves his words.

The passage has also been understood as a reference to persons and not Scripture. The New International Version reads, "And the words of the LORD are flawless, like silver refined in a furnace of clay, purified seven times. O LORD, you will keep us safe and protect us from such people forever." The Revised Standard Version agrees with this reading. The New American Standard Version changes "us" to "him," yet the focus is still on a person and not the preservation of God's words. The question then arises as to which translation is correct. That is a debate that has been persisting for centuries.[311]

The great reformer, John Calvin, noted that this passage could be understood to refer to either the words of God or God's people. Calvin himself thought the context had reference to the preservation of God's people.[312] Other great theologians of the past believed the passage referred to God's words. John Wesley, scholar and founder of the Methodist Church, writes that Psalm 12:6-7 concern the "words or promises (of God): these thou wilt observe and keep, both now, and from this generation for ever."[313] Dr. G. Campbell Morgan, while using the American Standard Version, claimed this passage was a promise for biblical preservation:

> The psalmist breaks out into praise of the purity of His words, and declares that Jehovah will "keep them," and "preserve

---

[311] It is interesting to note that some creeds following the Reformation included biblical preservation. The Westminster Confession of Faith in 1646 states that Scripture "being immediately inspired by God, and, by His singular care and providence kept pure in all ages." S. W. Carruthers, *The Westminster Confession of Faith*, 7th ed. (Manchester: R. Aikman and Son, n.d.), 92.

[312] John Calvin, *Calvin's Commentary on Psalms* (Grand Rapids: Eerdmans), 178-179

[313] John Wesley, "Wesley's Notes On The Bible" *The Master Christian Library*, version 7 (Rio, WI: Ages Software, 1999 ed.), disc 1.

them." The "them" here refers to the words. There is no promise made of widespread revival or renewal. It is the salvation of a remnant and the preservation of His own words which Jehovah promises.[314]

The Hebrew can be understood to refer to either "them" or "him." The Greek LXX uses the word *hemas* (us), yet the Greek versions of Aquila and Theodotian use the word *autous* (them). The argument as to the meaning of this passage, therefore, is open for discussion. Nevertheless, the first half of this passage is without question as to its meaning. The words of the Lord are pure, and the whole of Scripture testifies to this truth. It somewhat lacks consistency to think that God's words would be pure in their inception and yet lost in their transmission. If the Almighty takes time to purify his words, it would seem he would take just as much care to preserve them. Otherwise, why purify them at all? Of course, the truth of biblical preservation is not confined to this one biblical passage, as has already been noted.

The Fullness Of Time

In addition to the promise of preservation, it should also be noted that God does things in accordance with his own schedule. Concerning Jesus Christ, we are told when "the fullness of the time was come, God sent forth his Son, made of a woman" (Galatians 4:4). We are also told that all things will be accomplished by Christ "in the dispensation of the fullness of times" (Ephesians 1:10). There are no coincidences in regard to Christ. He fulfills things according to his purpose and in his timing. What is true of the Living Word is reflected in the written word. The Authorized Version came into being at just the right time. If we accept the Sovereignty of God, we must also believe his hand was in producing the world's most loved translation of the Bible.

---

[314] G. Campbell Morgan, *Notes On The Psalms* (Grand Rapids: Revell, 1958), 32.

Before the late sixteenth century and the early seventeenth century, the church in power was the Roman Catholic Church. Catholicism at that time prohibited the reading of the Bible in any language but Latin. However, by the late sixteenth century and early seventeenth century the Protestant Church became the major religious force in the English-speaking world. At this time, when the KJV was translated, the printing press was being refined. England was on the threshold of becoming a world empire, and the Protestant Reformation was in full swing.

Approximately one hundred fifty years before the KJV was printed, Bibles were all handwritten. One can begin to imagine the impossible task of reaching the world when all Scripture had to be copied in this fashion. By the seventeenth century printed books were common, and the desire of Christians to have their own copy of Scripture was rapidly growing. This is one of the reasons the Geneva Bible was so popular. Although the Puritans loved the Geneva Bible and brought it with them to the New World, by 1637 the King James Bible had replaced it throughout the Massachusetts Bay Colony.[315] In fact, the KJV was universally accepted in the New World "as the word of God and no question was raised as to its infallibility."[316]

The English language is divided into three periods. Old English, (700 to 1100 AD); Middle English, (1100 to 1500 AD); and Modern English (1500 to the present).[317] As a pioneer work of the Modern English era, the KJV has helped in the shaping and developing of the English language, and is the only modern translation of which this can be said. Dr. William Rosenau has correctly observed that the KJV has "molded new forms and

---

[315] Nathan O. Hatch and Mark A. Noll, eds., *The Bible in America: Essays in Cultural History* (New York: Oxford University Press: 1982) 27-33.

[316] Oliver Perry Chitwood, *A History of Colonial America* (New York: Harper and Brothers, Publishers, 1961 ed.) 441.

[317] Marjorie Anderson and Blanche C. Williams, *Old English Handbook* (New York: Houghton Mifflin Company, 1935), 6-7.

phrases, which, while foreign to the English, became with it flesh and bone."[318] Many great literary works that followed have been greatly influenced by the Authorized Version. This speaks of the importance of this great version in regard to the English language.

Although its beauty has been compared to the writings of Shakespeare, it is vastly easier read than Shakespeare, with equal influence upon our native tongue. Contemporary scholars of the English language have observed that:

> The King James Bible was published in the year Shakespeare began work on his last play, *The Tempest*. Both the play and the Bible are masterpieces of English, but there is one crucial difference between them. Whereas Shakespeare ransacked the lexicon, the King James Bible employs a bare 8000 words—God's teaching in homely English for everyman. From that day to this, the Shakespearian cornucopia and the biblical iron rations represent, as it were, the North and South Poles of the language, reference points for writers and speakers throughout the world, from the Shakespearian splendor of a Joyce or a Dickens to the biblical rigor of a Bunyan, or a Hemingway..[319]

The history and effect the KJV has had on our language not only speaks of its great literary value, but of the divine hand upon it that shaped our language, our culture, our history, and our thought.

---

[318] William Rosenau, *Hebraisms In The Authorized Version* (Baltimore: The Friedenwald Company, 1903), 31.

[319] Robert McCrum, William Cran, and Robert MacNeil, *The Story Of English* (New York: Viking Penguin Inc, 1986), 113. This book is a companion to the PBS television series on the history of the English language.

The Testimony Of The Translators

Although the testimony of the King's translators is often ignored, it stands as a unique tribute to their enterprise. In their second and third paragraphs of the original preface, titled *The Translators To The Reader*, the KJV translators make some very interesting comparisons. They liken their work to David delivering the ark of the Lord to Jerusalem, to Solomon building the temple of God, and even to Moses receiving the Law.[320]

The preface makes a case for providing individuals with Holy Scriptures in their native tongues. The translators listed the objections raised by the Catholic Church of that day: "Was their [i.e., Protestant] translation good before? Why do they now mend it? Was it not good? Why then was it obtruded to the people?"[321] Responding to such questions, the translators wrote:

> Yet for all that, as nothing is begun and perfected at the same time, and the later thoughts are thought to be the wiser: so, if we building upon their foundation that went before us, and being holpen by their labours, do endeavour to make that better which they left so good, no man, we are sure, hath cause to mislike us; they, we persuade ourselves, if they were alive, would thank us...And this is the word of God, which we translate...For by this means it cometh to pass, that whatsoever is sound already, (and all is sound for substance in one or other of our editions, and the worst of ours far better than their authentick Vulgar) the same will shine as gold more brightly, being rubbed and polished;...[322]

---

[320] "The Translators To The Reader," *The Holy Bible: King James Version* (Cambridge: Cambridge University Press), ix-xi.

[321] Ibid., xvii.

[322] Ibid., xviii-xix. Spelling matches that of the 1611 edition.

The translators saw their work as a completion of the earlier English translations. To them, the Authorized Version was the *perfecting* of these earlier works, hence the phrase "nothing is begun and perfected at the same time." Additionally, they believed that what they translated was the very "word of God." Finally, they state that even the worst of their early English versions (King James I considered the Geneva Bible a poor translation because of its marginal notes, which he saw as subversive) was far better than the Latin Catholic Bible. To the translators, theirs was the work of polishing what their forerunners produced, and thus the perfecting of the word of God. The translators also state:

> Now to the latter we answer, That we do not deny, nay, we affirm and avow, that the very meanest translation of the Bible in *English* set forth by men of our profession, (for we have seen none of theirs of the whole Bible as yet) containeth the word of God, nay, is the word of God.[323]

Why did the KJV translators alter these early works if they considered them the word of God? The translators write:

> Yet before we end, we must answer a third cavil and objection of theirs against us, for altering and amending our Translations so oft; wherein truly they deal hardly and strangely with us. For to whom ever was it imputed for a fault (by such as were wise) to go over that which he had done, and to amend it where he saw cause?…If we will be sons of the truth, we must consider what it speaketh, and trample upon our own credit, yea, and upon other men's too, if either be any way an hinderance to it.[324]

As sons of Truth, they were more concerned with presenting the pure word of God than establishing their own theological beliefs.

---

323 Ibid., xix.
324 Ibid., xx.

Truly, good Christian Reader, we never thought from the beginning that we should need to make a new translation, nor yet to make of a bad one a good one; (for then the imputation of *Sixtus* had been true in some sort, that our people had been fed with gall of dragons instead of wine, with whey instead of milk;) but to make a good one better, or out of many good ones, one principal good one, not justly to be excepted against; that hath been our endeavour, that our mark.[325]

The translators' goal was to produce from the early English versions based on the Traditional Text one principal English translation. The paragraph ends with praise because "the good hand of the Lord upon us, brought the work to that pass that you see."[326]

Their final paragraph expresses their concern for the reader, and thankfulness to God for his help in producing this beloved version.

Many other things we might give thee warning of, gentle Reader, if we had not exceeded the measure of a preface already. It remaineth that we commend thee to God, and to the Spirit of his grace, which is able to build further than we can ask or think. He removeth the scales from our eyes, the vail from our hearts, opening our wits that we may understand his word, enlarging our hearts, yea, correcting our affections, that we may love it above gold and silver, yea, that we may love it to the end…It is a fearful thing to fall into the hands of the living God; but a blessed thing it is, and will bring us to everlasting blessedness in the end, when God speaketh unto us, to hearken; when he setteth his word before us, to read it; when he stretcheth out his hand and calleth, to answer, Here am I, here we are to do thy will, O God. The Lord work a care and conscience in us to know him and serve him, that we may be

---

[325] Ibid., xxii.
[326] Ibid., xxiii.

acknowledged of him at the appearing of our Lord JESUS CHRIST, to whom with the Holy Ghost, be all praise and thanksgiving. Amen.[327]

A Jewish Book

The Bible is a Jewish book. The Apostle Paul states of the Jews that, "unto them were committed the oracles of God" (Romans 3:2). Every writer in the Old Testament and in the New Testament, with the possible exception of Luke, was Jewish. The central person of the New Testament, the Lord Jesus Christ, was born a Jew.

The Bible, therefore, uses Jewish terms and expressions called *Hebraisms*. Any correct translation of the Bible must reflect its Jewish heritage. English translations that weaken or remove these Jewish Hebraisms weaken our understanding of the people of God and the meaning of Scripture.

The KJV retains these Hebraisms. In fact, because of the popularity of the KJV, many of these Jewish expressions have become our expressions. As mentioned before, Dr. William Rosenau, a biblical scholar who made a study of the Hebraisms, writes:

> [The King James Bible has] molded new forms and phrases, which, while foreign to the English, became with it flesh and bone. The origin of most of these forms and phrases is not difficult to trace. They are like the equivalents of which they were translations—Hebrew in character.[328]

Thus we have many common expressions taken from the Authorized Version that have their basis in Hebraisms. The following are a few examples:

---

[327] Ibid., xxv-xxvi.
[328] Rosenau, 31.

Hebraism	Reference
In the sweat of thy face	Genesis 3:19
Am I my brother's keeper	Genesis 4:9
Unstable as water	Genesis 49:4
A stranger in a strange land	Exodus 2:22
A land flowing with milk and honey	Exodus 3:8
Sheep which have no shepherd	Numbers 27:17
Man doth not live by bread alone	Deuteronomy 8:3
Whatsoever is right in his own eyes	Deuteronomy 12:8
The apple of his eye	Deuteronomy 32:10
The people arose as one man	Judges 20:8
A man after his own heart	1 Samuel 13:14
How are the mighty fallen	2 Samuel 1:25
Thou art the man	2 Samuel 12:7
From the sole of his foot to the crown of his head	2 Samuel 14:25
Steal the heart	2 Samuel 15:6
Horn of my salvation	2 Samuel 22:3
The sweet psalmist of Israel	2 Samuel 23:1
How long halt ye between two opinions?	1 Kings 18:21
A still small voice	1 Kings 19:2
The shadow of death	Job 10:21
With the skin of my teeth	Job 19:20
The land of the living	Job 28:13
My cup runneth over	Psalm 23:5
The pen of a ready writer	Psalm 45:1
Wings like a dove	Psalm 55:6
From strength to strength	Psalm 84:7
As a tale that is told	Psalm 90:9
At their wit's end	Psalm 107:27
To dwell together in unity	Psalm 133:1
The way of the transgressor is hard	Proverbs 13:15
Heap coals of fire upon his head	Proverbs 25:22
Answer a fool according to his folly	Proverbs 26:5
Boast not thyself of to-morrow	Proverbs 27:1
Iron sharpeneth iron	Proverbs 27:17
There is no new thing under the sun	Ecclesiastes 1:9
To every thing there is a season	Ecclesiastes 3:1
The race is not to the swift	Ecclesiastes 9:11
A weariness of the flesh	Ecclesiastes 12:12
Let us eat and drink, for to-morrow we shall die	Isaiah 22:13
As a drop of a bucket	Isaiah 40:15

Many of these have found their way into modern versions simply because they have become common English expressions. We owe this to the Jewish flavor of the KJV. There are also certain expressions that are certainly Jewish but fail to be reproduced in modern versions. The following are a few examples among the thousands of Jewish Hebraisms noted by Dr. Rosenau;[329] for purposes of comparison I have added the equivalent translations from one of the most widely used modern versions, the NIV.

Reference	Jewish Hebraisms	English Expression
1 Kings 5:10	According to all his desire	He wanted
Exodus 8:10	According to thy word	It will be as you say
Leviticus 11:16	After his kind	Any kind
Genesis 45:23	After this manner	This is what
Exodus 14:13	Again no more forever	Will never see again
Exodus 2:23	And it came to pass	During that long period
2 Samuel 1:9	Anguish is come upon me	I am in the throes of death
Proverbs 14:14	Backslider in heart	The faithless
Psalm 90:17	Beauty of the LORD	Favor of the Lord
2 Samuel 12:12	Before the sun	In broad daylight
Exodus 32:18	Being overcome	Defeat
Genesis 43:33	Birthright	Ages
2 Kings 25:26	Both small and great	Least to the greatest
Proverbs 2:7	Buckler to them	A shield to those
Numbers 9:23	By the hand of Moses	Through Moses
Jeremiah 7:10	Called by my name	Bears my Name
Genesis 6:4	Came in unto	Went to
1 Samuel 2:26	Child Samuel	Boy Samuel
Ezra 6:16	Children of the captivity	The rest of the exiles
2 Samuel 7:10	Children of wickedness	Wicked people
Haggai 1:7	Consider your ways	Give careful thought
Psalm 2:2	Counsel together	Gather together
Psalm 30:2	Cried	Called
Jonah 1:2	Cry against	Preached against
Exodus 23:23	Cut them off	Wipe them out

[329] Ibid., 169-283.

Even Jewish expressions from Psalm 23, such as "I shall not want," "the valley of the shadow of death," and "I will dwell in the house of the Lord for ever" are changed in many modern versions. Today's English Version alters these beloved Hebrew expressions; they become "I have everything I need," "if I go through the deepest darkness," and "your house will be my home as long as I live." English expressions such as those found in the NIV and TEV may be easier for some to understand. However, they have lost the influence of their Jewish heritage.

The Preeminence Of Christ

Some have proclaimed that modern versions or their Greek texts deny the deity of Jesus Christ. Certainly there are some, such as the *New World Translation*, that seek to diminish Christ's deity. It is also true that some versions are stronger regarding Christ's deity than others. While most translations clearly and strongly proclaim this basic biblical truth, the Traditional Text does present a stronger Christology regarding His deity (Matthew 19:16-17; Romans 14:10, 12; Philippians 2:6; 1 Timothy 3:16; 1 John 5:7; and Revelation 1:8, 11).

Additionally, other aspects of Christology are more strongly presented in the Traditional Text. For example, in Luke 2:33, 43 the Traditional Text calls the stepfather of Christ by his name and separates him from the person of Mary. We read, "Joseph and his mother marvelled" and "Joseph and his mother knew not of it." However, the Critical Text changes "Joseph" to "father," making the texts read "his father and mother marveled" and "his father and mother knew not of it." Such readings do not in themselves deny the virgin birth of Christ; still the reading found in the Traditional Text upholds this doctrine and removes any possible confusion in this regard.

The same may be said of Christ's redemption. Again, the truth of salvation is found in all Greek texts and English translations. Yet, certain aspects are presented more forcefully in the Traditional Text and the KJV in certain places. We are told that we have redemption "through his blood" in Colossians 1:14. The Critical Text does not contain this phrase at this place, though it does appear in all texts in Ephesians 1:7. This raises two questions. First, why would the phrase be found in Paul's letter to the Ephesians and not in his letter to the Colossians? Second, how is it possible to have redemption without divine payment for that redemption? Clearly the phrase should remain in regard to this doctrine. The Greek manuscripts are evenly divided as to its inclusion or omission. This can be demonstrated with the two editions of the Majority Text.[330] The internal evidence, based on Ephesians 1:7, would argue for its inclusion in that the phrase is used by Paul elsewhere and is consistent with what he would have written. Overall, when we consider other textual sources, the reading must remain because it is biblical and in character with Paul's other writings.

An additional example concerns 1 Peter 2:2. We are told in the Traditional Text that as newborn babies in Christ we should "desire the sincere milk of the word that ye may grow thereby." The Greek phrase found in the Traditional Text reads *ina en auto auxethete* (that ye may grow). The Critical Text adds *eis soterian* (to salvation) at the end of the phrase, suggesting that salvation is something we grow to. This is why the NRSV renders the phrase as "that by it you may grow into salvation." Certainly the reading of the Traditional Text omits the confusion and provides a stronger Christology here regarding redemption.

---

[330] Zane C. Hodges and Arthur L. Farstad, eds., *The Greek New Testament According To The Majority Text* (Nashville: Thomas Nelson Publishers, 1985), 605. The critical apparatus of this edition of the Majority Text shows that the phrase *dia tou aimatos autou* (through his blood) is found in about half of the Byzantine manuscripts consulted. However, the phrase is found in the Greek text of *The New Testament in the Original Greek According to the Byzantine/Majority Textform* (Original Word Publishers, 1991) by Maurice A. Robinson, William G. Pierpont, and William David McBrayer. Therefore, it is more likely to be the majority reading and should be maintained in the text.

In regard to Christ, Paul reminds us that "in all things he might have the preeminence" (Colossians 1:18). If Christ is to have the preeminence in all things, this would include Bible translations. Just as one can use a modern version to prove the deity of Christ, so modern versions proclaim the person of Jesus Christ. Though this may not be in question, divine names are not always as strongly proclaimed in the Critical Text. Instead of phrases such as "Lord Jesus Christ" we might find "Jesus Christ" or "Jesus." In fact, there are about two hundred such examples found in the New Testament where the expanded title is found in the Traditional Text.

Sometimes a simple omission has profound impact. 1 John 1:7 is a good illustration of this. The Traditional Text reads, "But if we walk in the light, as he is in the light, we have fellowship one with another, and the blood of Jesus Christ his Son cleanseth us from all sin." Modern versions based on the Alexandrian textual line read "Jesus" instead of "Jesus Christ."[331] The difference seems small on the surface, but we must remember that John wrote this epistle to confront the heresy of Gnosticism. The Gnostics taught that *Jesus* and *Christ* were two separate entities. Jesus, they said, was born of Joseph and Mary and was physical. At his baptism *the Christ*, who was spiritual, was said to have entered into him. At this point, according to the Gnostics, Jesus became Jesus Christ. At his crucifixion, the Gnostics claimed that the Christ left, leaving only Jesus to die. At the resurrection, the disciples saw the *spirit Christ*, but the mortal Jesus remained dead. Once we understand the heresy John was confronting, the differences between the two readings becomes abundantly clear. If John had written "the blood of Jesus" he would have been making a statement that the Gnostics would have been in agreement with. After all, they believed that it was Jesus who shed his blood. But by writing "the blood of Jesus Christ," John was making a direct assault on this Gnostic heresy.

---

[331] The reading *Iesou Christou* (Jesus Christ) is found in over four hundred seventy-five manuscripts. The reading Iesou (Jesus) is found in about twenty-five manuscripts.

The Nature Of God

The Bible proclaims that God is truth (John 4:24). Without this fact, the whole Bible is a lie as well as all of Christianity. So, we must look for a Bible that reflects what God is since the Bible is his word. There are several places where the KJV and its underlining texts are more truthful in their proclamation of the word of truth. For example, in 2 Samuel 21:19 we read: "And there was again a battle in Gob with the Philistines, where Elhanan the son of Jaare-oregim, a Bethlehemite, slew *the brother of* Goliath the Gittite, the staff of whose spear was like a weaver's beam." This is a truthful statement supported by 1 Chronicles 20:5. Unfortunately, modern versions omit the phrase "the brother of," suggesting that Elhanan killed Goliath. Such a suggestion is biblically untrue, for the Scriptures are clear that David killed Goliath (1 Samuel 17).

The only place where the name *Lucifer* is given is Isaiah 14:12, "How art thou fallen from heaven, O Lucifer, son of the morning!" The verse is changed by some to read, "O morning star" instead of "O Lucifer." Is the one who fell from heaven *Lucifer* or *morning star*? The problem is compounded when we read in the New Testament that Jesus Christ is the morning star (Revelation 22:16). One may wish to argue the Latin derivative of the name *Lucifer*; however, the one who fell was not Jesus Christ.

In Matthew 5:22 the Traditional Text states, "But I say unto you, That whosoever is angry with his brother without a cause shall be in danger of the judgment." The Critical Text does not contain the phrase "without a cause." Therefore, if one is angry he is sinning. Since Christ was angry and chased the moneychangers out of the temple, he would be guilty of sinning. But we know that Christ did not sin, so the more truthful statement is found in the Traditional Text.

These arguments are not presented to defame, discredit, or disparage anyone's translation. As the King's translators reminded us, even the meanest translation of the Bible contains the word of God. When anyone sits down with his or her translation and reads what God has given, all

Christians rejoice. Nevertheless, one's personal choice in translation does not negate the promise of preservation. Nor should it cause any to speak ill of what has so wonderfully and beautifully been given. When we consider these things with respect to the traditional Hebrew and Greek texts and the English Authorized Version, we may find that God has truly crowned them with glory.

Scriptura est vitae magistra

About the Author

For over twenty years, Dr. Thomas Holland has been a pastor and scholar. He earned his B.A. from Cedarville College and later his Th.M and Th.D from Immanuel Baptist Theological Seminary. He has taught courses on the subject of biblical textual criticism and preservation, theology, and Christian apologetics at various Bible Institutes. Several of his courses are on numerous web sites. In 1996, *A Critique of The King James Only Controversy* by Dr. Holland was published through Bible Believers Press in Pensacola, Florida. Dr. Holland is an ordained minister with the American Baptist Churches (ABC-USA) where he and his wife, Amy, continue to labor for the Lord in the ministry to which they have been called.

E-mail address:
DrTHolland@aol.com

Appendix A

KJV Translators And Governing Rules

Westminster Group
Old Testament (Genesis-Kings)
Dr. Lancelot Andrewes, Dean of Westminster.
Mr. William Bedwell, St. John's College, Cambridge.
Dr. Francis Burleigh, Pembroke Hall, Cambridge.
Dr. Richard Clarke, Fellow of Christ's College, Cambridge.
Mr. Jeffrey King, Fellow of King's College, Cambridge.
Dr. John Layfield, Fellow of Trinity College.
Dr. John Overall, Dean of St. Paul's.
Dr. Hadrian Saravia, Canon of Canterbury.
Dr. Robert Tigue, Archdeacon of Middlesex.
Mr. Richard Thomson, Clare Hall, Cambridge.

New Testament (Romans-Jude)
Dr. William Barlow, Dean of Chester.
Mr. William Dakins, Fellow of Trinity College, Cambridge.
Dr. Roger Fenton, Fellow of Pembroke Hall, Cambridge.
Dr. Ralph Hutchinson, Archbishop of St. Alban's.
Mr. Michael Rabbett, Trinity College, Cambridge.
Dr. Thomas Sanderson, Balliol College, Oxford.
Dr. John Spenser, President of Corpus Christi College, Oxford.

Oxford Group
Old Testament (Isaiah-Malachi)
Dr. Richard Brett, Fellow of Lincoln College.
Dr. Daniel Featley (also know as Daniel Fairclough), Fellow of New College.
Dr. John Harding, President of Magdalen College.
Dr. Thomas Holland (no known relation to present author), Rector of Exeter College.
Mr. Richard Kilby, Rector of Lincoln College.
Dr. John Rainolds, President of Corpus Christi College.
Dr. Miles Smith, Canon of Hereford.

New Testament (Matthew-Acts and Revelation)
Dr. George Abbot, Dean of Winchester.
Dr. John Aglionby, Rector of Blechindon.
Dr. John Harmer, Fellow of New College.
Dr. Leonard Hutton, Bishop of Gloucester.
Dr. John Perin, Fellow of St. John's College.
Dr. Thomas Ravis, Fellow of St. John's College.
Sir Henry Savile, Provost of Eaton.
Dr. Giles Thomson, Dean of Windsor.

Cambridge Group
Old Testament (1 Chronicles- Ecclesiastes)
Mr. Roger Andrews, Master of Jesus College.
Mr. Andrew Bing, Fellow of St. Peter's College.
Mr. Laurence Chaderton, Master of Emmanuel College.
Mr. Francis Dillingham, Fellow of Christ's College.
Mr. Thomas Harrison, Vice-Master of Trinity College.
Mr. Edward Lively, Fellow of Trinity College.
Mr. John Richardson, Master of Trinity College.
Mr. Robert Spalding, Fellow of St. John's College.

Apocrypha
Dr. John Bois, Fellow of St. John's College (later edited Romans-Revelation).
Dr. William Branthwaite, Master of Caius College.
Mr. Andrew Downes, Fellow of St. John's College.
Dr. John Duport, Master of Jesus College.
Dr. Jeremy Radcliffe, Fellow of Trinity College.
Dr. Samuel Ward, Master of Sidney College.
Mr. Robert Ward, Fellow of King's College.

The Rules Framed By The KJV Translators

1. The ordinary Bible read in the Church, commonly called the Bishops' Bible, to be followed, and as little altered as the truth of the original will admit.

2. The names of the prophets and the holy writers, with the other names of the text, to be retained as nigh as may be, accordingly as they were vulgarly used.

3. The old ecclesiastical words to be kept, viz., the word *church* not to be translated *congregation*, &c.

4. When a word hath divers significations, that to be kept which hath been most commonly used by the most of the ancient fathers, being agreeable to the propriety of the place and the analogy of the faith.

5. The division of the chapters to be altered either not at all, or as little as may be, if necessity so require.

6. No marginal notes at all to be affixed, but only for the explanation of the Hebrew or Greek words which cannot, without some circumlocution, so briefly and fitly be expressed in the text.

7. Such quotations of places to be marginally set down as shall serve for the fit reference of one Scripture to another.

8. Every particular man of each company to take the same chapter or chapters; and having translated or amended them severally by himself where he thinketh good, all to meet together, confer what they have done, and agree for their parts what shall stand.

9. As any one company hath dispatched any one book in this manner, they shall send it to the rest to be considered of seriously and judiciously, for his Majesty is very careful in this point.

10. If any company, upon the review of the book so sent, doubt or differ upon any place, to send them word thereof, note the place, and withal send the reasons; to which if they consent not, the difference to be compounded at the general meeting, which is to be of the chief persons of each company at the end of the work.

11. When any place of special obscurity is doubted of, letters to be directed by authority to send to any learned man in the land for his judgment of such a place.

12. Letters to be sent from every bishop to the rest of his clergy, admonishing them of this translation in hand, and to move and charge as many as being skillful in the tongues, and having taken pains in the kind, to send his particular observations to the company either at Westminster, Cambridge, or Oxford.

13. The director in each company to be the Deans of Westminster and Chester for that place, and the king's professors in the Hebrew or Greek in either university.

14. These translations to be used when they agree better with the text than the Bishops' Bible: Tyndale's, Matthew's, Coverdale's, Whitchurch's, Geneva.

15. Besides the said directors before mentioned, three or four of the most ancient and grave divines in either of the universities, not employed in translating, to be assigned by the Vice-Chancellor upon conference with the rest of the Heads to be overseers of the translations, as well Hebrew as Greek, for the better observation of the fourth rule above specified.

Appendix B

Internal Evidence for Mark 16:9-20

The external evidence for the so-called longer ending of Mark (Mark 16:9-20) is substantial and overwhelming. It is the reading of the vast majority of the existing Greek manuscripts and lectionaries. It has ancient support from church fathers dating to the middle of the second century, and is also contained in a number of ancient versions including the Old Latin manuscripts, the Latin Vulgate, the Peshitta, and part of the Coptic versions.

More importantly, those who reject the longer reading do not, for the most part, replace it with any viable textual variant. Instead, it is the conclusion of most textual scholars that either Mark did not finish his Gospel or that the original ending was lost in the process of transmission. Neither view agrees with the doctrine of biblical inspiration, or the character of the New Testament as a whole. Sadly, the dominant position among textual critics is that the original ending was lost. This, of course, would nullify biblical preservation and would logically require us to ask if other sections have likewise been lost. It would also cause us to approach the Bible as we would any other book of antiquity without regard to its divine significance. In so doing, higher criticism gives way to lower criticism and questions the very foundations of biblical inspiration, infallibility, and preservation.

With the inexorable external evidence for the passage coupled with a high regard for biblical inspiration and preservation, what is the basis for considering the longer ending anything but original? The answer provided by some scholars concerns the internal evidence. To them the words and style do not correlate with what John Mark had already written. Dr. Bruce Metzger notes some of the internal evidence that causes the majority of scholars to reject this passage as genuine. Metzger writes:

> The long ending, though present in a variety of witnesses, some of them ancient, must also be judged by internal evidence to be secondary. For example, the presence of seventeen non-Marcan words or words used in a non-Marcan sense; the lack of a smooth juncture between verses 8 and 9 (the subject in vs. 8 is the women, whereas Jesus is the presumed subject in vs. 9); and the way in which Mary is identified in verse 9 even though she has been mentioned previously (vs. 1)—all these features indicate that the section was added by someone who knew a form of Mark which ended abruptly with verse 8 and who wished to provide a more appropriate conclusion.[332]

Let us first consider these points more closely and then establish the internal evidence that speaks in favor of the longer ending. The first point raised by Metzger sounds, on the surface, solid and convincing. The second two points are minor because they do not establish a pattern that is non-biblical in nature or one that could not be applied to other writers as well. For example, it is true that Mary is identified twice as "Mary Magdalene" in Mark chapter sixteen. However, since another Mary is identified in verse one with her, Mary the mother of James, then it would be logical to once again identify which Mary is spoken of in verse nine. Further, the connection of "Magdalene" with Mary is found elsewhere in the New Testament (Matthew 27:56, 61; 28:1; Mark 15:40, 47; Luke 8:2; 24:10; John 19:25; 20:1, 18). It is not abnormal to identify her as the one

---

[332] Bruce M. Metzger, *The Text Of The New Testament*, 3rd ed. (New York: Oxford University Press, 1992), 227.

of whom Christ had cast out seven devils. Luke likewise identifies her in this fashion (Luke 8:2), the significance of which will be emphasized later.

Additionally, the "lack of a smooth juncture" between verses eight and nine plays little significance. Verse nine focuses on the witness of Mary after seeing the empty tomb, understandable in light of the previous comments in verses one through eight. The Gospels are presented in a narrative providing a historical record of events occurring within the life of Christ. When such a record is supplied it is to be expected to find several junctures that are not smooth in transition; in fact, this is exactly what we find within all of the Gospels. For example, the Gospels present the raising of Jairus' daughter from death. Yet in the midst of the story the subject is changed to the healing of the woman with the issue of blood (Mark 5:22-43). Another example concerns Peter's denials. In the first three Gospels his denials are presented in one discourse (Matthew 26:60-75; Mark 14:66-72; Luke 22:54-62). Yet there is a change of subject in both Matthew and Mark regarding Peter following the crowd that arrested Jesus in that they present this fact earlier (Matthew 26:58; Mark 14:54). Further, John presents the event and then continues through Peter's first denial, only later to record the other two times he denies Christ (John 18:15-18, 25-27). These are all junctures that lack a smooth transition, yet are faithful to the historical events that occurred. Regardless, the final two points raised by Metzger are minor.

What is of much more significance is Metzger's first point, the non-Marcan words found in the longer ending. Depending on which text one uses, there are about one hundred eighty-three words found in the longer ending of Mark. Of these there are fifty-three words used that do not appear elsewhere in Mark's Gospel (at least in the form presented in the longer ending). Of these, all but twenty-one are found elsewhere in the New Testament in the exact form as presented by Mark. To find such a high number of unique words within twelve verses may on the surface seem to be strong evidence that Mark did not author this section. However, if this is true how does one explain the fact that the same thing occurs elsewhere in the New Testament? For example, in the first twelve verses of Luke there are twenty words used by Luke that are not found in the same form anywhere else in the New Testament. The following charts present the words unique to Mark 16:9-20 and those unique to Luke 1:1-12.

Reference In Mark	Greek Word[333]
Mark 16:9	Μαρια τη Μαγδαληνη
Mark 16:9	εκβεβληκει
Mark 16:10	πορευθεισα
Mark 16:10	πενθουσι
Mark 16:11	εθεαθη
Mark 16:11	ηπιστησαν
Mark 16:12	πορευομενοις
Mark 16:14	ωνειδισε
Mark 16:14	θεασαμενοις
Mark 16:16	απιστησας
Mark 16:16	κατακπιθησεται
Mark 16:17	παρακολουθησει
Mark 16:17	εκβαλουσιν
Mark 16:17	καιναις
Mark 16:18	θανασιμον
Mark 16:18	πιωσιν
Mark 16:18	βλαψη or βλαψει in the TR
Mark 16:18	επιθησουσιν
Mark 16:20	συνερψουντος
Mark 16:20	βεβαιουντος
Mark 16:20	επακολουθουντων

---

[333] Due to the nature of this thesis I have not transliterated the Greek words used.

Reference In Luke	Greek Word
Luke 1:1	Επειδηπερ
Luke 1:1	αναταξασθαι
Luke 1:1	διηγησιν
Luke 1:1	πεπληροφορημενων
Luke 1:2	παρεδοσαν
Luke 1:2	αυτοπται
Luke 1:3	παρηκολουθηκοτι
Luke 1:4	επιγνως
Luke 1:4	κατηξηθης
Luke 1:4	ασφαλειαν
Luke 1:5	εφημεριας
Luke 1:5	θυγατερων
Luke 1:6	δικαιωμασιν
Luke 1:7	προβεβηκοτες
Luke 1:8	ιερατευειν
Luke 1:8	ταξει
Luke 1:9	ιεπατειας
Luke 1:9	ελαχε
Luke 1:9	θυμιασαι
Luke 1:10	θυμιαματος

The fact that Mark has a number of words that appear only in this form in Mark 16:9-20 is not as unique as one would think; in Luke we have virtually the same number of words that appear only in this form, and are only found in Luke 1:1-12.

Of the twenty-one words unique to Mark, none of them are unique words in and of themselves. Instead, they are forms of words found elsewhere in the New Testament. For example, in Mark 16:9 we have the word εκβεβληκει (he had cast out) which is simply the third person singular pluperfect aorist of the word εκβαλλω, a word found throughout the New Testament. Likewise, the word πορευθεισα (went) found in Mark 16:10 is a form of the word πορευομαι that appears about a dozen times elsewhere in Scripture. Another form of this very word, πορευομενοις, appears in Mark 16:12, 15. So also the word wneidise (upbraided) of Mark 16:14, which is the aorist of ονειδιζω that appears about ten times in the New Testament including Mark 15:32 where it appears as ωνειδιζον (reviled).

Additionally, even if these unique words were found only in Mark 16:9-20 (in both form and occurrence), that would not establish that someone else wrote the conclusion of this Gospel. Excluding the longer ending, there are no less than one hundred two words that are unique to Mark. Likewise, the same can be said of the other New Testament writers. Matthew has one hundred thirty-seven words that are unique to that Gospel, Luke has three hundred twelve in his Gospel, and John has one hundred fourteen words unique to his Gospel. Therefore, unique words (or even forms of words) do not establish that Mark did not write the last twelve verses of his Gospel. Instead, we find this to be commonplace within the New Testament.

Having presented this evidence, the question then must be asked: "Is there any internal evidence that substantiate Mark as the writer of the longer ending?" The answer is yes. However, before we consider the evidence we must recall something about John Mark. The New Testament reveals that Mark was related to Barnabas and traveled with him and the Apostle Paul early in the ministry of Paul (Acts 12:25). Mark, a young man at the time, returned from the mission voyage. Later, when Barnabas wanted to take Mark with him on the next trip, Paul refused, causing a rift between Barnabas and Paul (Acts 15:37-39). This occurs around 46 AD. Paul then travels on with Silas and Luke. Later in life, Paul asks for Mark to rejoin him, with Luke still at his side (2 Timothy 4:11). We see from Scripture that Mark was a traveling companion of Paul's, and later a friend and fellow minister with this mission minded apostle and the beloved physician, Luke. Mark writes his Gospel (between 57 and 63 AD) before Luke writes either his Gospel or the book of Acts (both written between 63 and 68 AD). When Paul asks Timothy to bring Mark with him it is around 66 AD and the context indicates that Mark had been with them for sometime. It is reasonable to conclude that Mark had first hand information from Luke and Paul regarding events in their lives that are later revealed in the book of Acts.

With this in mind, it comes as no surprise to find in Mark 16:9-20 an association with Luke and Paul. To begin with, the sign gifts found in the longer ending are all fulfilled in Luke's record of Acts with the exception of the one conditional sign gift ("if they drink any deadly thing"). The gifts of casting out devils, speaking with new tongues, healing the sick, and taking up serpents are all fulfilled in Acts (16:18; 2:4; 9:32-35; 28:3-6). The account of the two on the road to Emmaus is not only recorded in Mark 16:12 but is also found in Luke 24:13-35. As noted earlier in this thesis, Mark identifies Mary Magdalene as the one of whom Christ cast out seven devils, an event that is noted again only in Luke (8:2). The ascension of Christ is found in Mark 16:19-20 as well as Luke's two books (Luke 24:50-53; Acts 1:6-11). Just as the book of Matthew expands the condensed events in the Gospel of Mark, so the longer ending of Mark is a condensed presentation of what Luke later expands. This indicates that the writer of the longer ending was associated with Luke and knew him personally, highlighting some of the very events Luke later emphasizes under his inspiration. John Mark would certainly fit this position.

We have those unique words found in Mark 16:9-20. Many of these have a very strong association with Luke and Paul, both of whom were associates of John Mark. For example, in Mark 16:10 we find the word aphggeilen (reported/told) that appears nowhere else in Mark's Gospel in that form. The same word in the same form appears nine other times in the New Testament, all in Luke's writings (Luke 8:47; 14:21; Acts 5:25; 11:13; 12:14; 16:36; 22:26; 23:16; 28:21). The word pisteusaV (believing) appears in this form only twice in the New Testament, once in Mark 16:16 and then again by Luke in Acts 11:21. The Critical Text uses the word blayh in Mark 16:18 while the Textus Receptus uses the form blayei (shall it hurt). Both are a form of the word blayan (hurt) which is found only once in the New Testament and that by Luke in his Gospel (4:35). In Mark 16:11 we have the word hpisthsan (believed it not) which is a form of the Greek word apistew that is found only five times in the New Testament, all either by Luke (24:11, 41; Acts 28:24) or Paul (Romans 3:3; 2 Timothy 2:13). The word πορευομενοις (went) of Mark 16:12 is a form of the word πορευομαι that is used eighty-six times by Luke in his Gospel and the book of Acts.

Below are some additional examples of words that are used by Mark only in the longer ending and yet appear in the same form heavily in the writings of both Luke and Paul.

Greek Word	Only Occurrence In Same Form
κακεινοι	Mark 16:11, 13; John 17:24; Acts 15:11; Romans 11:23; 1 Corinthians 10:6; Hebrews 4:2
ζη	Mark 16:11; John 4:50, 51; Romans 6:10; 7:1; 14:7; 1 Corinthians 7:39; 2 Corinthians 13:4; Galatians 2:20; Hebrews 7:8; 9:17
ετεπα	Mark 16:12; Acts 20:15; 27:3; James 2:25
λοιποις	Mark 16:13; Luke 8:10; 24:9; Romans 1:13; 1 Corinthians 7:12; 2 Corinthians 13:2; Philippians 1:13; Revelation 2:24
ενδεκα	Mark 16:14; Matthew 28:16; Luke 24:9, 33; Acts 1:26; 2:14
παση	Mark 16:15; Matthew 6:29; Luke 7:17; 12:27; John 16:13; Acts 1:8; 2:43; 5:23; 7:22; 23:1 Romans 1:29; 9:17; 1 Corinthians 1:5; 4:17; 2 Corinthians 1:4; 7:4; 8:7; 12:12; Ephesians 1:3, 8; 4:31; 5:9; 6:18; Philippians 1:3, 4, 9, 20; Colossians 1:9, 11, 23, 28; 3:16; 1 Thessalonians 3:7, 9; 2 Thessalonians 2:10; 3:17; 1 Timothy 2:2, 11; 5:2; 2 Timothy 4:2; 1 Peter 1:15; 2:13; Revelation 11:6
πιστευσασιν	Mark 16:17; Acts 11:17; 2 Thessalonians 1:10
γλωσσαισ	Mark 16:17; Acts 2:4, 11; 10:46; 19:6; Romans 3:13; 1 Corinthians 12:30; 13:1; 14:5, 6, 18, 23, 39; Revelation 10:11
ανελημφθη	Mark 16:19; Acts 1:2, 22; 10:16; 1 Timothy 3:16

None of these establish that Mark wrote the longer ending. However, when we consider all of this in light of the contextual evidence within the longer ending, we can certainly see that whoever wrote the longer ending had a unique awareness of the events and vocabulary of both Luke and Paul. As we have seen, this would certainly be consistent with what we historically know of John Mark. It is enough to say that there is nothing in the longer ending to dispel it from the Gospel of Mark, and everything in it that would call for its inclusion. It certainly should not be rejected because of the faulty witnesses of Vaticanus and Sinaiticus. And, as can be seen, it should not be rejected because of the internal evidence. Instead, both the external and internal evidence reveals that the longer ending was penned by John Mark and is part of the divine record.

Appendix C

Textual Evidence

The following information is provided to allow the reader a quick glance at some of the manuscripts used as textual support. It is not an in-depth listing of all material.

Some Biblical Manuscripts Among The Dead Sea Scrolls

Cave 1	1QGen., 1QExod., 1QDeut.*a*, 1QDeut.*b*, 1QJudg., 1QSam., 1QPs.*a*, 1QPs.*b*, 1QPs.*c*, 1QIsa.*a*, 1QIsa.*b*, 1QEzek., 1QDan.*b*
Cave 2	2QGen., 2QExod.*a*, 2QExod.*b*, 2QExod.*c*, 2QNumb.*a*, 2QNumb.*b*, 2QNumb.*c*, 2QNumb.*d*, 2QDeut.*a*, 2QDeut.*b*, 2QDeut.*c*, 2QRuth.*a*, 2QRuth.*b*, 2QJob, 2QPs., 2QJer.
Cave 3	3QEzek., 3QPs., 3QLam.
Cave 4	4QGen-Exod.*a*, 4QGen.*b*, 4QGen.*c*, 4QGen.*d*, 4QGen.*e*, 4QGen.*f*, 4QExod.*b*, 4QExod.*c*, 4QExod.*d*, 4QExod.*e*, 4QExod-Lev.*f*, 4Qlev-Num.*a*, 4QLev.*b*, 4QLev.*c*, 4QLev.*d*, 4QLev.*e*, 4QLev.*g*, 4QNumb.*b*, 4QDeut.*a*, 4QDeut.*b*, 4QDeut.*c*, 4QDeut.*d*
Cave 5	5QDeut, 5QKings, 5QPs., 5QIsa., 5QLam.*a*, 5QLam.*b*, 5QAmos
Cave 6	6QpalaeoGen., 6QpalaeoLev, 6QDeut (?), 6QKgs., 6QDan.
Cave 7 (all in Greek)	7QLXXExod, 7Q4 (?), 7Q5 (?)
Cave 8	8QGen., 8QPs.
Cave 11	11QpalaeoLev.*a*, 11QpalaeoLev.*b*, 11QDeut., 11QEzek., 11QPs.*a*, 11QPs.*b*, 11QPs.*c*, 11QPs.*d*, 11QPs.*e*, 11QPs.

Some Old Testament Masoretic Manuscripts

4445 (820-850 AD)	Cairo Codex (895 AD)	Petersburg Codex (916 AD)	Aleppo Codex (900-950 AD)	Leningrad Codex (1008 AD)

Some Greek Manuscripts Of The New Testament[334]

Papyrus	Approximate Number: 100
First century	P4, P46, P64, P67
Second century	P52, P66, P90, P98
Third century	P1, P5, P9, P12, P15, P20, P22, P23, P27, P28, P29, P30, P32, P38, P39, P40, P45, P47, P48, P49, P53, P65, P69, P70, P75, P77, P80, P87, P91, P95
Fourth century	P6, P7, P8, P10, P13, P16, P17, P18, P24, P25, P35, P37, P51, P62, P71, P72, P78, P81, P83, P84, P86, P88, P89, P92
Fifth century	P14, P19, P21, P50, P51, P57, P63, P82, P85, P93
Sixth century	P2, P26, P33, P36, P54, P56, P58, P63, P68, P76, P83, P84, P94, P96
Seventh century	P3, P11, P31, P34, P43, P44, P55, P59, P60, P61, P68, P73, P74, P79, P97
Eighth century	P41, P42, P61

---

[334] If a manuscript is listed between centuries (such as fourth and fifth) it is placed in the latter century (in this example the fifth century).

Uncials	Approximate Number: 300
Third century	0189, 0212, 0220
Fourth century	01, 03, 058, 0162, 0169, 0171, 0185, 0188, 0206, 0207, 0221, 0228, 0230, 0231, 0242, 0258
Fifth century	02, 04, 05, 016, 026, 029, 032, 048, 057, 059, 061, 062, 068, 069, 077, 0113, 0125, 0139, 0160, 0163, 0165, 0166, 0172, 0173, 0174, 0175, 0176, 0181, 0182, 0201, 0214, 0215, 0216, 0217, 0218, 0219, 0226, 0227, 0236, 0240, 0244, 0252, 0254, 0261, 0264, 0267, 0270, 0274, 0301
Sixth century	06, 08, 022, 023, 024, 027, 035, 040, 042, 043, 060, 064, 065, 066, 067, 070, 071, 072, 073, 074, 076, 078, 079, 080, 081, 082, 084, 085, 086, 087, 088, 089, 090, 091, 092a, 092b, 093, 094, 0110, 0124, 0143, 0147, 0158, 0159, 0170, 0178, 0179, 0180, 0184, 0186, 0187, 0190, 0191, 0193, 0198, 0202, 0208, 0213, 0222, 0223, 0224, 0225, 0232, 0237, 0241, 0245, 0246, 0247, 0251, 0253, 0260, 0263, 0265, 0266, 0282, 0285, 0292, 0293, 0296,
Seventh century	083, 096, 097, 098, 099, 0103, 0104, 0106, 0107, 0108, 0109, 0111, 0112, 0119, 0138, 0144, 0145, 0164, 0167, 0183, 0199, 0200, 0204, 0209, 0210, 0211, 0235, 0239, 0259, 0262, 0268, 0275, 0289, 0294, 0300
Eighth century	07, 019, 047, 054, 095, 0101, 0102, 0116, 0118, 0123, 0126, 0127, 0134, 0146, 0148, 0156, 0157, 0161, 0168, 0205, 0229, 0233, 0234, 0238, 0250, 0256, 0277, 0281, 0291
Ninth century	09, 010, 011, 012, 013, 014, 015, 017, 018, 020, 025, 030, 031, 034, 037, 038, 039, 041, 049, 050, 053, 063, 0117, 0120, 0122, 0128, 0130, 0131, 0132, 0133, 0135, 0136, 0137, 0150, 0151, 0154, 0155, 0196, 0197, 0248, 0255, 0257, 0269, 0271, 0272, 0273, 0278, 0279, 0298
Tenth century	021, 028, 033, 036, 044, 045, 046, 051, 052, 056, 075, 0105, 0115, 0121, 0121b, 0140, 0141, 0142, 0177, 0243, 0249
Eleventh century	0299

Minuscule	Approximate Number: 2,800
Ninth century	33, 461, 565, 892, 1080, 1295, 1862, 1895,2142, 2464, 2500
Tenth century	14, 29, 34, 36e, 27, 63, 82, 100, 115, 135, 144, 151, 161, 175, 221, 237, 262, 274, 278b, 307, 314, 326, 344, 364, 371, 398, 399, 405, 411, 436, 450, 454, 456, 457, 478, 481, 564, 568, 584, 602, 605, 619, 626, 627, 669, 832, 920, 1055, 1066, 1076, 1077, 1078, 1079, 1203, 1220, 1223, 1225, 1347, 1351, 1357, 1392, 1417, 1424, 1452, 1458, 1582, 1611, 1662, 1720, 1735, 1739, 1756, 1760, 1829, 1836, 1841, 1845, 1851, 1874, 1875, 1880, 1891, 1905, 1912, 1920, 1927, 1954, 1997, 2110, 2125, 2193, 2324, 2329, 2351, 2373, 2414, 2424, 2545, 2722 2768, 2789, 2790, 2811, 2812
Eleventh century	7p, 8, 12, 20, 23, 24, 25, 28, 35, 37, 39, 40, 42, 50, 65, 68, 72, 75, 77, 81, 83, 89, 98, 104, 108, 112, 123, 124, 125, 126, 127, 133, 137, 142, 143, 148, 150, 158, 174, 177, 186, 194, 195, 197, 200, 207, 208, 210, 213, 212, 215, 230, 236, 237, 238, 241, 250, 259, 272, 276, 277, 300, 301, 302, 314, 323, 325, 331, 343, 348, 350, 352, 354, 357, 360, 375, 376, 422, 424, 451, 458, 459, 465, 466, 470, 473, 474, 475, 476, 490, 491, 497, 504, 506, 507, 516, 526, 527, 528, 530, 532, 547, 548, 549, 559, 560, 569, 583, 585, 596, 607, 623, 624, 625, 638, 639, 640, 651, 672, 699, 700, 707, 708, 711, 717, 746, 754, 756, 773, 785, 788, 809, 831, 870, 884, 887, 894, 901,910, 919, 937, 942, 943, 944, 945, 964, 965, 991, 994, 1006, 1012, 1014, 1028, 1045, 1054, 1056, 1073, 1074, 1110, 1123, 1168, 1174, 1175, 1187, 1192, 1194, 1207, 1209, 1210, 1211, 1212, 1214, 1216, 1219, 1221, 1222, 1243, 1244, 1277, 1300, 1312, 1313, 1314, 1317, 1320, 1324, 1340, 1343, 1346, 1373, 1384, 1438, 1443, 1444, 1448, 1449, 1470, 1493, 1505, 1510, 1513, 1514, 1517, 1520, 1521, 1545, 1556, 1570, 1579, 1607, 1668, 1672, 1691, 1693, 1701, 1730, 1734, 1738, 1770, 1828, 1835, 1838, 1846, 1847, 1849, 1854, 1870, 1878, 1879, 1888, 1906, 1907, 1908, 1916, 1919, 1921, 1923, 1924, 1925, 1932, 1933, 1934, 1946, 1955, 1980, 1981, 1982, 2001, 2007, 2081, 2098, 2132, 2133, 2138, 2144, 2172, 2176, 2181, 2183, 2199, 2275, 2277, 2281, 2396, 2295, 2307, 2344, 2346, 2381, 2386, 2387, 2430, 2442, 2447, 2451, 2458, 2468, 2475, 2539, 2547, 2559, 2563, 2567, 2571, 2587, 2596, 2613, 2637, 2649, 2661, 2723, 2746, 2760, 2782, 2787

Twelfth century	1r, 1, 2e, 2ap, 3, 9, 11, 15, 21, 22, 32, 36, 44, 46, 57, 64, 71, 73, 76, 80, 84, 88, 95, 97, 98, 103, 105, 110, 111, 116, 119, 120, 122, 129, 132, 134, 138, 139, 140, 156, 157, 159, 162, 179, 183, 187, 193, 196, 199, 202, 203, 217, 224, 225, 226, 229, 231, 240, 242, 244, 245, 247, 251, 261, 264, 265, 267, 268, 269, 270, 275, 280, 281, 282, 297, 304, 321, 306, 319, 320, 329, 330, 334, 337, 346, 347, 351, 353, 355, 356, 365, 366, 374, 378, 387, 392, 395, 396, 401, 407, 408, 419, 431, 438, 439, 440, 443, 452, 462, 471, 485, 499, 502, 505, 509, 510, 514, 517, 518, 520, 524, 529, 531, 535, 538, 543, 550, 551, 556, 570, 571, 580, 587, 610, 618, 620, 622, 637, 650, 655, 657, 660, 662, 673, 674, 688, 692, 713, 720, 736, 748, 750, 760, 765, 768, 770, 774, 777, 778, 779, 782, 787, 793, 799, 808, 826, 828, 843, 857, 860, 877, 896, 902, 911, 916, 917, 922, 936, 950, 967, 971, 973, 975, 980, 983, 987, 993, 998, 1007, 1010, 1013, 1046, 1071, 1081, 1083, 1085, 1088, 1112, 1169, 1176, 1186, 1190, 1191, 1193, 1195, 1197, 1198, 1199, 1200, 1217, 1218, 1224, 1230, 1231, 1240, 1241, 1301, 1309, 1315, 1316, 1318, 1319, 1323, 1329, 1338, 1344, 1350a, 1355, 1358, 1359, 1360, 1364, 1365, 1375, 1385, 1437, 1539, 1540, 1542b, 1566, 1583, 1646, 1673, 1683, 1709, 1714, 1718, 1737, 1752, 1754, 1755a, 1755b, 1800, 1821, 1826, 1828, 1872, 1889, 1910, 1914, 1915, 1917, 1926, 1942, 1951, 1962, 1970, 1971, 1974, 1986, 1988, 2013, 2030, 2050, 2096, 2126, 2127, 2135, 2139, 2143, 2145, 2147, 2173, 2177, 2189, 2191, 2289, 2298, 2382, 2389, 2412, 2415, 2426, 2437, 2445, 2459, 2490, 2507, 2536, 2541, 2549, 2550, 2552, 2562, 2639, 2650, 2657, 2671, 2700, 2712, 2725, 2727, 2744, 2781, 2784, 2785, 2791, 2792, 2794, 2814, 2815, 2818
Thirteenth century	4, 6, 13, 51, 52, 55, 60, 65, 74, 94, 107, 118, 121, 128, 136, 141, 147, 167, 170, 180, 192, 198, 204, 206, 218, 219, 220, 227, 248, 260, 263, 283, 284, 291, 292, 293, 303, 305, 309, 327, 328, 342, 359, 361, 362, 384, 388, 390, 410, 435, 441, 442, 449, 460, 469, 472, 473, 477, 479, 482, 483, 484, 496, 500, 501, 511, 519, 533, 534, 544, 546, 553, 554, 558, 573, 574, 579, 592, 593, 597, 601, 614, 663, 666, 677, 684, 685, 689, 691, 696, 705, 714, 715, 725, 726, 729, 737, 757, 759, 775, 811, 820, 825, 827, 830, 835, 840, 897, 898, 900, 905, 906, 912, 914, 915, 966, 969, 970, 981, 995, 997, 999, 1000, 1004, 1008, 1009, 1011, 1015, 1016, 1031, 1050, 1052, 1053, 1057, 1069, 1070, 1072, 1087, 1089, 1094, 1103, 1107, 1129, 1148, 1149, 1150, 1161, 1177, 1201, 1205, 1206, 1208, 1213, 1215, 1226, 1229, 1238, 1242, 1251, 1255, 1285, 1310, 1339, 1341, 1352a, 1398, 1400, 1542a, 1546, 1555, 1563, 1573, 1594, 1597, 1604, 1622, 1642, 1685, 1689, 1717,1727, 1728, 1731, 1736, 1740, 1742, 1758, 1772, 1827, 1852, 1855, 1858, 1887, 1922, 1938, 1941, 1956, 1972, 1992, 2027, 2053, 2062, 2111, 2119, 2140, 2141, 2236, 2311, 2322, 2353, 2372, 2374, 2376, 2380, 2390, 2400, 2409, 2420, 2423, 2457, 2479, 2483, 2502, 2516, 2534, 2540, 2542, 2558, 2568, 2600, 2624, 2627, 2633, 2643, 2645, 2658, 2660, 2665, 2696, 2699, 2718, 2724, 2757, 2766, 2761, 2788, 2796, 2804, 2805, 2807

Fourteenth century	5, 16, 18, 45, 53, 54, 66, 76, 109, 131, 155, 171, 172, 182, 185, 189, 190, 201, 214, 223, 232, 235, 243, 246, 254, 255, 257, 266, 290, 308, 316, 324, 349, 358, 367, 369, 381, 386, 393, 394, 402, 404, 409, 412, 413, 414, 415, 417, 425, 426, 453, 480, 489, 492, 494, 512, 521, 523, 540, 577, 578, 586, 588, 594, 600, 603, 604, 621, 628, 629, 630, 633, 634, 642, 644, 645, 648, 649, 656, 668, 680, 686, 690, 698, 716, 718, 727, 730, 731, 734, 741, 758, 761, 762, 763, 764, 769, 781, 783, 784, 786, 789, 790, 794, 797, 798, 802, 806, 818, 819, 824, 833, 834, 836, 839, 845, 846, 848, 858, 864, 866a, 867, 889, 890, 903, 904, 921, 928, 938, 951, 952, 953, 959, 960, 977, 978, 1005, 1020, 1023, 1032, 1033, 1036, 1038, 1061, 1062, 1067, 1075, 1093, 1099, 1100, 1119, 1121, 1185, 1189, 1196, 1234, 1235, 1236, 1248, 1249, 1252, 1254, 1283, 1328, 1330, 1331, 1334, 1342, 1345, 1350b, 1356, 1377, 1395, 1409, 1445, 1447, 1476, 1492, 1503, 1504, 1506, 1518, 1523, 1524, 1543, 1547, 1548, 1572, 1574, 1577, 1605, 1613, 1614, 1619, 1630, 1637, 1654, 1675, 1678, 1723, 1725, 1726, 1732, 1733, 1741, 1746, 1747, 1761, 1762, 1771, 1831, 1832, 1842, 1856, 1859, 1877, 1881, 1899, 1902, 1918, 1928, 1929, 1952, 1975, 1984, 2005, 2036, 2042, 2060, 2073, 2080, 2085, 2148, 2160, 2161, 2174, 2200, 2266, 2273, 2303, 2309, 2310, 2355, 2356, 2377, 2399, 2407, 2427, 2431, 2432, 2441, 2454, 2466, 2584, 2492, 2499, 2503, 2578, 2593, 2626, 2629, 2634, 2651, 2653, 2666, 2668, 2679, 2698, 2716, 2765, 2767, 2773, 2774, 2775, 2780, 2783, 2786, 2793, 2803, 2808, 2809
Fifteenth century	4ap, 17, 30, 47, 56, 58, 69, 70, 117, 149, 181, 205, 209, 285, 268, 287, 288, 313, 322, 368, 375, 379, 380, 385, 418, 429, 432, 446, 448, 467, 493, 525, 541, 575, 616, 636, 664, 694, 739, 801, 841, 844, 853, 880, 954, 955, 958, 961, 962, 1003, 1017, 1018, 1024, 1026, 1059, 1060, 1105, 1202, 1232, 1233, 1247, 1250, 1253, 1260, 1264, 1482, 1508, 1617, 1626, 1628, 1636, 1649, 1656, 1729, 1745, 1450, 1751, 1757, 1763, 1767, 1844, 1876, 1882, 1948, 1957, 1958, 1959, 1964, 1978, 2003, 2014, 2015, 2016, 2020, 2028, 2065, 2067, 2069, 2175, 2178, 2221, 2352, 2418, 2452, 2455, 2495, 2523, 2554, 2652, 2675, 2691, 2729, 2816
Sixteenth century	61, 90, 99, 335, 372, 445, 522, 724, 755, 867, 918, 957, 1019, 1030, 1065, 1088, 1239, 1362, 1367, 1370, 1374, 1618, 1704, 1749, 1768, 1861, 1883, 1884, 1911, 1930, 1931, 1936, 1937, 1979, 1985, 2009, 2218, 2378, 2422, 2496, 2501, 2555, 2572, 2573, 2579, 2635, 2636, 2690, 2711, 2721, 2779, 2806, 2810
Seventeenth century	849, 2544
Eighteenth century	1325, 2318

Greek Lectionaries	Approximate Number: 2,200
Eighth century	L563, L1602
Ninth century	L292, L249, L490, L514, L672, L844, L846, L965, L1575, 1599
Tenth century	L1, L2, L5, L150, L156, L309, L597, L770, L813, L847, L1231, L1356, L1552, L2211
Eleventh century	L3, L4, L32, L48, L60, L165, L185, L253, L381, L384, L590, L591, L598, L599, L603, L617, L751, L755, L853, L859, L883, L963, L991, L995, L1178, L1298, L1443, L1627, L1750
Twelfth century	L44, L59, L68, L69, L70, L76, L80, L147, L211, L303, L384, L513, L524, L596, L673, L809, L852, L854, L858, L866, L867, L921, L961, L1016, L1021, L1127, L1154, L1364, L1365, L1439, L1634, L1780, L1977
Thirteenth century	L10, L12, L299, L333, L547, L680, L884, L895, L1223, L1590, L950, L1056, L1074, L1084, L1642
Fourteenth century	L170, L184, L185, L313, L422, L1153, L1156, L1159, L1579, L1663

Dates And Contents Of Some Early Manuscripts[335]

---

[335] As of the publication of this book, these are the oldest known manuscripts. However, their dates have been questioned, as have some of the contents of some of these manuscripts. The majority of these are fragmentary.

Manuscript	Date	Contents
P4 (Paris Papyrus)	Before 66 AD	Luke 3:23, 5:36
P64 (Magdalen Papyrus)	Before 66 AD	Matthew 26:7-8, 10, 14-15, 22-23, 31
P67 (Barcelona Papyrus)	Before 66 AD	Matthew 3:9, 15; 5:20-22, 25-28
7Q4 (Dead Sea Scrolls)	Before 68 AD	1 Timothy 3:16-4:3
7Q5 (Dead Sea Scrolls)	Before 68 AD	Mark 6:52-53
P46 (Pauline Codex)	Around 85 AD	Paul's Epistles
P52 (John Rylands Papyrus)	Around 100-125 AD	John 18:31-33, 37-38
P66 (Bodmer Papyrus II)	Around 125 AD	Almost all of the Gospel of John

Some Latin Manuscripts Important In Textual Criticism

Fourth century	*a, m*
Fifth century	*a2, b, e, ff2, h, k, μ, n, φ*
Sixth century	*d, f, i, j, s, t, w, gue*
Seventh century	*aur, β, o, π, l, q, r1, r, t, v, gat, u*
Eighth century	*ff1, p, s, z, r2, ρ,*
Ninth century	*g1, λ, ar*
Tenth century	*δ, ro, sin, g2, mon, comp*
Twelfth century	*ph, div*
Thirteenth century	*c, gig, sa, dem*

Some Early Latin Vulgate Manuscripts

Fifth century	N, Σ
Sixth century	M, P, san, U
Seventh century	durmach, Δ, I, J, O, S, X, Z
Eighth century	A, Ep, L, Ma, Q, R, theo, Y

Glossary

Aeons—A created god or gods of the Gnostic heresy.

Alexandrian Text—The family of Greek manuscripts upon which most modern version are based. The three main manuscripts of the Alexandrian line are Alexandrinus (except in the Gospels), Sinaiticus, and Vaticanus. The name is derived from Alexandria, Egypt.

Allegoricalism—To interpret Scripture spiritually and not literally.

Ancient Versions—Used as a source for establishing a Greek text or to support a reading in a Greek manuscript. Such versions include Jerome's Latin Vulgate, the Old Latin, Old Syrian, Coptic, Gothic and other versions.

Apocrypha—Religious books of the Old Testament written between the Testaments which are not considered canonical.

Apostolic Constitutions—The largest liturgical collection of writings from Antioch, Syria dating to around 380 AD.

Autographs—The written manuscripts of the Old and New Testaments. The term "original autographs" would refer to the manuscript in its original form written by the inspired writer.

Brevior Lectio Potior—The maxim of modern textual critics which means, "the shorter reading is preferred."

Byzantine Text—Also called the Traditional Text, the Syrian Text, and sometimes the Majority Text. The largest family of Greek manuscripts draws its name from the Byzantine monks who copied the text. The Greek Textus Receptus, the text on which the Authorized Version is based, is from the Byzantine line of manuscripts.

Caesarean Text—A mixture of the Western and Alexandrian line of Greek manuscripts. It is thought to have originated in Egypt and was transported to Caesarea by Origen. Later, it was taken to Jerusalem. While at Caesarea it is thought to have been further developed.

Canonicity—The character that allows certain Old Testament and New Testament books to be part of the Biblical canon. This characteristic is divine inspiration.

Cappadocian Fathers—Early church fathers consisting of Basil of Caesarea, Gregory of Nazianzus, and Gregory of Nyssa. The Cappadocian fathers were strong theologians who supported the doctrine of the Trinity and whose manuscripts reflect the Traditional Text line.

Codex—A written manuscript with sheets bound together to form a book, as opposed to a scroll.

Conflation—The mixing of two textual lines to form one reading.

Conjectural Emendation—The classical method of textual criticism in which the editor of a Greek text attempts to restore what is considered the original reading based on the information at hand. This is applied when a reading in the Greek text is either missing or limited and the editor feels the need to supply what is lacking based on other information.

Critical Apparatus—A devise found in many modern Greek texts explaining the reason for various readings as well as supplying textual information for or against a certain reading. It usually lists what Greek manuscripts were consulted, what early translations were used, and which of the Church Fathers quoted the questioned reading in its various form.

Critical Text—One of several Greek texts based on the Alexandrian textual line, usually containing a critical apparatus within its contents.

Dead Sea Scrolls—Manuscripts found in the caves at Qumran near the Dead Sea that contain Biblical and non-Biblical writings.

Diatessaron—A harmony of the Gospels compiled by Tatian in the second century.

Didache—Known as the *Teaching of the Twelve Apostles*, this ancient catechism dating to the early second century contains a form of the Lord's Prayer that supports the reading found in the Textus Receptus.

Dittography—A scribal error involving the repetition of a letter, syllable, word, or phrase.

Docetism—A form of Gnosticism which taught that Christ's body was a phantom and not physical.

Dynamic Equivalent—A thought for thought translation to provide overall meaning. The New International Version, New Revised Standard Version, and Today's English Version are all examples of dynamic equivalent translations.

Essenes—A strict Jewish sect, which lived in piety and isolation, and is considered by many scholars to have been responsible for the Dead Sea Scrolls.

External Evidence—The approach to textual criticism that considers the age of a manuscript, its geographical distribution, and its relationship with other textual families.

Formal Equivalent—A word for word translation, also known as a literal translation. The King James Version, New American Standard Version, and Revised Standard Version are all examples of formal equivalent translations.

Geniza—A type of storage room for worn or faulty manuscripts.

Gnosticism—A heretical teaching that everything physical was evil and everything spiritual was good. The Gnostics taught that God, who was spiritual, could not have created the physical world, which was evil. Therefore, the Gnostic god created other beings known as "aeons" that in turn created the physical world. Some Christian Gnostics taught that Christ was one of these created aeons.

Granville Sharp Rule—A Greek grammatical rule stating that two nouns of the same case that are personal descriptions which are separated by the Greek word kai (and) refer to the same person if the first noun has a definite article preceding it and the second noun does not have the definite article before it.

Greek Manuscripts—Manuscripts existing in the form of papyrus, vellum, or paper written in Greek. They are classified into one of four textual types: Byzantine, Alexandrian, Western, and Caesarean.

Greek Texts—Books that are formed from various Greek manuscripts that mostly represent a certain textual line. The Textus Receptus and Majority Text are Greek texts that represent the Byzantine line of manuscripts. The United Bible Societies' Greek Text and the Nestle-Aland Greek Text are Greek texts that represent the Alexandrian line of manuscripts.

Haplography—A scribal error consisting of the omission of a pair of letters or group of letters.

Hebraism—Jewish expressions or phrases translated into English that retain their original Jewish character.

Hexapla—A version of the Old Testament containing six translations in parallel form, including the Greek Septuagint.

Higher Criticism—The process of establishing or denying the authenticity of a certain book based on its authorship, date of writing, and general information. Higher criticism, as it relates to Biblical studies, often denies the inspiration, historical statements, or doctrinal teaching of various canonical books.

Homoeoteleution—A scribal error resulting when two phrases in a given text are alike and the scribe skips over the portion between the two phrases, omitting what is between two like phrases.

Internal Evidence—The approach to textual criticism which considers a textual variant in light of the original writer's style and vocabulary, the context, and how the variant harmonies with other passages by the same writer.

Johannine Comma—The passage from 1 John 5:7 that supports the Trinity. The verse reads: "For there are three that bear record in heaven, the Father, the Word, and the Holy Ghost: and these three are one."

Lectionaries—Books used by the early church that contained lessons, hymns, and citations from passages of Scripture.

Lower Criticism—The same as textual criticism.

Lucian Recension—The theory that Lucian of Antioch, Syria, led a group of scholars to edit texts to produce what became the Byzantine text.

Marcionism—The teaching that proclaimed Jehovah as an evil god who created the world, and that all created flesh is therefore evil.

Majority Text—A consensus text reflecting a majority of the existing Greek manuscripts that have been cataloged and collated.

Middle English—Period of English language dating from 1100 to 1500 AD.

Miniscules—Also known as "cursives." A style of writing that consists of small letters with spacing between the words.

Minority Text—A text from the Alexandrian line based on a few early manuscripts.

Modern English—Period of English language dating from 1500 to the present.

Old English—Period of English language dating from 700 to 1100 AD.

Paleography—The science of dating manuscripts by the shape and style of the letters used in writings.

Paper—The writing surface used since the fourteenth century.

Papyrus—A plant from which the bark was cut into thin strips and dried to produce a writing surface. This form of paper was used for manuscripts until about the seventh century.

Patristic Citations—Quotations of the early church fathers.

Pericope De Adultera—The passage from John 7:53-8:11 referring to the woman caught in the act of adultery.

Peshers—Commentaries or interpretations on Biblical writings, usually associated only with the Hebrew Old Testament.

Peshitta—The standard Syriac version. The word means "clear" or "simple."

Proto-Masoretic Text—Manuscripts that agree with the Masoretic text, yet date before the Masoretic text became the official Hebrew Bible as recognized by scholarship.

Proto-Samaritan Text—Manuscripts of the Samaritan Pentateuch, the five books of Moses, where the Hebrew text is often the same as the Masoretic text with differences in spelling rather than textual variants.

Proto-Septuagint Text—Manuscripts written in Hebrew that reflect a reading more like the Greek Septuagint than the Masoretic or Traditional Text.

Pseudepigraphal Books—Religious books that are not considered canonical by Protestants, Catholics, or Jews.

Qumran—Ruins located in the northwest corner of the Dead Sea. In 1947, the first of what became known as the Dead Sea Scrolls were discovered there.

Septuagint—Most noted Old Testament translated into Greek. The name literally means *seventy* and is sometimes signified as LXX. It is thought to have been translated in Alexandria, Egypt, around 250 BC. Some, however, suggest that it was translated much later.

Scroll—A manuscript written on sheets bound side by side and then rolled together as opposed to a codex.

Talmud—A body of Jewish civil and religious laws that also provided commentary on the Hebrew Old Testament.

Tenacity—The persistency of textual variants that appear in early manuscripts and reappear in later manuscripts.

Textual Criticism—Sometimes called "lower criticism." The science that seeks to reconstruct the original text of Scripture based on the existing manuscripts and Biblical citations within the patriarchs of Church history.

Textus Receptus—The Greek text used by Protestant translators during the Reformation. Desiderius Erasmus first produced this text in 1516 based on Greek manuscripts available to him. It was later revised by Robert Estienne (Stephanus), the royal printer of Paris, who issued various editions from 1546 to 1557. In his last edition, Stephanus proclaimed his conversion to Protestantism. Theodore de Beza, the successor of John Calvin, later revised the Testus Receptus based on additional manuscripts he possessed or to which he had access. Beza also included his own Latin translation that was placed between the Greek text and Jerome's Latin Vulgate. It also encluded various notes on every page, providing some additional textual information and insight. His last two editions, 1589 and 1598, were used by the translators of the King James Version as the basis for their translation. Finally, Bonaventure Elzevir and his nephew Abraham produced a very popular edition in 1624 that contained the following Latin phrase in its preface: "*Textum ergo habes, nunc ab ominibus receptum; in quo nihil immutatum aut corruptum damus.*" The name "Textus Receptus" comes from this phrase, "*Textum…receptum…*" (the text received by all). The Textus Receptus was the standard Greek text for almost 400 years.

Textual Variant—A difference between two manuscripts.

Uncials—A style of writing which consists of all capital letters written without accent marks, punctuation, or separation of words or sentences.

Vellum—Dried animal skins used as a writing surface. This period lasted from the end of the third century to the fifteenth century.

Western Text—A text longer than the Alexandrian text and close to the Byzantine textual line. Codex Bezae in the Gospels and Acts, and Codex Claromontarus in the Epistles reflect the Western text, as do the Old Latin manuscripts. It derives its name from the western Church and is thought to have originated in Syria.

Bibliography

Books

Aland, Kurt and Aland, Barbara. *The Text of the New Testament*. 2nd edition. Translated by Erroll F. Rodes. Grand Rapids: Eerdmans,1989.

Aland, Kurt, Benduhn-Mertz, Annette and Mink, Gerd. *Text und Textwert der Griechischen Handschriften des Neuen Testaments: I. Die Katholischen Briefe Band 1: Das Material*. Berlin: Walter De Gruyter, 1987.

Alexander, David and Alexander, Pat, editors. *Eerdmans' Handbook to the Bible*. Grand Rapids: Eerdmans, 1973.

Anderson, Marjorie and Williams, Blanche C. *Old English Handbook*. New York: Houghton Mifflin Company, 1935.

Barker, Kenneth. *The NIV: The Making of a Contemporary Translation*. Grand Rapids: Zondervan, 1985.

Bates, Ernest Sutherland. *The Bible: Designed to be Read as Living Literature*. 1936; reprint, New York: Simon and Schuster, 1965.

Bauer, Walter. *A Greek-English Lexicon Of The New Testament And Other Early Christian Literature*. Chicago: The University of Chicago Press, 1957.

Bingham, Caroline. *The Making of a King*. Garden City, NY: Doubleday, 1969.

Bois, John. *Translating For King James*. Translated by Ward Allen. Vanderbilt University Press, 1969.

Brown, Harold O. J. *Heresies*. New York: Doubleday & Company, Inc., 1984.

Bruce, F. F. *The English Bible: A History of Translation*. New York: University Press, 1961.

Burgon, John W. *The Revision Revised*. Paradise, PA: Conservative Classics, 1883.

Burrows, Millar. *The Dead Sea Scrolls*. New York: Viking Press, 1955.

Cairns, Earle E. *Christianity Through the Centuries.* 1954; reprint, Grand Rapids: Zondervan, 1976.

Carson, Donald A. *The King James Version Debate: A Plea for Realism.* Grand Rapids: Baker Book House, 1979.

Carty, Charles M. and Rumble, L. *Bible Quizzes to a Street Preacher.* Rockford, IL: Tan Books and Publishers, 1976.

Chitwood, Oliver Perry. *A History of Colonial America.* New York: Harper and Brothers, 1961.

Clifton, Chas S. *Encyclopedia Of Heresies And Heretics.* New York: Barnes & Noble, 1992.

Dana, H. E. and Mantey, Julius R. *A Manual Grammar of the Greek New Testament.* Toronto: Macmillan, 1927.

Dore, John R. *Old Bibles: An Account of the Early Versions of the English Bible.* London: Eyre and Spottiswoode, 1888.

Durant, Will and Durant, Ariel. *Caesar and Christ. The Story Of Civilization.* 6 vols. New York: Simon and Schuster, 1944.

Ehrman, Bart. *The Orthodox Corruption Of Scripture.* New York: Oxford University Press, 1993.

Ehrman, Bart and Holmes, Michael, editors. *The Text Of The New Testament In Contemporary Research.* Grand Rapids: Eerdmans, 1995.

Eisenman, Robert and Wise, Michael. *The Dead Sea Scrolls Uncovered.* New York: Barnes & Noble, 1992.

Epp, Eldon J. and Fee, Gordon D. *Studies in the Theory and Method of New Testament Textual Criticism.* Grand Rapids: Eerdmans, 1993.

Eusebius. *Ecclesiastical History.* Translated by Kirsopp Lake. London: Heinemann, 1926.

Farstad, Arthur. *The New King James Version In The Great Tradition.* Nashville: Thomas Nelson Publishers, 1989.

Finegan, Jack. *Encountering New Testament Manuscripts.* Grand Rapids: Eerdmans, 1974.

Foxe, John. *Foxe's Book Of Christian Martyrs.* 1559; reprint, Springdale, PA: Whitaker House, 1981.

Fraser, Lady Antonia. *King James VI of Scotland: I of England.* New York: Alfred A. Knopf, Inc., 1974.

Fuller, David Otis, editor. *Counterfeit or Genuine.* Grand Rapids: Grand Rapids International Publications, 1975.

_____. *Which Bible?* Grand Rapids: Grand Rapids International Publication, 1970.

Gaster, Theodor H. *The Dead Sea Scriptures: An English Translation.* Garden City, NY: Doubleday Anchor Books, 1956.

Geisler, Norman L. and Nix, William E. *A General Introduction to the Bible.* Chicago: Moody Press, 1968.

Golb, Norman. *Who Wrote the Dead Sea Scrolls?* New York: Scribner, 1995.

Graham, Henry G. *Where We Got the Bible: Our Debt to the Catholic Church.* Rockford: Tan Books and Publishers, 1987.

Green, Michael. *Evangelism in the Early Church.* Grand Rapids: Eerdmans, 1975.

Greenslade, S. L. *The Cambridge History of the Bible.* New York: Cambridge University Press, 1983.

Haley, John W. *Alleged Discrepancies of the Bible.* 1874; reprint, Grand Rapids: Baker Book House, 1977.

Hatch, Nathan O. and Noll, Mark A., editors. *The Bible in America: Essays in Cultural History.* New York: Oxford University Press: 1982.

Hills, Edward F. *The King James Version Defended.* Des Moines: The Christian Research Press, 1956.

Hort, F. J. A. *The Apocalypse of St. John 1-3: The Greek Text with Introduction, Commentary, and Additional Notes.* 1908; reprint, Minneapolis: James and Klock Publishing, 1976.

_____. *The First Epistle of St. Peter 1:1-2:17: The Greek Text with Introductory Lecture, Commentary, and Additional Notes.* 1898; reprint, Minneapolis: James and Klock Publishing, 1976.

Hoskier, H. C. *Concerning the Text of the Apocalypse.* 2 vols. London: Bernard Quaritch, Ltd., 1929.

James, M. R., translator. *The Apocryphal New Testament.* Oxford: Clarendon Press, 1924.

Josephus, Flavius. *The Works of Josephus.* Translation by William Whiston. Peabody, MA: Hendrickson Publishers, 1987.

Jurgens, W. A. *The Faith of the Early Fathers.* Collegeville: The Liturgical Press, 1970.

Kenyon, Frederic G. *The Chester Beatty Biblical Papyri: Fasciculus I.* London: Emory Walker, 1933.

_____. *Handbook to the Textual Criticism of the New Testament.* Grand Rapids: Eerdmans, 1912.

_____. *The Story of the Bible.* 1936; reprint, Grand Rapids: Eerdmans, 1967.

_____. *The Text of the Greek Bible.* London: Gerald Duckworth and Company, 1949.

Kohlenberger, John R. III. *All About Bibles.* New York: Oxford University Press, 1985.

Kilpatrick, George D. *The Principles and Practice of New Testament Textual Criticism.* Leuven: University Press, 1990.

Kittel, Gerhard. *Theological Dictionary of the New Testament.* Grand Rapids: Eerdmans, 1965.

Klein, Ralph W. *Textual Criticism of the Old Testament: The Septuagint After Qumran.* Philadelphia: Fortress Press, 1974.

Knowles, David and Obolensky, Dimitri. *The Christian Centuries.* Mahwah, NJ: Paulist Press, 1969.

Kohlenberger, John R. *All About Bibles.* New York: Oxford University Press, 1985.

Kubo, Sakae, and Specht, Walter. *So Many Versions?* Grand Rapids: Zondervan Publishing House, 1975.

Lampe, G. W. H. *A Patristic Greek Lexicon.* Oxford: Clarendon Press, 1961.

Letis, Theodore, editor. *The Majority Text: Essays and Reviews in the Continuing Debate*. Fort Wayne, IN: The Institute for Reformation Biblical Studies, 1987.

Lewis, Jack P. *The English Bible From KJV to NIV.* Grand Rapids: Baker Book House, 1982.

Lightfoot, J. B. *The Apostolic Fathers*. London: Macmillan, 1891.

Maier, John and Tollers, Vincent, editors. *The Bible in its Literary Milieu*. Grand Rapids: Eerdmans, 1979.

Mansoor, Menahem. *The Dead Sea Scrolls*. Grand Rapids: Eerdmans, 1964.

Millard, Alan. *Discoveries From The Time of Jesus*. Oxford: Lion, 1990.

Metzger, Bruce M. *A Textual Commentary on The Greek New Testament*. New York: United Bible Societies, 1992.

_____. *The Early Versions of the New Testament*. New York: Clarendon, 1977.

_____. *The Text of the New Testament*. 3rd edition. Oxford: Oxford University Press, 1992.

Metzger, Bruce M. and Coogan, Michael D., editors. *The Oxford Companion To The Bible*. New York: Oxford University Press, 1993.

McCrum, Robert, Cran, William, and MacNeil, Robert. *The Story of English*. New York: Viking Penguin Inc, 1986.

Milligan, George. *Sections From the Greek Papyri*. Cambridge: University Press, 1912.

Moulton, Harold K. *The Analytical Greek Lexicon*. 1852; reprint, Grand Rapids: Zondervan. 1978.

Moulton, James H. and Milligan, George. *The Vocabulary Of The Greek Testament*. Grand Rapids: Eerdmans, 1949.

Murdock, James. *The Syriac New Testament from the Peshitta Version*. Boston: H. L. Hastings, 1896.

Opfell, Olga S. *The King James Bible Translators*. London: McFarland, 1982.

Pagels, Elaine. *The Gnostic Gospels*. New York: Vintage Books, 1981.

Paine, Gustavus S. *The Men Behind the King James Version.* 1959; reprint, Grand Rapids: Baker Book House, 1982.

Peter,Edward. *Inquistion.* The Free Press; 1988.

Pfeiffer, Charles F. and Harrison, Everett F., editors. *The Wycliffe Bible Commentary.* Nashville: The Southwestern Company, 1968.

Pickering, Wilbur N. *The Identity of the New Testament Text.* Nashville: Thomas Nelson, 1980.

Roberts, Alexander and Donaldson, James. *The Ante-Nicene Fathers.* The Master Christian Library: Ages Software, Version 7, 1999.

Robinson, James M., editor. *The Nag Hammadi Library.* San Francisco: Harper San Francisco, 1988.

Rosenau, William. *Hebraisms In The Authorized Version.* Baltimore: The Friedenwald Company, 1903.

Rummel, Erika. *Erasmus' Annotations on the New Testament: From Philologist to Theologian.* Toronto: University of Toronto Press, 1986.

Scrivener, F. H. *A Plain Introduction to the Criticism of the New Testament.* Edited by E. Miller. 2 vols. London: George Bell and Sons, 1894.

_____. *The New Testament in the Original Greek, together with the Variations Adopted in the Revised Version.* Cambridge: Cambridge University Press, 1880.

Soden, Hermann F. Von. *Die Schriften des Neuen Testaments.* 2 vols. Gottingen: Vandenhoech und Ruprecht, 1911.

Souter, Alexander. *The Text and Canon of the New Testament.* New York: Charles Scribner's Sons, 1917.

Sturz, Harry A. *The Byzantine Text-Type and New Testament Textual Criticism.* Nashville: Thomas Nelson Publishers, 1984.

Thayer, Joseph. *A Greek-English Lexicon of the New Testament.* 1901; reprint, Grand Rapids: Baker Book, 1977.

Thiede, Carsten Peter and D'Ancona, Matthew. *Eyewitness To Jesus.* New York: Doubleday, 1996.

Van Bruggen, Jakob. *The Ancient Text of the New Testament.* Winnipeg: Premier, 1976.

VanderKam, James C. *The Dead Sea Scrolls Today.* Grand Rapids: Eerdmans, 1994.

Vedder, Henry C. *A Short History of the Baptists.* 1907; reprint, Valley Forge: The Judson Press, 1969.

Vermes, Geza. *The Dead Sea Scrolls in English.* Middlesex, England: Penguin Books, 1962.

Westcott, Arthur. *The Life and Letters of Brook Foss Westcott.* London: Macmillan, 1903.

Westcott, B. F. *The Gospel According to St. John: The Authorized Version with Introduction and Notes.* 1881; reprint, Grand Rapids: Eerdmans, 1975.

_____. *The Historic Faith.* London: Macmillan, 1885.

White, James R. *The King James Only Controversy: Can You Trust the Modern Translations?* Minneapolis: Bethany House, 1995.

_____. *The Forgotten Trinity.* Minneapolis: Bethany House, 1998.

Whyte, Alexander. *Lancelot Andrewes and his Private Devotions.* Grand Rapids: Baker Book House, 1981.

Wisse, Frederik. *The Profile Method for Classifying and Evaluating Manuscript Evidence.* Grand Rapids: Eerdmans, 1982.

Wurthwein, Ernst. *The Text of the Old Testament.* Translated by Errol F. Rhodes, Grand Rapids: Eerdmans, 1979.

Bible Translation and Greek Texts

American Standard Version. New York: Thomas Nelson & Sons, 1901.

Authorized (King James) Version. London: Robert Barker, 1611.

Contempory English Version. New York: American Bible Society, 1995.

Douay Rheims Version. Rockford, Illinois: Tan Books And Publishers, Inc., 1971 reprint of the 1610 edition.

New American Version. Nashville: Thomas Nelson Publishers, 1971.

New American Standard Version. Nashville: Thomas Nelson Publishers, 1971.

New English Bible. New York: Oxford University Press, 1971.

The Greek New Testament. Edited by Kurt Aland, Matthew Black, Carlo M. Martini, Bruce M. Metzger, and Allen Wikgren. New York: United Bible Societies, 1998.

The Greek New Testament According to the Majority Text. Edited by Zane C. Hodges and Arthur L. Farstad. Nashville: Thomas Nelson, 1985.

The New Testament In The Original Greek. (Westcott and Hort). 2 vols. London: Macmillan and Co. Ltd., 1881.

The New Testament in the Original Greek According to the Byzantine/Majority Textform. Edited by Maurice A. Robinson, William G. Pierpont, and William David McBrayer. Original Word Publishers, 1991.

New Testament: The Greek Text Underlying the English Authorized Version of 1611. London: The Trinitarian Bible Society, [n.d].

New International Version. Grand Rapids: Zondervan Bible Publishers, 1978,

New King James Version. Nashville: Thomas Nelson Publishers, 1982.

New Living Translation. Wheaton: Tyndale House Publishers, Inc., 1996.

New Revised Standard Version. Iowa Falls: World Bible Publishers, Inc., 1989.

New World Translation. New York: Watchtower Bible And Tract Soceity, 1984.

Novum Testamentum Graece. Edited by Barbara and Kurt Aland, Johannes Karavidopoulos, Carlo M. Martini, and Bruce M. Metzger. Stuttgart: Deutsche Bibelstiftung, 1995.

Novum Testamentum Graece. Edited by Alexander Souter. Great Britain, E Typographeo Clarendoniano, 1910.

Revised Standard Version. New York: Oxford University Press, Inc., 1973.

Revised Version. San Francisco: J. Dewing & Co., 1881.

Today's English Version. Nashville: Thomas Nelson Inc., 1976.

Periodicals

Aland, Kurt. "The Text of the Church," *Trinity Journal*, (Fall, 1987).

American Bible Society, *Committee on Versions to the Board of Managers.* 1852.

Bonani, George. "Carbon-14 Tests Substantiate Scrolls Dates." *Biblical Archaeology Review.* (November/December, 1991).

Crim, Keith R. "Translating The Bible Into English: The First Thousand Years." *The Bible Translator.* (April, 1974).

Hodges, Zane. "The Greek Text of the King James Version." *Bibliotheca Sacra* (124 Fall, 1968).

————. "Rationalism and Contemporary New Testament Criticism." *Bibliotheca Sacra.* (128, January/March, 1971).

Hunger, Herbert. "Zur Datierung des Papyrus Bodmer II (P66)." *Anzeiger der Osterreichischen Akademie der Wissenschaften.* (1960).

Katzman, Avi. "The Dead Sea Scrolls Update: Chief Dead Sea Scroll Editor Denounces Judaism, Israel; Claims He's Seen Four More Scrolls Found by Bedouin." *Biblical Archaeology Review.* (January/February, 1991).

Kim, Youn Kyu. "Palaeographical Dating of P46 to the Later First Century." *Biblica.* (lxix, 1988).

Moody, Dale. "God's Only Son: The Translation Of John 3:16 In The Revised Standard Version." *Journal Of Biblical Literature.* (72, 1973).

Nelson, Wilton. "New Light From An Old Lamp." *Latin American Evangelist.* (January/February, 1970).

O'Callaghan, Jose. *Journal of Biblical Literature.* (91: 1972).

Ostling, Richard. "Is Jesus in the Dead Sea Scrolls?" *Time.* (September 21, 1992).

Shanks, Hershel. "Dead Sea Scrolls Updated: Scholars, Scrolls, Secrets and 'Crimes'." *Biblical Archaeology Review.* (November/December, 1991).

_____. "Is the Vatican Suppressing the Dead Sea Scrolls?" *Biblical Archaeology Review.* (November/December, 1991).

_____. "Who Controls the Scrolls?" *Biblical Archaeology Review.* (March/April, 1991).

Tov, Emanual. "The Unpublished Qumran Texts From Cave 4 and 11." *Biblical Archaeologist.* (June, 1992).

Scripture Index

General Index

Printed in Great Britain
by Amazon